GREECE

THE WORLD IN COLOUR SERIES

THE WORLD IN COLOUR

GREECE

EDITED BY

DORÉ OGRIZEK

McGRAW-HILL PUBLISHING COMPANY LTD
NEW YORK   LONDON   TORONTO

GREECE

Copyright 1955

Printed in the Netherlands

This book has been prepared under the editorship of
DORÉ OGRIZEK

Translation by
PADDY O'HANLON

Illustrations by
BEUVILLE - JEANNE CUSENIER - JACQUEMOT
EDY LEGRAND - JACQUES LIOZU - PIERRE NOEL
MARIANNE PERETTI

We should like to acknowledge with thanks the assistance given to us in the preparation of this book by the Greek National Tourist Organization *and the* Greek Information Office

PREFACE

I HAVE always regarded the charioteer of Delphi as a blind man walking without progressing, a sign of the times that deceives us, a votive column with enamel eyes and bronze eyelashes, a proof of the continuity of Greece. Whilst there is no need for me to comment on the role she plays in this disorderly world, by virtue of my prerogative as a poet I confer on Greece the Order of the Myth, an invisible, sovereign order.

All soil inevitably dries up in the end, and by the time of Plato's death Greece was already confronted with geographical and social troubles. Despite the dearth of water, there was never any lack of that strange sap thanks to which fables take root in the rock, blossom and perfume the air.

I visited the Islands on a friend's yacht. There I observed that what appeared to be obstacles in our eyes never formed a stumbling block for the navigators of old, and the problem of simply journeying to Delphi by road did not prevent the building of temples there, or carrying statues to and from the city.

Poor little charioteer! With his toes aligned in a horse-drawn chariot he used to be the crowning glory of the amphitheatre in Delphi.

Though amputated and deprived of his chariot, he still goes on. He makes no attempt to "hitch a lift". He drives statically on a pedestal. Only, all that he lacks testifies to a void as mysterious as that of the future. He seems to be saying: "My reins are a blind man's stick. Time is a sham. It is deceiving you. Don't ever be taken in."

Having consulted this oracle, not far from the Sibyl's lair, I visited Greece in quest of something more than traces of the legends and the gods which the Greeks created in their image: they lived in the same building, so to speak, where mortals and immortals used to cross each other on the stairs.

Everywhere I found the sources of the significant magnificence with which this wise race amplified the merest gesture. One source alone escaped me and held me bewitched—the fountain of Medusa's blood from which Pegasus was born when the monster was beheaded.

Unless it were that Perseus—invisible, armed with a sword and a mirror—found in the sublime ugliness of a Gorgon the sign of true beauty? Thus Pegasus was born to our stupefaction, as if Medusa had petrified us all. This would explain his action. And as a result we were all bewitched by Medusa, and we still are, whilst the horse still beats the buoyant air of the Peloponnese with his great wings.

Greece is swathed in an impenetrable purple cloak of fables. But the genealogy of mythologists is less open to doubt than that of historiographers, since time deforms History and forms myth, and since History is truth turned false, whilst myth is falsehood incarnate.

Amongst the oleanders bordering the road to Mycenae, we hardly expect to stumble upon those rugged blocks of stone, that welter of tombs, the foundations of a vanished sumptuousness. We expect the shadows of Clytemnestra and her son and daughter to welcome us, whilst the hillside echoes their quarrels like the screams of birds of prey.

The marshes in Nauplia exhale breath from the Hydra's mouths. The hives in Knossos reveal to us the secret of a decadent way of life—the climax of a civilization. In Epidaurus, we can follow the elegant crowd seen in any health resort. And the theatre of Dionysos at the foot of the Acropolis produces spectacles such as we dream of.

I leave the specialists to talk to you in detail of this land drawn through the air by exquisite monsters. Whenever I go there, I fall under the spell, and blush at my youthful blunder in scoffing at Maurras for embracing a column in the Parthenon. There was nothing to laugh at. Rosy fire courses those marble veins. The marble speaks. If the cicadas kept silent, one would hear its voice. Alas, all those statues of maidens murmur is Edgar Allan Poe's "Nevermore".

JEAN COCTEAU
of the *Académie Française*

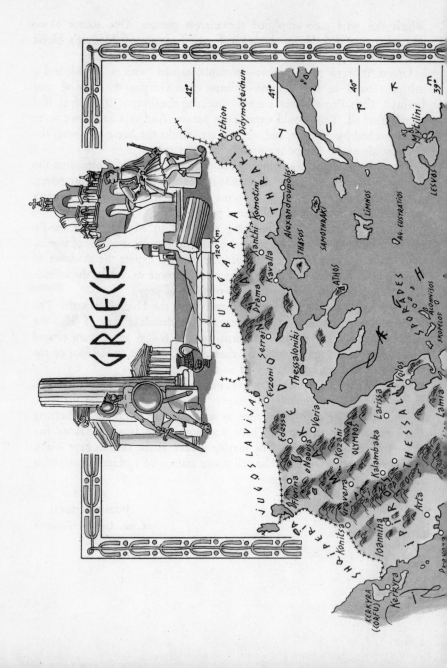

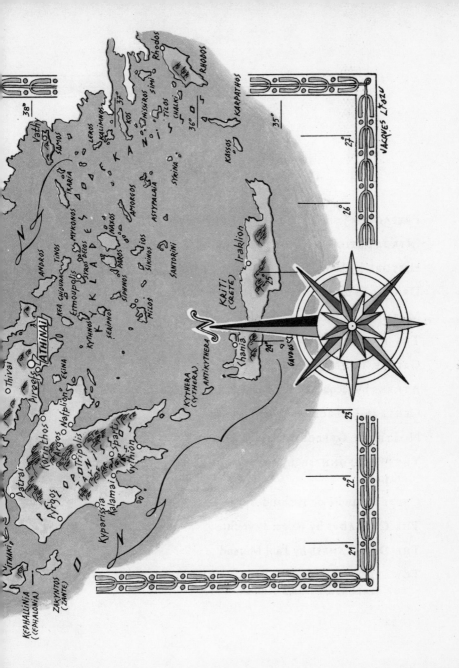

CONTENTS

INTRODUCTION TO THE VOYAGE

G REECE is a land as fair as she is poor. Myth and legend, the beauty of her mountains and shores, the blue sea that hems her and the brilliance of her skies comprise her major assets.

Countless wars, scourges, and catastrophes laid waste the country time and again. During the last war, her courage paid a heavy tribute in the form of destroyed ports, broken roads, demolished bridges....

Yet, thanks to the vitality of her people, spurred by their consciousness of the mission History has imperatively assigned them, and their inexhaustible capacity for work, the country has been completely rebuilt.

In Greece today thousands of miles of roadways (asphalt, for the most part) interlink every corner of the country. Motor-car and rail-car are the most common means of transport. Newly constructed boats assure communication by sea. A network of airlines links the main centres in the Greek mainland as well as the islands.

Moreover, in the most frequented tourist centres, visitors will find every comfort in recently modernized hotels or in well-run Tourist Guest-houses. Since 1950, establishments of this kind have been built in Athens, Olympia, Delphi, Nauplia, Rhodes, Corfu, Mykonos, etc., as well as Mycenae, Epidaurus, Corinth, Xylocastro, Paleokastritsa, etc.

The main gateways to Greece are: by sea, Piraeus and Patras; by road, Evzoni (on the Yugoslav frontier), and by air, Athens (Elliniko Airport). It has been decided to set up Reception Centres of the National Tourist Office at each of these gateways, where visitors can apply on arrival for information, and obtain maps, pamphlets, etc.

Greece is the ideal country for excursions, and the most convenient way of travel is by car. Tourists arriving from the West (especially those who bring their own car) would be well advised to disembark in Patras rather than Piraeus. Patras, the capital of the Peloponnese, is a port of call on the Venice-

Brindisi-Piraeus line, regularly serviced by four Greek shipping companies. Each week there are three Brindisi-Piraeus trips, and one Venice-Brindisi-Piraeus crossing.

Landing in Patras effects an economy on the traveller's ticket and on transport of the car, not to mention a saving of time. There are excellent hotels and restaurants in Patras, and the tourist arriving there can continue his journey to Athens by skirting the wonderful coast of the Gulf of Corinth, or set off immediately on a tour of the Peloponnese (Olympia, etc.)—which the majority of visitors to Greece prefer—or again, head for Delphi (by way of Rhion, Antirhion, and the attractive little town of Natpaktos).

We do not promise our visitors the luxury and perfect organization they will find in great countries such as France, Switzerland, Italy, etc., whose touristic treasures have long been turned to advantage. The exacting traveller will find a great deal to be desired. By way of compensation he will find life cheap—Greece being, at the time of writing, the least expensive country in Europe—and enjoy the cordial atmosphere and hospitable spirit that have characterized the Greek race for thousands of years.

One of the many epithets attributed by our distant forebears to the greatest of their Gods, Zeus, was *Xenios*, meaning "hospitable" or "protector of strangers". And whereas the rich Greek language often comprises two or three words expressing the same idea, there is only one word, *xenos*, to designate both "stranger" and "guest". This identification of the two meanings is intentional, and true to life: it clearly denotes the people's natural tendency to consider every stranger as an impatiently awaited friend.

And it is in this spirit that I extend a welcome to all the readers of this book who come to visit Greece.

R. AGATHOCLES
*President
of the National Tourist Office of Greece*

HISTORY

INSTITUTIONS OF ATHENS AND SPARTA

ATHENS—Prior to Solon's time, power was divided amongst nine *archons* (elected for a year from the *Eupatridae*) and the *Areopagus*.

In 594 B.C. Solon modified this state of affairs on increasingly democratic lines. In 507 Clisthenes continued the good work by dividing Attica into a hundred *demes*, grouped in ten tribes, without distinction of wealth. In addition to the archons he appointed ten *strategi*, elected by the people, and entrusted each in turn with command of the army. The Areopagus was brought up to full strength by the Helius, a kind of immense jury of the people composed of 5,000 members drawn by lots each year from amongst the citizens as a whole, and divided into ten *dikasteries*.

Under Pericles, an indemnity of one obol was attributed to the Heliasts for each day's attendance. This indemnity was later extended to every citizen attending the people's Assembly. Thus even the poorest citizen was able to discuss, and vote on in person, the laws he was to obey. It was truly democratic government in the highest sense of the word.

SPARTA—The institutions granted to Sparta in the 9th century B.C. by her semi-legendary king Lycurgus are, on the contrary, remarkable for their aristocratic and immutable character.

Although the king was both religious and military leader, in private life he was a common citizen. Power was in the hands of five *Ephori* (inspectors) elected for one year, supervised by the Council of Elders (twenty-eight members over sixty years of age, elected for life).

Lycurgus had parcelled the land of Lacedaemon into equal lots. Each Spartan received one of these lots, together with a certain number of *Hiloti* (serfs) to cultivate it. The Spartan himself was not allowed to be a labourer, or a craftsman, or a tradesman, but only a soldier (and in order to remove him from all temptation to do business, Lycurgus made the money so heavy that it was practically unusable). According to Spartan custom, deformed children were thrown at birth into the Gulf of Taygetus; the others were trained to hard living and stoic endurance of suffering. Military training as such began at the age of eighteen. At twenty years of age the Spartan became a soldier and received his uniform, a red tunic which would not show the blood. On being named citizen, at thirty, he married a young girl who had been brought up just as rigorously. Marriage exempted him from sleeping in barracks, but he was still obliged to take all his evening meals (consisting basically of black broth) with his comrades. He remained under arms until the age of sixty, and was not allowed to

The Cretans invent bullfighting

leave his town without authorization. In return, his old age was handsomely provided for.

History or Story?—In Greece, more than any other country of ancient times, History made her *début* chaperoned by Legend.

What is the origin of the acorn-eating Pelasgians, the first known inhabitants of the earth, who drained the marshes, cultivated the plains, and built towns on the heights? They worshipped the powers of Nature and, to protect themselves, built those crude walls which the Greeks subsequently christened *cyclopean*.

What was the origin of the Cretans who, between the 14th and 15th centuries B.C., founded a civilization in Knossos which achieved a harmonious balance between utilitarian activities, artistic pleasures, sports (they invented bullfighting), and the acme of comfort?

How much should be attributed to chronicle, and how much to fable, in what is known of the first leaders: the Cretan Minos, husband of Pasiphae, father of Ariadne, of Phaedra, and—reputedly, at least—of the Minotaur (thanks to the understanding of human feelings he acquired through contact with his boisterous family, he was later designated first Judge of Hades); the Phoenicians Cadmus (founder of Cadmea, the citadel around which Thebes subsequently grew up) and Pelops who landed in the 14th century B.C. in the south of Greece in the region which became known as the Peloponnese?

Egypt, for her part, sent Greece two illustrious colonizers: Danaos,

Agamemnon tragically ends a life heaped with honours

father of the Danaïds, and Cecrops who divided Attica into twelve boroughs, introduced olive growing, and founded the citadel of Cecropia on the site of the future city of Athens.

ARRIVAL OF THE HELLENES—Pelasgians, Phoenicians, Cretans, and Egyptians were soon to withdraw and generally disappear in the face of the onslaught of Aryan peoples—the Hellenes—who came down from the plateaux of Asia. The first of the invaders, the Achaeans, entrenched themselves behind mighty fortresses on the natural bastions with which Greece is so generously provided. The Achaean kings of Tiryns and Mycenae lived in sumptuous palaces, decorated in Cretan fashion with frescoes and beautiful pottery. In hunting and war, the kings themselves wore richly embossed bronze weapons and heavy golden jewels. So great was the power of Mycenae that during the Trojan War her leader, Agamemnon, was designated by the Achaeans as King

17

of Kings—an honour which was to heap misfortunes on him, as we know!

The existence of Mycenae, Agamemnon, and Troy herself was long open to doubt. But excavations undertaken in 1870, solely on the strength of Homer's texts, by the German Schliemann (shortly before the discoveries of the Englishman Evans in Crete) corroborated the poet's accounts and made Legend cede her place to History.

After the Achaeans, three new groups of Hellenes invaded Greece. The Iolians, driven back by subsequent groups, finally crossed the Aegean Sea and settled on the north coast of Asia Minor and a number of islands, the

Codrus sacrifices himself for his country

most renowned of which was Lesbos, the home of Sappho. Then came the Dorians and Ionians who were of primary importance.

Driving the Barbarians and Hellenes of other clans indiscriminately before them, the uncouth Dorians thrust right into the Peloponnese, where they subjugated most of the Pelasgians—except those from Arcady—and where the warlike genius of their race was incarnated in one of the most extraordinary towns in history, Sparta, the rival of Athens, of which she was the living antithesis.

Meanwhile the Ionians settled on the open plains beside the sea—such as Attica—or on the Aegean coast of Asia, south of the Iolians. There, in prosperous towns—Smyrna, Phocica, Ephesus, Miletus—and islands such as Chios and Samos, a highly refined form of civilization rapidly developed. Whilst ten towns vie for the honour of bringing Homer into the world, Chios would seem to present the strongest claim.

But the foremost Ionian city was indisputably Athens, where the people's taste for art, speculation, and criticism reached its zenith.

KINGS AND TYRANTS—The legendary hero Theseus united the twelve boroughs of Attica in a single nation, taking as capital the ancient city of Cecropia, which he consecrated to the goddess Athena. Cecropia thus became Athens, and Theseus was her first king. The last was Codrus. During a war against the Corians, the Oracle had revealed that the victory would be won by the side whose king fell in battle. Disguised as a peasant, Codrus

By a ruse, Pisistratus establishes a pleasant form of tyranny

provoked an enemy soldier and let himself be stabbed, to assure his country's triumph. Thereupon the Athenians abolished royalty, ostensibly because they despaired of ever finding an equal to Codrus.

As a matter of fact, never was a people less fitted for monarchy. Power passed into the hands of the aristocracy or *Eupatridae* (the well-born), but they soon aroused the hatred of the peasant and working-classes, who revolted on several occasions. The tyranny of the Eupatridae was not merely political, but financial and juridical as well. They made loans at high rates of interest to the common people who being unable to repay, were reduced to slavery. And only the Eupatridae were entitled to know and interpret the laws, until the end of the 7th century. At that time the first legal code comprehensible to the man in the street was drawn up by the archon Drachon. It was far from earning him a reputation for indulgence.

After several uprisings of the people, in 594 Solon suppressed slavery for debts and diminished the amount of indebtedness by effecting the first devaluation (he reduced the rate of the drachma from six grams of silver to 4.36 grams). At the same time, he endowed Athens with a wise and moderate constitution. He lived until the day one of his relatives, Pisistratus, artfully seized power (after wounding himself intentionally in order to procure a bodyguard) and became *tyrant*, or absolute master.

In actual fact, Pisistratus' tyranny was a golden age for the Athenians. Their new master made no changes in Solon's wise laws; he simply made sure they were observed. He possessed a large personal fortune, which he

The two major episodes in the Median Wars

put to intelligent and generous use. At his instigation, the Athenian countryside was clad with olive groves and vineyards, the town with monuments, the sea with sails.

On the literary plane, two important events took place during this period: the first theatrical performance, and the establishing of the final text of the homeric poems, which until then had been handed down by the bards, through word of mouth, with wide variations.

GREEKS VERSUS PERSIANS—The King of the Medes and Persians, Cyrus, had conquered the whole of Asia Minor, including the Ionian colonies in the Aegean Sea. In 499 one of these colonies, Miletus, revolted against Cyrus' successor, Darius, and Athens was bold enough to send her reinforcements. Darius never forgot. He even had one of his servants repeat to him before each meal: "King, remember the Athenians."

In 490, six hundred of his ships landed a mighty army of 110,000 men in Attica; they massed on the Marathon plain 25 miles from Athens. The Athenians numbered one against ten; but they had a strategist of merit, Miltiades. Their victory, won at a run with a song on their lips, was as complete as it was unexpected. Placed literally under the sign of the running race, it was announced in Athens that very evening by one of the combatants, who dropped dead from exhaustion once he had accomplished his mission.

Marathon won the Greeks ten years' respite, during which time Themistocles built a powerful, well-trained fleet in Athens.

Marathon and Salamis

The war was resumed in 480 under Darius' son, Xerxes. Leonidas, King of Sparta, vainly attempted to halt the Persian hordes at the narrow Thermopylae pass, and was slaughtered there with three hundred of his compatriots, in the purest Spartan tradition. But the Persians swooped down on Attica and penetrated into the Acropolis, burning and massacring. Most of the Athenians took refuge in the neighbouring islands, threatened by the Great King's twelve hundred warships. The Greeks had only four hundred triremes to oppose them. It was then that, in the narrow rocks of Salamis, thanks to Themistocles' audacious ruse, the miracle of Marathon was repeated, in an even more extraordinary way. Overcrowded in a narrow space, the Persians collided with each other, breaking their oars and rudders one against another, and thus became an easy prey. "Only a plaint mingled with sobs reigned over the sea" said Aeschylus describing the twilight at Salamis where the Persians perished by the thousand, dispatched by the Greeks "like a school of tunny-fish." Xerxes, who had a throne of gold erected on a headland so that he might watch the rout of the Greeks, had a grandstand view of his own defeat.

The following year the Persians endured further rebuffs at Plataea, and again at Mycalae on the coast of Asia. Their home territory was now to become the battlefield.

Through the great victories of Marathon and Salamis, the Athenians derived moral benefits from the Median Wars, which they turned to material advantage. They persuaded the Greeks of the islands and the coast

The century of Pericles sees the apogee of Athenian civilization

of Asia to entrust them with their defence, in return for payment in silver and ships. Thus was formed the Confederation of Delos, whose seat, as its name implies, was situated on Apollo's sacred island. The Confederation's treasury was for the most part used to fortify and embellish Athens. In particular, Themistocles fitted out the port of Piraeus to replace the former roads of Phalerum, now inadequate.

Despite the services he had rendered, the victor of Salamis in turn fell victim to the fickleness of his fellow-citizens, who voted him into ostracism. It was then that he joined the household of his former rival, the Great King, where he was to end his days. Political influence passed into the hands of Miltiades' son Cimon, who harried the Persians even in Asia, and died in 449 B.C. too soon to witness the signing of the Treaty of Kallias (448) which put an end to the Median wars.

THE CENTURY OF PERICLES—No sooner had the Persian danger been averted than Sparta and Athens, which until then had vied only in valour, began to tear each other limb from limb in a struggle to dominate the Greek world.

However, before the great conflict known as the "Peloponnesian War" was unleashed, the efforts of Cimon and Pericles culminated in truces during which Athens was to reach the zenith of her power and glory.

The longest of these truces lasted 14 years, throughout which Pericles continued to wield power, without ever holding or soliciting a title other than that of Strategus. His eloquence was the real instrument of his power.

The feast of the Panatheneans

Under his impulse, and that of his friend the sculptor Phidias, the Athenians undertook to enrich themselves and their town, which became a peerless artistic, literary, and intellectual centre, the meeting-place of brains and beauty in the Mediterranean world. The most renowned monuments of the Acropolis date from the "century of Pericles". Herodotus, Thucydides, and Xenophon belong to the same Golden Age. Festivals took on a new lustre, and the theatres staged the works of contemporaries by the names of Aeschylus, Sophocles, Euripides, and Aristophanes.

"You are a dolt", wrote a Greek, "if you haven't seen Athens. But if, having set eyes on her, you have not sworn to live there, you are a dunce."

On a more practical plane, Pericles built the Long Walls to protect the road linking Piraeus to Athens, and thus assured her food supply at all times.

GREEK AGAINST GREEK—The war between Athens and Sparta was resumed in 413 B.C. It was to last 27 years.

At an early stage it was aggravated in Athens by the plague, brought in by an oriental ship. The epidemic lasted two years and took toll of thousands of victims, one of whom was Pericles. The Spartans, on the other hand, were demoralized by the Sphagia affair, in which 300 of their men—the same number as at Thermopylae—let themselves be captured *alive*, as hostages for the Athenians. The peace concluded in 421 could have endured, were it not for the intervention of one of the most brilliant and least reliable

The Peloponnesian War was revived by Alcibiades

Athenians, Alcibiades. The main thing we remember about him is that he had his dog's tails clipped, in order to set people talking. Unfortunately for his country, his activities did not stop at that. Although they condemned Miltiades to irons, exiled Aristides and Themistocles, and fined Pericles, the Athenians long forgave Alcibiades everything: the mutilation of Hermes, the disastrous Sicilian expedition undertaken on his advice, and even his stay with the Spartans.

They showed less clemency to the leaders of their victorious fleet in the Islands of Arginusae, who were condemned to death for abandoning the bodies of their dead in a tempest. This ill-rewarded victory was the last to be won by Athens. In 405, the Bay of Aegos-Potamos (the river of the kid), the Spartan Lysander took the Athenian fleet by surprise, destroyed it, and massacred 3,000 prisoners.

Vanquished, to the accompaniment of flutes Athens was obliged to tear down Pericles' Long Walls, destroy part of Piraeus, and accept a Spartan garrison in the Acropolis. From the aristocrats Sparta appointed thirty tyrants who took their revenge for their previous loss of power by wreaking terrible reprisals on their fellow-citizens.

The tyranny of the Thirty was overcome only in 403 by Thrasybulus. His first act was to proclaim a general amnesty, the most generous initiative to be taken in Greece for many years. By refusing to fawn on the people, Socrates was the last to fall victim to those troubled times.

The defeat of the Athenians at Aegos-Potamos

THE PERSIANS' GOLD—After Aegos-Potamos, Sparta might well deem herself mistress of Greece. She occupied Cadmea, the citadel of Thebes, whilst her young king Agesilaus resumed the ancient war against the Persians, this time as conqueror. But the Persians, who had learnt to know the Greeks, financed the uprising of Athens, Thebes, and Corinth against Sparta. Despite his victories in Asia, Agesilaus had to hasten back to succour his homeland.

So it was with the Greeks until the Macedonian conquest. When warring as one man against the foreign foe, they were invincible (witness the extraordinary epic of the Ten Thousand, as recounted by one of their leaders, Xenophon), but they exhausted their strength and abased their finest qualities in an endless series of town-to-town wars, carefully supported by Persian funds.

For a few years, it looked as if union would be achieved under the Theban hero Epaminondas. After recapturing Cadmea from the Spartans, with the

25

help of his friend Pelopidas, Epaminondas carried the day at Leuctra and won the confidence of the Peloponnese peoples. But his death at Mantinea (in 362) dashed all hopes.

Moreover, without realizing it Pelopidas had just sewn the seeds of his homeland's defeat. At the issue of a skirmish with belligerent Macedonia, he had brought back a young Macedonian prince, Philip, as hostage. The prince was educated by Greek masters in Thebes, but he learnt even more by observing the rivalry of the great cities, their sterile quarrels, and their growing weakness. He was never to forget the lesson taught by captivity.

The Great King is vanquished by Alexander

PHILIP—He became king of Macedonia in 360, and had at his command a redoubtable army of massive phalanxes, bristling with lances, light infantry peltasts, archers and slingers, heavy cavalry and engineers.

His first annexations (Amphipolis and Potidaea) were carried out on widely different pretexts. In 352 the Amphictyons of Delphi decreed a holy war against the Phocians, accused of tilling a field consecrated to Apollo. They appealed to Philip to punish this sacrilege. He did not wait to be told twice. Crowned with laurels, as befits the champions of a holy cause, his soldiers crossed Thessaly, invaded Phocia, defied the Phocians.... and Philip retained Thessaly.

Preoccupied with killing each other, the Greeks were blind to the Macedonian peril. Alone in Athens, Demosthenes attempted to stir his fellow citizens out of their apathy, proclaiming in his booming voice: "How long will you continue to stroll about asking each other 'What's the news?'

Ah! What could be more novel than a Macedonian who has conquered Athens and is master of Greek affairs?"

But Demosthenes was opposed by two contradicting voices, almost as powerful as his own—his rival Aeschines, deluded or bribed by Philip, and Phocion, a general who, though courageous and upright, was held in such contempt by his contemporaries that whenever anyone applauded him in the tribune, he would pause to ask: "Have I said something silly?"

Still full of religious zeal, the Amphictyons precipitated events by calling on Philip once more for help. This time it was the Locrians who had com-

The Great King abandons his treasures and his wives

mitted sacrilege in one way or another. As usual, Philip hastened to their aid. But, deeming the time ripe to unmask his batteries, he left the Locrians to fight it out with the Gods, and turned his attention to occupying the town of Elataeus, a key position in Boeotia and Attica. Rising at Demosthenes' back, the Athenians and Thebans, united too tardily, attempted to bar the Macedonian advance. They were crushed at Cheronea in 338. Philip was master of Greece.

Two years later, whilst preparing an expedition against the Persians, he was assassinated by one of his generals. Power was transmitted to his eldest son, a youth of twenty—Alexander.

ALEXANDER THE GREAT—All he inherited from his barbarian forebears, was their incoercible mettle, which drove him recklessly into the thick of battle, and later incited him to kill his friend Clitus, only to regret it bitterly afterwards. But by upbringing, education, and language he was Greek, and his father provided him with the finest tutor of his day, Aristotle.

After Philip's death, Athens and Thebes attempted to reconquer their independence. Alexander hastened to quell the rising. On the strength of her name alone, Athens had always been treated with clemency by her conquerors. Alexander made no exception to the rule; but, as an exemplary measure, he razed Thebes to the ground, sparing only the poet Pindar's house. Then, without wasting an instant, he turned his attention to Asia.

The Fourth Crusade revives a semblance of unity

In a temple in Gordion there was a famous chariot, the shafts of which were attached by an inextricable knot. The Empire of Asia was promised to whoever could untie it. With one stroke of his sword, Alexander severed the Gordian knot. At Issos and Arbela he vanquished Darius, who abandoned his tents and treasures and fled his generous conqueror, only to fall victim to a treacherous satrap. Alexander treated the Great King's corpse with royal honours and excuted the assassin. Subsequently he married one of Darius' daughters, and the majority of Macedonian nobles followed suit, taking Persian girls as wives.

The next four years led Alexander right to the borders of India, where he conquered King Porus. When questioned as to how he wished to be treated, Porus made a reply that must have pleased his victor: "Like a king", he said—and so he was.

But the conqueror's soldiers were exhausted and refused to follow him further east, so he was obliged to return to Babylon. He planned to make her the mighty capital of his Empire, but in the midst of this gigantic undertaking he caught a fever, and died at the age of 32 (in 323). During the twelve years of his reign he had intermingled peoples, founded towns, created a great commercial and cultural movement and, in short, changed the face of the known world.

His generals began to fight for power when his body was hardly cold. After a series of long, confused battles, Alexander's Empire was split into three kingdoms: Egypt, ruled by the Ptolemies (sons of Lagos), the dynasty

under the leadership of the Christian Barons

of Cleopatra; Asia, under Seleucus' sons, the Seleucidae; and lastly Macedonia, where Antigone's sons, the Antigonidae, ruled.

ROMAN GREECE—After Alexander's death, the Greeks made several fresh attempts to regain their independence. But neither the Aetolian League nor the Achaean League succeeded in preventing civil wars from rekindling with renewed fire, fanned from within the majority of cities by social wars in which the poor rebelled against the rich in outbursts of unbelievable cruelty.

Meanwhile Philip V of Macedonia, who had committed the crime of extending hospitality to Hannibal, the enemy of Rome, was beaten by the Romans at Cynocephalae (197). The following year, in the course of the Isthmic Games at Corinth the Consul Flamininus proclaimed the independence of Greece, and was nearly stifled to death by the delirious mob.

It did not take the Greeks long to realize that their freedom was nothing but an illusion. They contracted a series of alliances with the enemies of the Romans (Perseus, King of Macedonia, Mithridates, King of Pontus), only to be repressed each time and treated somewhat more severely than before. In 148, Greece was annexed to the Roman province of Macedonia. Later she became a separate province—Achaia.

Although eventually, as Horace sang, "conquered Greece conquered her uncouth victor" and although her fervent admirers comprised the *élite* of Rome, including even emperors such as Hadrian who prided himself on his

Athens, in turn, falls into the hands of the Turks

title of "honorary Athenian"; although her philosophers, architects, and artists, encouraged by Mycenae such as Herodes Atticus (2nd century B.C.) continued to enrich her soil and astound the world.... for all that, her political power was long dead.

Greece continued to be the theatre of major battles, but the Greeks no longer had a role to play. It was at Pharsala in Thessaly that Caesar's triumph over Pompey was consecrated; at Philippi that Caesar's murderer, Brutus, perished; at Actium, on the Ionian coast, that Cleopatra's galleys took flight and Antony took his life....

PAGANS, CHRISTIANS, AND MOSLEMS—As early as the 1st century A.D., Greece became a hotbed of Christianity, fertilized for the most part by Saint Paul's sermons in Athens and Corinth. As for the little Island of Patmos in the Dodecanese, she found her way into religious history when

Saint John, who was exiled there, experienced the terrifying visions recorded in his *Apocalypse*.

At the decline of the Roman Empire of the West, Greece naturally remained united to the Eastern Empire, whose capital was Constantinople, the former Megarian colony of Byzantium, enlarged and renamed by Constantine in 330.

For a long time Paganism and Christianity co-existed in Greece in comparative tranquillity. The feast of the Panathanaea was still held in Athens, whilst the people continued to consult the Oracle in Delphi until the 4th

The Erechtheon is turned into a seraglio

century. Schools of philosophers grew up beside the churches—the Neo-Platonists in particular—and their teachings and customs grew more and more akin to those of the Christians.

The Emperor of the Orient, Theodosius, was the first to declare war openly on paganism, but it was not until the advent of Justinian, in the 6th century, that the philosophic schools in Greece were closed and the temples—including the Parthenon—converted into churches.

Throughout this period, Greece was in no way spared the barbarian invasions that sacked the ancient Roman world—Visigoths in the 4th century, and Avars in the 6th century. Justinian built a series of fortifications, but to no avail. Slavs from further east founded large colonies in Greece.

In the 8th century Athens gave the Empire of the Orient yet another great empress, Irene, who fiercely opposed the iconoclasts and took her place amongst the saints of the Orthodox Church. Throughout the 10th and 11th centuries the Normans ravaged the Greek coast and took Piraeus by storm. Bit by bit Greece fell into the hands of the West.

The Fourth Crusade in 1204 revived a semblance of unity under the authority of the Christian barons Baudouin de Flandres, Emperor of Constantinople; Boniface de Montferrat, king of Salonica; Geoffroy de Villehardouin, prince of Achaia (Morea); Guy de la Roche and Gauthier de Brienne, dukes of Athens. These Christian kingdoms were for the most part short-lived. The Greeks recaptured Constantinople, and remained there under the Paleologus dynasty until 1453. The duchy of Athens fell

In 1687, Morosini bombards the Acropolis

first to the Catalans, then to the kings of Aragon and Sicily, and finally, in 1395, to the Venetians.

Then the great Turkish tide was unleashed. The fall of Constantinople —in 1453—marked the end of the Middle Ages and the beginning of Modern Times. Greece, in her turn, fell into the Moslems' power. In 1456 the Turks seized Athens. The Parthenon was crowned with a minaret and converted into a mosque, whilst the Erechtheon served as seraglio for the *disdar* (governor).

Rhodes, where the Knights of Saint John had entrenched themselves, held out until 1522. But eventually she too fell.

The 16th and 17th centuries number amongst the darkest in the whole of Greek history. The towns were depopulated, the countryside ravaged by war. Turkish soldiers, or *Timariots*, settled on the choicest lands. Wherever they managed to survive, the Greeks were crushed by taxes. For all that, they succeeded in safeguarding their language, their religion, and their traditions.

In 1687 the doge Francesco Morosini laid siege to Athens (then reduced to 9,000 inhabitants), and, with an only too well-aimed bomb, blew up the Parthenon which had been transformed into a powder-mill.

And yet the Sublime Porte welcomed writers, artists, and sightseers to Greece. Her past, and her misfortunes, aroused growing interest throughout the world. In 1800 Lord Elgin requested firmans permitting him to study the ruins of the Parthenon. He took advantage of this opportunity to carry off works of inestimable worth, such as the Panathenean frieze.

In 1821 the Greeks take up arms to to reconquer their freedom

INDEPENDENCE—The great revolutionary movements of the 17th century whetted the Greek's thirst for freedom. Outstanding intellectuals for the most part resident in large European centres—including Adamandios Korais in Paris and Constantine Kounas in Vienna—contributed by their writings to the diffusion of liberal ideas in Greece. A philosopher-bard, Righas Pheraeos—the "apostle of the Nation", and the herald of freedom —drew up a plan of liberation of all the Christian peoples bent beneath the Turkish yoke; he was arrested by the Austrians and executed at the Sultans' request. Numerous pamphlets in Greek, published continuously in important centres such as Paris, Vienna, Trieste, and Venice, were distributed by patriots within the country. Abroad, in Russia a small group of proletarians (all Greek) formed the "Society of Friends", with the aim of propagating the idea of revolution, raising the necessary funds, and organizing the uprising. The hotbeds from which the first flames sprang

—at the instigation of Alexander Ypsilantis—were the Danube countries, then governed by Greek princes accredited by the Sublime Porte. The conflagration was quelled (1821), but from its sparks other fires were lit that same year from one end of Greece to another (both on the mainland and on the islands). The revolution spread. It lasted seven years and, despite opposition from the Holy Alliance, the Greeks' love of freedom and their resolution to die for it carried the day. Marko Botzaris, Kolokotronis, Karaiskakis, and the naval heroes Kanaris, Miaoulis, La Bouboulina, wreathed themselves in glory.

Incapable of crushing the Greeks singlehanded, the Ottomans appealed to Mahomet Ali, Sultan of Egypt, who was beholden to them. In 1827 Rechid Pacha recaptured Athens despite the magnificent defence organized by one of Napoleon's ex-officers, Colonel Fabvier, who had been won over to the Greek cause. Bloody reprisals ensued, but in the West public opinion was roused. Lord Byron organized the defence of Missolonghi, and perished there of fever, whilst in *Les Orientales* Victor Hugo depicted the Ottoman atrocities—"The Turks have passed this way, leaving ruins and death in their wake...."—and Greek courage:

> *Friend, said the Child, the blue-eyed child of Greece,*
> *All I ask is powder, powder and shot.*

At last, on the 20th October, 1827, forcing their governments' hesitant hands, the French, English, and Russian fleets destroyed the Turko-Egyptian fleet at Navarino. And on 3rd February, 1830, Greek Independence was officially recognized by the European powers, and the Greek crown entrusted to the King of Bavaria's second son, Otto.

THE RECONQUEST—At birth, the young "Kingdom of Greece" was incomplete, since only a small number of her provinces had been liberated and the majority of Greeks were still oppressed. Consequently, the liberators' first concern was to deliver their brothers by a series of wars, which happily resulted in independence for nearly all the Greeks. Thus in 1864, on the occasion of George I's accession to the throne as head of the New Dynasty, the Ionian Islands were united to the kingdom; in 1881 came the turn of Thessaly and part of Epirus; in 1913 another part of Epirus, Macedonia, Western Thrace, the Aegean Islands, and Crete; in 1920 Eastern Thrace; and finally, after the last world war, the Dodecanese.

Greece courageously played her part in both world wars. In the last war, she held the Italians at bay, and Italy had to appeal to the Germans in order to break down Greek resistance. Hardly had she begun to rise from her ruins, than a terrible civil war was unleashed upon her. Pacified by Marshal Papagos, under the reign of King Paul and Queen Frederika Greece, now presents to the world the picture of a young and energetic land. Thanks to her youthful spirit she can face the future with a smile, and lightheartedly bear the burden of a sumptuous past which is still her greatest source of wealth.

A FEW DEFINITIONS

AMPHICTYON: A kind of League of Nations before its time (probably more efficient). Its origin was traced back to Deucalion's son, Amphictyon. There were several Amphictyonic Councils in Greece, but the most famous was that of Delphi, which grouped twelve cities. At the beginning of Greek History the Amphictyons played an important political role. Later they dealt only with questions of a religious nature.

AREOPAGUS (hill of Ares): A hilltop near the Acropolis and, in a wider sense, the Assembly that used to meet there, comprising both a kind of Senate and a supreme court. The Areopagus was composed of retired archons, and maintained an aristocratic character within the bosom of the Athenian democracy. Under Pericles' reign, its prerogatives were restricted.

DIKASTERY: A section of 500 members of the people's tribunal or Helius. Each case was tried by a dikastery drawn by lots the same morning, in order to ensure against corruption, and presided over by an archon.

LITURGY (Literally, *public service*): An astute Athenian method of reducing the State's expenses by consigning them to the richest citizen. The main liturgies consisted of trierarchy, or equipping a trireme, and choregy, or the organization of public entertainment. Generally speaking, the citizen so designated made it a point of honour to discharge his liturgies as handsomely as possible. He could, however, refuse, on the grounds that another was richer than he. The new nominee then had to perform his duty, or exchange his fortune with his predecessor.

METIC (Literally, *outside the house*): A foreigner established in Athens, where he could ply his trade under the protection of special laws, but was obliged to pay more taxes than the citizen, without enjoying any political rights.

OSTRACISM: An Athenian custom fostered by Clisthenes to forestall the return of tyranny. Whenever a citizen's actions or merits threatened to make him overpopular, the people had the right to exile him for 10 years. The sentence was originally inscribed on an oyster-shell (ostrakon): 6,000 votes entailed banishment (which by no means implied dishonour or confiscation of possessions).

DRAMA
AND LITERATURE

DRAMA AND LITERATURE

THE soil of Greece might well be termed the literary sanctuary of the human race. But, once it is stripped of the prejudices fostered by ignorance, routine, and—what is worse—pedantism, the fearsome respect it always inspires (known of old as "holy terror") is readily transformed into friendly familiarity. Erudition is by no means a prerequisite for admittance to this charming temple. Quite the contrary: all one need know is that Greek writers amassed the fortune on which modern civilization—deemed ungrateful and spendthrift—is still living.

There is no imagining what would have become of the history of thought, not to mention art, if in the distant past a Balkan peninsula flanked by a handful of islands had not, throughout a thousand years, sheltered a small predestined people who taught "mankind to sing, to think, and, in fact, to speak...." For the Greek language is still one of the basic elements of every European tongue, and even today it helps to form a great many words used in science, industry, and medicine. Despite the confusion of Babel, Greek is the cement that holds together all the international and universal elements in our languages. As the great linguist Meillet said: Europe's common vocabulary is built entirely on Greco-Latin foundations, i.e., an extremely hellenized form of Latin.

Needless to say, we have no intention of outlining a course in philology at this stage. However, it should be pointed out that—although English-speaking people arriving in Greece may at first be disconcerted by the Greek alphabet, the sound of everyday speech, the headlines in the papers, the printing on posters—they should all bear in mind that, willynilly, they carry a great deal of Greek in their heads. Melancholy, democracy, telegram, evangelist, polytechnic.... yes, it's all Greek. And, were Greece not one of our linguistic forebears, hundreds of other simple words—cream, pain, pheasant, paper.... to mention only a few of the most diverse and familiar words in our native tongue—would not be as they are. We mention this banal fact in order to impress on every civilized man that, in visiting Greece, he should not feel completely out of his element.

Homer and Calliopes (Louvre)

THE GREEK LANGUAGE—There are historic reasons to explain why the Greek way of speech is the most beautiful in the world. As much as twenty-two centuries ago, Greek was no longer a turmoil of dialects. It had already been reduced to a common language, *koine*, and the Eastern Mediterranean as a whole had adopted it as an auxiliary tongue, and as the literary and administrative language. In fact, it left its mark on all the countries bordering on the Mediterranean; even in Provence, the rare Gallic inscriptions to be found are in Greek characters, or interspersed with Greek words. Latin, as spoken by the Romans, was intermingled with words from Greek rhetors and philosophers. The Christian scriptures, drawn up solely in Greek, popularized the former pagan tongue to such an extent that it wormed its way into the soul of the entire West. What is even more extraordinary, ancient Greek continued to be spoken throughout the Turkish occupation of ancient Hellade. Although as far as the common people were concerned it became an artificial tongue, it never fell into disuse. Consequently, when the country was liberated in 1827 there was no need to revive the language: it simply had to be reinstated in literary and official circles. Nowadays we all know the Greeks have two forms of expression: popular speech (*demotic*), and the language of the purists (*katharevousa*).

However, there is only a shade of difference between the two. The notices in the underground between Athens and Piraeus could be read by a contemporary of Plato, or of Cleopatra at least. Anyone with a classical education would require only a brief initiation in order to understand the newspapers.

But this continuity would be contrary to nature, had the vitality of Greek not been assured by another persistent trend: as in German or Italian, articulation and phonetics have advanced hand in hand throughout the ages. On considering the rapid—and often disastrous—way in which the English, and even French, languages develop, we respectfully bow to the language of Homer which, after two and a half millenaries of maturity, is as young as ever, whilst the texts provide a solid guarantee against decrepitude. On entering Greece, one should say to oneself: "Now I am in the domain of the incorruptible, the eternal."

In order to revive all the memories of ancient literature, we should have to

Dancer from Myrina (Louvre)

41

Ulysses and the Sirens (British Museum)

follow the itinerary of the Scythian described by the French priest Barthé-lémy at the end of the 18th century in his *Voyage du Jeune Anacharsis en Grèce*. The young Barbarian's travels reputedly led him through the land of gods, heroes, and great writers. He encountered Plato chatting with his disciples at Cape Sounion, Sophocles staging his version of Antigone in the theatre of Dionysos, the poet Pindar in Thebes, the poetess Sappho in Lesbos, and Xenophon the historian in retirement in Elis where he used to organize hunts. The book served as a manual of Hellenism for several generations. Since then, modern travel has assumed such proportions that it should in turn give birth to similar works.

But it should not be forgotten that the sphere of Greek civilization spread far beyond the present limits of the kingdom of the Hellenes. It encompassed Thrace and part of present-day Macedonia, a large sector of Asia Minor, Egypt, and Sicily. By birth, Greek writers often belonged to territories which are no longer officially Greek. It is therefore not surprising that, in order to take a census of them, we have to ransack the entire Eastern Mediterranean.

This is substantiated by the fact that the great periods in the literary history of the Greeks correspond to widely diverse geographic centres.

The most ancient goes by the name of Iono-Dorian, since it spread across the Asian shores known as Ionia, and encompassed the great writers who flourished in the Aeolian Isles, as well as the Dorian poets from the Peloponnese, scattered throughout Sicily. This first period began a thousand years before our era and endured until the end of the 6th century B.C.

The second period is described as Attic; it represents the golden age of the 5th and 4th centuries B.C., centred round Athens and Attica, the unforgettable hub. Every style of literature and every mode of thought achieved perfection therein.

The third, or Alexandrinian, comprised the following two centuries, during which the Greek world expanded, thanks to the primacy of the Macedonian kings. Although they subjugated Hellas, they raised Hellenism to the pinnacle of the civilized world. In those days the intellectual capitals were Alexandria, Pergamos, Antioch (now Turkish), Syracuse (now Italian). And, as the famous saying goes, Greece, conquered by the Romans, morally assimilated her fierce conqueror.

Briseis and Achilles (Louvre)

Hermes, Orpheus, and Eurydice (Naples)

The next six hundred years, from the 1st century B.C. to the 5th century A.D., embraced the fourth, or *Roman* period. By that time literature was no longer rooted to a specific soil—hence the predominance of abstract or didactic writings by historians, philosophers, orators, and theologians.

This period naturally opened the door to the Byzantine era, which extended through the Middle Ages. Although comparatively little known, except to specialists, it was extremely fertile. It witnessed the birth of countless chroniclers, encyclopaedists, and jurists who rank in the history of the human mind; but their writings remained a closed book to Europe, who was still waiting for Hellenism to sow the seeds that were to germinate in the Renaissance of the 16th century.

Beginning with the Homeric age, and continuing through that of the Paleologist emperors, we have covered a triumphal span of two thousand years. It would then be no exaggeration to proclaim Greece and her literature the champions of endurance and models of longevity. No civilization or literature of today would dare to challenge such a record.

HOMERIC POETRY—All literature begins with poetry. If the legends are to be believed, Greek poetry was born in Pieria, a mountain range forming the northern foothills of Mount Olympus. It then moved on to Boeotia (whose

44

ill-repute is hard to justify), where Apollo and Mars were said to dwell on Mount Helicon. It first took shape in the guise of religious lyrics, attributed to illustrious masters who may never have existed. Orpheus and his brother Linos were priests or initiates. We all know that Orpheus lost his young wife, Eurydice, set off to claim her in hell, lost her again, and was himself massacred by frenzied Maenads. But he survived mainly through the Orphic hymns ascribed to him; they resemble the great Hindu poems, glorifying a kind of Pantheist god, sovereignly good and fertile. And then came Thamyris, the poet to defy the Muses, the demi-goddesses of poetry, who put out his eyes for this sacrilege.

As early as the 9th century B.C., the Greeks colonized the Asian shores facing their peninsula. The ensuing wars engendered epic accounts of the heroes' exploits: hence the cycle celebrating the war of Troy or that of Ilion which took place in Anatolia, north of Smyrna. The Homeric poetry it inspired thus originated in Asia. The name is derived from that of the

Homer (Louvre)

fabulous blind poet Homer, whose birthplace is disputed by as many as seven towns. Many tales are told of his misfortunes as an orphan, his travels as an infirm beggar, and his success as a wandering minstrel, but they are of symbolic value only. Homer was probably a Smyrniote, although attempts have also been made to demonstrate that he came from Chios, the Greek island off the Ottoman coast, famed for its excellent wine. Be that as it may, Homer flourished on the borders of the Hellenic world, and the *aedes*, or narrative poets who succeeded him, travelled mainly round the archipelago.

For Westerners such as ourselves, the *Iliad* and the *Odyssey* have retained a human element, a

45

romantic limpidity, and a wealth of symbolism with which no other primitive epic can vie. Compared with the German *Nibelungen* or the Finnish *Kalevala*, there is an appreciable difference. These old fables can be

read time and again, like adventure stories, or philosophic essays, or psychological studies, for each of them rings true. Homer is probably the most easily intelligible and rejuvenating author of any nation—the universal master, and this is the secret of his worldwide popularity.

His successors, the rhapsodes, merely botched heroic tales, embroidering endlessly on the theme of the wars of Ilion. From them were born countless poems woven from mythology and history, known as cyclics; few masterpieces have survived, but they served to inspire the great tragic authors and the Latin poets, not to mention the romance-writers of the Middle Ages.

HESIOD—Hesiod is the greatest name of the following period, which dates approximately from the 7th century B.C. Though his father came from Asia, Hesiod belonged intrinsically to the mainland of Greece. He prided himself on being a Boeotian peasant, steeped in the atmosphere of farm life, and boasted that he had sued for his rights like peasants all the world over. He is primarily known for his great poem, *Works and Days*, a treatise on agriculture, skilfully portraying the life of beasts, plants, and the men of

Hesiod (Vatican)

the soil. It forms an anthology of moral truths, expressed with the eternal wisdom of a virile mind, as ageless as Nature herself.

Hesiod is also given credit for the *Theogony*, a history of the gods and of their only too human rivalries. This mythological epic doubtless served as a textbook of religious instruction for believers, and developed into a series of picturesque fables for poets and philosophers. Literary tradition has conserved the gist of it throughout the ages. Hesiod thus deserves to be venerated as a creator of immortal images which even the Christians have adopted to symbolize the dreams and passions of mankind.

POETRY—After this era of impersonal poems began the age of individual lyrics, sung to the accompaniment of flutes and zithers. Thanks to their talent and their artistic minds, it was really the Greeks who invented all we know about melody, choral singing, polyphony, etc. The art is believed to have been born in Phrygia and Lydia (Asiatic provinces again). It triumphed in Lesbos at the dawn of the 7th century B.C., and then conquered the rest of Greece. The elegies, odes, war ballads, moral and sentimental songs, the dithyrambs, paeons, and parthanaea compose a museum rich in masterpieces, despite the mutilation it has undergone. The masters of each of these styles have found their way into legend or history: Amphion, who charmed the very stones with his lyre; Arion, who was saved from a watery grave by an entranced porpoise; Alcman, who, when enslaved in Sparta, learnt from the birds the art of singing; Alcaeus, the political conspirator and warrior who, voluptuous to the last, begged to be anointed with perfume even on his deathbed; Sappho, who fell prey to more than one type of love, and reputedly hurled herself into the sea from the Leucadian rock when spurned by handsome Phaon; Anacreon of Teos (another Asiatic island), who faithfully served the tyrants in Samos and Athens, where he sang so sublimely of sensual pleasures that for fifteen or twenty centuries thereafter he was echoed by Horace, Ronsard, Omar-Khayyám, Fong-Che, and all the Chinese poets....

Side by side with these great poets in a minor key, the names of the founders of official lyricism are usually inscribed: Simonides, who was almost Athenian but lived in Sicily; and above all Pindar, the glory of Thebes, who was forty years old at the time of the Battle of Salamis in 480 B.C., and whose triumph was such that in his lifetime he was already a classic. In his *Odes to Victory*, this great poet and moralist established a definite pattern for pure lyricism. His name is the emblem of civic enthusiasm, sublime style, and bold but harmonious genius.

HERODOTUS—Greek prose made her debut as early as the 6th century B.C. Her world-famed philosophers and scientists form a chain of ever-burning torches along the road of thought: Thales, Anaximander, Pythagoras—who also came from Samos, and lived in Greater Greece, that is to say Southern Italy and, like Confucius, founded a quasi-religion—Heraclitus, Parmenides. And then there were the chroniclers or logographers, the last and most famous of whom was Herodotus, the true father of history. He was born in Asia, at Halicarnassus, and hence Ionian. Having travelled widely in Asia and Africa, been welcomed to Athens by Pericles himself, and witnessed the building of the Propylaea in the Acropolis, he may be regarded as the synthesis of the Greek mind at the dawn of the great classical age. In his *Histories*, abounding in trifling details and sweeping truths, mingling *naïveté* and critical wit, picturesqueness and austerity, he is the most amusing and intelligent of chroniclers. This reminds us of the fabulist Aesop who, a century earlier, embroidered anecdotes into stories with a moral, by no means lacking in humour.

DRAMA—But it was in the 5th and 4th centuries B.C. that Greek genius reached its apogee, and Athens was the focal point. It was exactly as if the gods had decided to make this tiny State the sanctuary of literature and art, under the safeguard of a refined and enthusiastic society, and a population of aristocrats. Endless wars and serious political crises in no way hindered the city of Pallas from exercising her intellectual hegemony: Atticism, named after Attica of which Athens was the capital, still remained the symbol of clear thinking and perfect taste.

For two hundred years Greek literature became an apanage of Athens. It was made famous by the birth of dramatic art which, as elsewhere, developed from religious rites, inspired by a gloomy, barbarous mythology in which the poets sought the human element. The great feasts in honour of Dionysos and Bacchus were popular entertainments as much as religious ceremonies; the authors of Greek dramas also wrote tragedies and opera scores, and were probably producers as well.

Sappho Playing on her Lyre (Louvre)

Herodotus (Naples)

TRAGEDY—The three great names immortalized by the history of tragedy are: Aeschylus, Sophocles, and Euripides.

AESCHYLUS—This nobleman from Eleusis fought in the two Median Wars against the Persians, rose to glory, and died in Sicily, his land of adoption. He composed eighty plays, seven of which have survived intact, together with a number of fragments. Although his tragedies were merely a form of cantata for several voices, they attained perfection. Horror and tenderness, greatness and simplicity vie with each other in *The Persians*, *Prometheus Bound*, and *Agamemnon*. It was Aeschylus who painted Greek mythology for us in its symbolic colours, providing an inexhaustible fund of superhuman types and human truths.

SOPHOCLES—The poet laureate Sophocles was born at Colonus near Athens. This great public servant was a friend of Herodotus. To all accounts, he had an active amatory career. He died at the age of ninety odd, and the city erected altars in his honour. Universally acclaimed as the perfect tragedian, he is credited with 123 plays. Through Sophocles' pen, Electra, Oedipus, Antigone, Philoctetes, and Ajax are even more alive today than if they were people of flesh and blood. He puts us on familiar terms with superhuman greatness, in a purified world, which, though fired by noble passions alone, still bears traces of human nature; his treatment of great themes, in which mortal will matches with fate and pity with rancour, are beyond compare. Sophocles is at one and the same time a stirring dramatist, a high-minded philosopher, and a bold but sensitive lyricist—a poet to the finger-tips, eternally envied by his successors.

He alone is capable of expressing pity, sadness, the joy of living, and love, in one and the same breath.

EURIPIDES—Euripides was a native of Salamis, where he reputedly came into the world the very day when the enemy fleet waged the famous battle. He was one of the first strictly professional writers; after an unhappy marital life, he left Athens for Macedonia, where one of Alexander's predecessors was already attracting the great Greek artists, and there he died. His works comprise a score of tetralogies, making a total of at least 80, and possibly 92 plays. He brought the art of tragedy back to earth by transforming the legendary heroes into simple mortals, and at times he seems to vent his irony on the situations created by an archaic tradition. Helen, Hecuba, Iphigenia, Medea, and Andromache play the female roles in his repertory, whilst the curious male characters Hippolytus and Ion inspired the French classics *Phèdre* and *Athalie*.

Euripides had a truly modern outlook; he loved to discuss new ideas, and had a weakness for sentimentality and situations with a colour of truth; in short, he all but invented popular drama. In the space of a century Greek

Dionysos arriving in a Theatre (Louvre)

tragedy was already completing its cycle, and whilst second-rate plays and authors had abounded for the past two hundred years, this religious art, rapidly secularized, was on the decline. One of its offshoots was a more colloquial, almost comic type of "satyric" drama in which less sublime characters appeared on the scene—ogres, tyrants, satyrs, and cyclops—paving the way for the great comedies.

COMEDY—They also descended from the Dorian or Megarian peasant farces which provided entertainment during the feasts of Bacchus. Even Sicily had her share, Epicharme being the most famous. But it was Athens who brought comedy to a fine art, and yet succeeded in conserving its extravagant plebeian character, quite out of line with the scholarly conception of Greek literature formed in later years.

Aristophanes, who died at the beginning of the 4th century, almost gave his name to this refined but unbridled form of wit. He was primarily a political polemist who flouted fashionable ideas and men in high places—especially the democrats, and even Demos, the King Populo in person.... Plato depicted Aristophanes as a kind of Rabelais: easy-going, liberal-minded—not to say a free-thinker—blessed with an easy tongue and a fertile imagination. Eleven of his forty-four comedies have survived. To this day, the *Birds*, *Lysistrata*, and the *Assembly of Women*, continue to inspire imitations and adaptations. *Clouds*, *Wasps*, and *Peace* also paint a vivid picture of the customs and intrigues of two and a half millenaries ago and—paradoxically—this pamphleteer was also a great lyric poet, comparable to Shakespeare in this respect.

After Aristophanes, comedy became an agreeable portrait of customs, as we now see it—similar to modern "comedies of manners"—and its best exponent was Menander. The works of this elegant Athenian, epicurean, libertine, and "man-about-town" have disappeared. But it is certain that in this sphere too, Athens prefigured the whole art of modern drama.

PHILOSOPHY—Athens also created every form of serious literature: eloquence, philosophy, didactic works on science, medicine, history, art, and technology. It is therefore no surprise that every branch of civilization flourished within her shadow.

Athens witnessed the birth of the sophists, rhetors, and dialecticians who taught men the art of reasoning. They were, of course, preceded by the

Theatre of Epidaurus

great philosophers whose doctrines have survived better than their writings: men such as Heraclitus (of Ephesus in Asia) and Parmenides (from Greater Greece, like his successor Zenon) gave a definite form to the most abstract ideas of God, Being, the mutable and the immutable—in short, they originated all the controversial metaphysical ideas.... But the Socratic school of the 5th century was renowned for great writers as much as great thinkers, and even in the previous generation Democritus of Thrace, who lived in Egypt and Athens—a materialist and positivist before his time, and the inventor of atomic theory—acquired far-reaching fame as a stylist.

PLATO—Socrates was not himself a writer, but his disciples made up for this. Plato, the fountain-head of human thought, was the first. He was noble, rich, and a good citizen, but not very democratic. After witnessing his master's execution, he went into exile in Italy and Egypt, where the dictators welcomed him with open arms. He returned to teach in his homeland, where he apparently died during a wedding feast—which, by the way, was not the divine *Banquet.*

Sophocles (Lateran Museum, Rome)

Thirty dialogues and letters go to make up his work, in which the most exquisite familiarity, theatrical and romantic sense vie with masterly dialectic. In Plato modern religions sought their spiritual substance, which this pagan seemed to secrete like a premonition. It was Plato who gave a form to spiritualism and theism (which he freed of the crass legends of mythology), and to the theory of knowledge founded on the vision of pure Ideas as perceived by the Soul in eternity. Phaedrus, Phaedo, and Parmenides are as lastingly popular as any novel, and the *Republic*, in which the author describes the intellectuals' ideal city, is the dream of every social reformer to this day. In Renan's words, Plato was the best exponent of "the sacred music of thinking minds".

XENOPHON—His disciple—not to say emulator—Xenophon was an ex-warrior, and general of the Greek mercenaries that Cyrus raised against his own brother, hence a Persian soldier; he even fought in the Spartan camp against his homeland, Athens. After his fall, he was subjected to live in Olympia and Corinth. He died in about 350, after recording his theories and experiences as a philosopher, soldier, and great proprietor, and portraying his master Socrates in four famous tomes, including the *Memorabilia* and *Apologia*. His memoirs as a condottiere, the *Anabasis*, and his treatises on politics and economics combine severe criticism of Athens and a eulogy on Sparta. Under the name *Cyropaedia* he composed the first novel, in which he attempted to describe the young King of the Persians as a faultless monarch. The Greeks did not cry treason, since Xenophon's clear and simple art raised Atticism to the summit of realism, and, as a historian, he was second to Thucydides.

THUCYDIDES—This eminent Athenian mine-owner, an aristocrat to the finger-tips, and a general in his day (an office held by election), was also exiled by the demagogues and died in Thrace, doubtless assassinated. He found time to relate the Peloponnese War—which lasted over twenty years. In contrast to Herodotus, he is the historian pure: objective, even though bound to his party, a marvellous critic of facts and analyst of causes. Moreover, his addresses, which have been reconstituted, prove him to be a master of eloquence. He had a number of disciples and imitators such as Ephor and Theopompus, who was the first to conceive a *Universal History*, and whose glory was likewise universal; but their works are known only at second hand.

ARISTOTLE—The 4th Hellenic century was, in fact, renowned for its philosophers, the most illustrious of whom was Aristotle. He was a Greek born in Macedonia—then enemy territory; brought up in Athens, yet tutor to King Alexander; pursued as a traitor by the democrats, yet head of a school in democratic Greece and respected by the tyrants, he died in exile in Chalkis, Euboea. Though the fifty treatises he left were on very varied subjects, they form the cornerstones of ancient and modern philosophy. His prodigious mind embraced every subject, from physics to psychology and politics to natural sciences, including even aesthetics and literary criticism; this explains why for twenty centuries scholars have universally acclaimed him as erudite, dialectic, rich in concrete views and abstract theories. One might venture to say that human thought would not be what it is were it not for Aristotle. Two thousand years after his birth people were still debating in his name, and even today philosophers refer to him without false shame. This ex-patriate alone would have sufficed to raise his nation to glory.

ORATORS—Athenian eloquence in the 4th century assumed every form; judicial, political, and professorial alike. The amazing thing is that none of the subjects it touched on has waned in any way. It is universally agreed

Aristophanes (Louvre)

that the orators of those days attained the height of clarity and order, elegance and pathos in their speeches. The refreshing pleadings of Lysias, a Syracusan transplanted to Athens, are as entertaining reading as a short story by de Maupassant. He brings to life a whole world of delinquents as vivid as if they were tried only yesterday. Isaeus is on a par with him, but he concentrated on civil offences. Isocrates, the son of a flute-merchant, and an acquaintance of Socrates, lived to be over a hundred; he rose to the pitch of delivering great addresses in praise of the soldiers who fell on the field of honour, and preaching unity to the Greeks, if only under the hegemony of the former Barbarians from Macedonia.

Demosthenes bequeathed a great name to political history. This stammering son of an Athenian gunsmith eventually became the patron of orators. He led or inspired the anti-Macedonian party, shared their successes and defeats, and poisoned himself when captured by the enemy. He was a passionate, fanatic, and loyal hero (although accused of being corrupted by the Persians), and the greatest of demagogues in the true sense of the word. His public harangues were even more moving than his addresses to the court.

His ally Hyperides, a carefree youth famed for his greed and his passion for the courtesan Phryne, and his friend Lycurgus, the prince of lawyers in his day, were almost the equals of Demosthenes. His enemies (the most renowned of whom was Aeschines, clerk of the court, an impecunious actor, and possibly a foreign agent) were scarcely inferior to him, and their common talent has now reconciled them in the memory of mankind.

Thus ended a peerless golden age which coincided with the liberation of Athens, and extended through Greece whose frontiers were widened by Alexandrism: subjugated by the Macedonian, she became the mistress of the world, and even her conqueror, Rome, could not do other than follow her school.

STOICISM AND EPICUREANISM—Greek literature then thrived in several centres: apart from Athens there were Alexandria in Egypt, Pergamon in Asia Minor, Antioch, Syracuse, Rhodes, and Tarsus—not to mention the Phoenician and Carthaginian towns. Everywhere schools of rhetors and philosophers prospered, rivalling the Athenian Lyceum and Academy (the name has since been adopted by innumerable modern institutions, although they were simply the gardens or rooms where the disciples of Plato and Aristotle used to foregather). It was then that the doctrines of Stoicism (or the Porch), propounded by Zenon, a Cypriot scholar, and Epicureanism, founded by Epicurus, a professor of Samos and later Athens, spread throughout the world. There is far less difference between the two schools than is generally believed, since both were based on rationalism, and both preached moderation in pleasure and resignation to pain. In the third century less refined philosophers, the cynics or sceptics, gave definite expression to the tendencies of the human mind which have since been named after them. Here, as elsewhere, Greece held the torch.

Plato (Vatican)

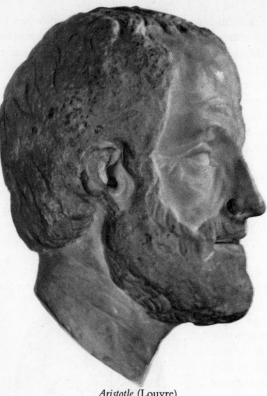

Aristotle (Louvre)

THE ALEXANDRIAN ERA—In the Alexandrian era all the secondary arts—grammar, geography, erudition, physics, and mathematics—also flourished under the general heading of literature, not forgetting the novel, which originated in the form of amusing fables or mythological tales (the "Milesian fables" for instance, typify what we now class as broad jokes), and were to meet with great success in the West.... Minor poets—composers of amatory poems or farcical dialogues—also began to appear, such as the Sicilian Herondas. Another Sicilian, Theocritus, brought into vogue the pastoral idylls which eternally enchant townspeople and scholars by their portrayal of rustic life and communion with nature.

The glory of Theocritus alone would suffice to extol Alexandrinian Greece, but it is magnified still further by Bion, Moschos, Meleager, the Asiatics, and all the passionate or licentious poems which have been collected throughout the centuries in *Anthologies* (literally "collections of flowers"). The higher forms of lyricism and obscure poetry also made their appearance in this era (Lycophron is the famous champion), as well as personal lyricism and sentimental poetry which have endured to this day, outliving the tragedies, epics, and the great set odes.

PLUTARCH AND LUCIAN—For all that, Alexandrian Greece was not yet on the wane. She witnessed the translation of the Bible into Greek (the *Septuagint* version), and the birth of a great historian, Polybius. This soldier from Arcady, held hostage in Rome—where he became a friend of the Roman generals, including Scipion himself—travelled widely throughout Gaul and Africa, and was probably the first to conceive history as a positive science. He recorded the death of free Greece, and acclaimed her resurrection in the Roman universe.

After him Diodorus of Sicily, a great scholar, contemporary of Augustus, and Strabo of Asia Minor, a contemporary of Tiberius, became the masters of critical history and human geography: later scholars have simply expounded their principles; the Jewish chronicler Philo who settled in Egypt and remained loyal to his race despite terrible persecutions, and Flavius-Joseph, his co-religionist, extolled in Greek the greatness of Israel, her misfortunes and divine predestination as the chosen race. Thus the influence of Greece gradually spread in political as well as religious spheres.

Little Hellas—Boeotia and Cheronea where the Greeks met crushing defeat—gave birth to Plutarch, a subject of Trajan and Hadrian who was fêted in Rome. His *Parallel Lives*, and his religious, moral, and scientific essays gave the second century of our era the synthesis of civilization.

This encyclopaedically minded polygraph has served as professor to humanists for fifteen hundred years, and as a mine of information for every adept of Greco-Latin culture. In his field he is on an equal footing with the greatest men of all time. The contrast to this historian of heroes

Demosthenes (Vatican)

is Lucian, the Syrian Voltaire, the type of man of letters—one might even say journalist—who had no respect either for mortals or for gods. One might think he wrote for a world that was dead, but no, he was contemporary with Marcus Aurelius, the emperor who used to write in Greek, as did Hadrian and Julian the Apostate. Literary Greek still had centuries to live.

PLOTINIUS AND JOHN CHRYSOSTOM—There is no end to the list of authors who continued to honour her until the 4th century, through the decline of paganism and the rise of Christianity. Although the myriad apologists, doctors of theology such as Justinius and Clement of Alexandria, bantering poets, novelists, philosophers, scholars, philologists, and rhetors, now live only on library shelves, they still haunt the Elysian Fields of the mind. The neo-Platonist Plotinius would seem to have put pagan mysticism on a footing with the new form of spirituality, whilst moralists and theologians such as Gregory of Naziantium (in Asia) and John Chrysostom (of Antioch) brought the religion of Christ to the borders of ancient wisdom. Christian Greece, or Greece on the road to Christianity, composed the archives of great writers. In fact John Chrysostom, patriarch of Constantinople, exiled by the empress Eudoxia, figures as a confessor, and indeed almost a martyr.

THE BYZANTINE ERA—This scholar opened the door to Byzantine Greece, traditionally known as the epilogue of Hellenism proper. There remained a number of poets, dons, chroniclers, and above all religious orators, not forgetting a handful of philosophers surviving from the old Academy, some still mystical, some already scholastic. But the world had changed, and whilst the West was in the throes of the Middle Ages, the Greek intelligentsia was withdrawing into the monasteries of the East.

She did no more than slumber. The whole of Europe was awaiting her awakening, and for seven or eight centuries our Middle Ages honoured her without knowing her. The Renaissance rediscovered her without effort.

And since that time it is impossible to travel across the soil of Greece, and to land on an island or a shore of the peninsula, without stirring up the ghosts of all those who taught the West to appreciate beauty and seek for truth.

Aesop and the Wolf (Vatican)

MYTHOLOGY

THE GODS

in Greece	in Rome
ZEUS	JUPITER
HERA	JUNO
APHRODITE	VENUS
HERMES	MERCURY
HEPHAISTOS	VULCAN
APOLLO	PHOEBUS
ARES	MARS
ATHENA	MINERVA
POSEIDON	NEPTUNE
DEMETER	CERES
ARTEMIS	DIANA
HADES	PLUTO
EROS	CUPID
HERAKLES	HERCULES
ASKLEPIOS	AESCULAPIUS
DIONYSOS	BACCHUS
KRONOS	SATURN
RHEA	CYBELE
KORI *or* PERSEPHONE	PROSERPINA

AND THE HEROES

THE GODS ARE NOT YET DEAD

Paganisme immortel, es-tu mort? On le dit;
Mais Pan ne le croit pas et la Sirène en rit.

Art thou dead, immortal paganism?—So would they say;
But the Siren mockingly laughs and Pan cries nay.

THESE verses from Sainte-Beuve are the calm, irrefutable reply of every poet's heart to the terrifying voice that announced the death of the God Pan on the eve of the ancient world. No, the great Pan is not dead, nor have the Gods of Greece been swathed in a "purple shroud", to be buried without hope of awakening in the stark silence and rigid peace of their marble tombs. No, the gods are not dead and the very soil that gave them birth evokes them beneath the splendour of a sky which makes them vivid and familiar to us.

BIRTH OF THE GODS—At the first dawn the poetic imagination of the Greeks, their youthful sensitivity, their instinct for all that is divine, and their natural piety begot all the Gods they were to honour and serve from the wonderful scene that nature unfolded before them. In their youthful eyes everything on earth, under the earth and in the skies vibrated with life; everything around them was animated by a divine and active force, which they felt pulsating within them like the vitality in sap. This divine force appeared to them not only in the waving of trees, the flowers in the fields, and the orchards fragrant with fruit; they sensed its power in the sparkle of the springs, the song of the brooks, the cool of the woods enchanted by singing birds, and even in the inviolate silence of the steep mountains crowning the wild but august land of Cybele, mother of the first Gods and wild beasts.

THE GODS OF NATURE—Every spring spurting forth from the depths of the earth or the hollow in a rock was a bright-eyed Nymph, a fair Naïad pouring water to quench the cattle's thirst and refresh the weary shepherds with a cool drink. Streams and waterways were regarded as Divinities who nourished the soil and the plant life which clad it in springtime. In the forests and underwood, the Dryads or guardians of the trees used to dance in the moonlight. The Hamadryads, who lived in the bark of fir trees, came to birth and died simultaneously with the tree they chose as a home; they felt every blow of the woodcutter's impious axe, and avenged themselves to the full. The mountain slopes and summits tormented by the winds were inhabited by Oreads; these mountain Nymphs escorted Artemis whenever the chaste huntress ventured through their wild and rocky kingdom beneath the glowing moon. That elusive sprite, the fair Nymph Echo, always eager to chatter, repeated their cries and replied without respite to the barking pack unleashed in pursuit of startled doe or deer.

The shepherds' pipes one hears in the Greek mountains inevitably recall the sound of the reeds on which Pan used to play, to tease the Nymphs and entice them into his rocky retreat. In the depths of the valleys and gorges, he used to accompany the songs and dances of the Napaea who dwelt in the wooded dales. When the wind whistled through the pine forest, the shepherds in the Arcadian mountains thought they heard the pipes of Pan. To quote a Homeric Hymn, "No one can surpass the song of his pipes—not

Poseidon, Dionysos, and Demeter (Parthenon Frieze, British Museum)

66

Battle between Gods and Giants (Louvre)

even the bird whose gentle melody wafts through the leaves when spring blossoms. To the sound of his flute, the Mountain Nymphs hasten to the edge of the murky spring, and inspired by his song their voices resound to the very mountain-tops. Pan himself joins in their frolics and gambols back and forth, trampling the flowers into the lush meadow beneath his charmed feet." As guardian of the flocks, he used to wander through the thickets, pause beside a carefree brook, scramble up the steep rocks and survey his flocks from the summit. At night-fall he would regain the fold, playing on his pipes an air befitting the mellow witching hour. Beneath the arresting heat of high noon he would slumber in the shade of a tufted oak, whilst his herd, weary of seeking for pasture beneath the scorching sun, clustered beneath a nearby tree. Woe betide the shepherd who ventured to ruffle the God's siesta with the sound of his pipes! The horned brow, cloven feet, and bushy beard of Pan would suddenly appear, and his voice would ring so fiercely that the tactless pastor's herd would disperse, panic-stricken, amongst the rocks, and flee along the thorny track through a cloud of golden dust. When winter constrained the shepherd to laze beside the hob, warming himself at a fire of vine-shoots, yearning for the return of blossom-time, he would while away the hours by modulating on the flute the airs Pan had played to him in the valleys and woods.

THE GODS OF THE SEA—Since every aspect of nature was deified, from the poetry of plant life and the copses of rustling leaves, so were the sea and her blessings, her shifting scenes, and her sparkling, magic grace. In a country whose regions were more often than not divided by tall mountains, the sea was more than a mere watery belt. Winding deeply inland and scooping out long waterways, she opened up trade routes and carried the mariner right into the heart of the country.

The divine king of the waters and the absolute ruler of the empire of the seas was Poseidon. So great was his strength that with a blow of his trident he made the waves swell, shook the foundations of the earth, wrenched up mountains and scattered their fragments over the waters, forming barren islets and solitary rocks girt by a pliant belt of salt foam. His wife was the divine Amphitrite, who left her palace in the watery depths to wander with her august spouse through the vast expanses of their joint realm. Their chariot was drawn by horses with bronze feet, and golden manes floating in the winds. The sea-monsters emerged from their retreats and gambolled around them. Astride Dolphins, Nereids with tresses of seaweed and Tritons blowing conches heralded the arrival of this brilliant retinue. The jubilant sea smoothed her billows, and the horses glided so swiftly that the briny waves did not even moisten the bronze axle of the chariot bearing the king of the waves and the queen of the open sea across the azure plain.

Were the sea as blue as the sky or as green as an emerald, it was the sea God, Glaucos, reflecting the subtle shades of the Grecian sky. Should she change in colour or aspect, it was Proteus, the old shepherd of the elusive waves perpetually varying the face of the waters. And if, on a clear and radiant day, the sun spread a cloth of gold over the glittering sea, it was Aphrodite beaming at the calm waves from which she emerged.

Pan (Louvre)

THE GODS OF THE SKY, AND OF NIGHT AND DAY—Zeus the all-seeing was the God of day, the mighty author of all the phenomena enacted in the ether. He had power to darken the sky at will, gather clouds, unleash storms, hurl his lightning in every direction, make the dread thunder roar and shake the earth to its foundations. The heavenly bodies which served as night's apparel and brightened the day—the Sun, the Moon, the Evening and Morning Stars—were also Gods who travelled each day through the azure skies, or twinkled in the velvet shade of every peaceful night.

The very winds of north and south, east and west, were Deities who brought in their breath heat or cold, malefic drought or beneficial rain.

TREES AND FLOWERS AS GIFTS OF THE GODS—Fertilized by the Sky, the earth gave birth and nourishment to every living being. Beasts and plants alike sprang from her maternal womb. Each Divinity planted his own tree and made it thrive. The olive tree came from Athena; the laurel grew to wreathe Apollo's brow and the Muses' locks; and the heavily laden vine was Dionysos' gift to unhappy mortals, bringing them oblivion of their worries in the joy of drunkenness. The flowers too were a divine gift; they sprang up in Aphrodite's steps as her dainty feet, emerging from the briny waves, advanced across the enchanted sands on the seashore.

ANIMALS AT THE SERVICE OF THE GODS—Like the trees and the flowers, the beasts also played their role in respect to the Divinity who had chosen them to serve him. As Sappho sang, the swift wings of cooing doves swept through the air "the golden chariot bearing immortal Aphrodite with her blissful smile". The owl, with its sea-green eyes glowing in the shadows, watched over Athena. The peacock, whose lustrous plumage recalls the splendour of the starry night, was the companion of Hera, the Goddess of the Sky. Poseidon reigned over the horses whose fiery gallop dragged him over the waves, which also came under his sway. That tireless huntress swift-footed Artemis drove with her a barking pack. Zeus despatched an eagle with wide red wings to carry his thunderbolts into the sky. And lastly, the song of the nightingale was so pure that it enchanted the Gods themselves. In a chorus in *The Birds*, Aristophanes extols this prodigy in the following words: "When from thy wild throat, clear melodies unfurl, the unsullied echo of their notes vibrates above the leaves, to the very throne of Zeus. When

golden-headed Phoebos hears thy voice, he answers thy plaint on his ivory lyre, and the Gods form choirs again and lead the chorus. Then, from their immortal lips the divine joy of the songs of the Blessed rise in unison."

THE GODS AS GUARDIANS OF HUMAN EFFORT —Just as the produce

Poseidon Chastising the Giant Polybotes (Bibliothèque Nationale, Paris)

70

of the Earth and the marvellous celestial phenomena were due to various Gods, the work of man's hands and mind were aided and abetted by them, and hallowed by their divine examples. Demeter, the Goddess of harvesting and tillage, taught the human race to live on bread and abandon their wild ways for family life. In discovering the vine and wine, Dionysos initiated mortals in the creative and lyrical joy which was one day to give birth to Greek tragedy by

Zeus (Vatican Museum)

inspiring Aeschylus, Sophocles, and Euripides. Athena, not content with making the olive grow and choosing its boughs as a symbol of victory and peace, also invented weaving. For this reason, during the feast of the Panathenaeans, a sacred peplos woven by the patient hands of the most skilful sempstresses in the city and adorned with the richest of embroidery, was consecrated to Saint Pallas, the patron of Athens. This grey-eyed Goddess also protected Attic pottery, and was credited with discovering the potter's wheel. Hephaistos, or Vulcan, the craftsman who forged the great Achilles' armour, the Sun Chariot, and Zeus' throne on his anvil, was revered as the God of blacksmiths. The herdsmen honoured the God Pan and played the flute, as he did, to prevent their flocks from straying.

Trade was protected by the Wind God, Hermes. Thanks to the swiftness of his winged heels he became the messenger of the Gods, presided over athletic games, and assembled souls with his wand, to drive them along the road to Hell. The music of the breezes in fields and woods inspired him to invent the lyre. By dint of imitating the voices of the forest on its sonorous chords, he became the God of oratory eloquence. Ever on the move, he directed the winds which swelled the sails, protected merchants travelling from one trading post to the next, safeguarded markets and trade routes

by land and sea. As God of bargaining, he blessed avid traders with glib tongues to convince or dupe buyer and seller alike.

Like agricultural labour and daintier handicrafts, intellectual work also enjoyed religious and divine consecration. The Muses presided over poetic creations, works of the mind, and the arts which ennobled and glorified life.

Athena, the peaceful and serene, guided intellects in quest of wisdom, set an example of moderation, calm courage, clear and serious thinking. By uniting the dance, music, and poetry, Dionysos created the art of tragedy, let the mind give vent to its enthusiasm, and opened the way to exultant lyricism and divine inebriety. Crowned with laurels and marching to the sound of his golden zither, Apollo accompanied the dances of the Charities and the song of the Muses. He was the God of poetic inspiration, the God of the prophets and wise bards, the creator of the rhythm of seasons and days; at daybreak his zither awoke the song of nature and conducted the eternal harmony of the universe throughout the livelong day.

THE GODS WATCH OVER THE HOME AND THE STATE—The Gods also reigned over Greek cities and families. Hestia was present in the fire in the hearth. As guardian and queen of every household, even the humblest, she assured harmony and stability, peace and goodwill; her benevolence was extended to each guest and stranger who crossed the threshold. Like the households, the cities possessed an altar where the holy fire of Hestia burned for everyman. The soul of the city took its spark from this fire, and each time a town set forth to found a distant colony, the sacred flame lit at the communal hearth accompanied the bold colonists. Zeus' chaste wife Hera—the model of womanly fidelity, inclined to be jealous only because her love got the better of her—safeguarded the laws of marriage and preserved the newborn.

Each city had its acropolis, to shelter the temple of her tutelary God and preserve the cult of the victorious Hero who had founded and valiantly defended her.

The moral qualities that make for generous hearts and minds also had their divine protectors. Athena, for instance—the warrior virgin armed from head to foot, whose gilded lance announced the approaches of Athens to sailors rounding Cape Sounion—detested any form of cruelty, and her magnanimous heart knew how to restrain the warlike ardour of her intrepid yet placid soul. One day, so the legend runs, when valorous Tydeus was mortally wounded during a lengthy battle, the indomitable Goddess Athena implored Zeus to intervene in his favour. From the all-powerful Sovereign of the Heavens she obtained a remedy which would not only heal and save him, but render him immortal. She then descended to the battlefield, where she found Tydeus in the act of wreaking the most inhuman vengeance. The head of his enemy had been brought to him, and after breaking the bones of the skull in a blind fury, Tydeus was devouring the gory head like a bloodthirsty barbarian! This hideous sight horrified the judicious Goddess. Instead of accomplishing her mission, she turned her back on the brutal soldier and sped her footsteps further afield.

Birth of Athena (Louvre)

73

REVELATION OF THE DIVINE THROUGH BEAUTY—In the beginning, the soul of the elements did not have a form of its own. It was only by a gradual process that artists and poets gave this nondescript soul a shape befitting the different aspects in which it was manifested. The Greek landscape was so beautiful in their eyes that they could only imagine, conceive, and create Gods in harmony with the pureness of contour of a countryside modelled each day by the subtle glow of a light which accentuated the minutest details. In creating his Zeus of Olympus in gold and ivory, Phidias was merely expressing in plastic form the majestic, forceful beauty, the perfect equity and the calm, compassionate gentleness that Homer described in the face of the Father of both Gods and mortals:

"With his dark eyebrows, Zeus gave a sign of assent. The Sovereign of the heavens shook the ambrosial locks on his immortal head, and mighty Olympus tottered."

After Phidias, in their marble statues of Gods and Goddesses Polycletus, Lysippus, and Praxiteles achieved the formal beauty and typical expression preserved for eternity in the irresistible grace of Aphrodite's lovely arms, the supple, robust elegance of Hermes' youthful body, the athletic vigour of warlike Area, the ecstasy of Dionysos with his long curls, and the poetic, dreamlike quality of Apollo.

To house the divine images incarnated in ivory or gold, marble or bronze by these gifted Greek artists, innumerable temples were built—in the citadels defending the towns, in public squares, and on headlands invisible from afar. In the sacred precincts of Delphi and Olympus, temples were erected one beside another. In their silent, leafy depths the grottoes in the woods concealed delightfully naïve representations of grotesque Satyrs and bright-eyed Nymphs, to ensure that the springs flowed plentifully and freely, that the sap rose in the trees, and the meadows blossomed in spring.

Everywhere the mind of Mother Nature and Man were closely inter-woven; the fertility of the land, the whim of the seas, and the dazzling mirage of the sky all illustrated the intimate union between the arts and divine forces. A religious, poetic harmony reigned on all sides, bringing the world the revelation of the Divine through the Beautiful, and confirming in advance Goethe's meditation on the fact that each monument of Greek antiquity was a pledge of faith: "Men are creative in poetry and art only as long as they are religious." The magnificence of the festivals in honour of Zeus in Olympus, Apollo in Delphi, and Poseidon on the isthmus of Corinth served only to enhance this revelation of God through beauty.

THE RELIGION OF MYSTERIES—In the philosophic era, this religion of the poetic age was in time to become a religion of practical wisdom and profound thought. Priests and philosophers used the legends of Gods and Heroes as a symbolic basis for their doctrines.

The rites previously performed in Saint Eleusinia to make the corn grow more quickly and revive the tarnished ears, were changed into Mysteries of perpetual life and immortality.

Just as after a sojourn in the earth the grain ploughed into the furrow received new life from the united forces of the Earth and the Heavens, Man's soul buried in the earth was also reborn and returned to the world of light. This doctrine of immortality found expression in a sacred drama based on the following legend. Demeter had a daughter, Kori, who was spirited away by the King of Hades. Stricken with grief,

Dionysos with Satyr
(Louvre)

Demeter wandered night and day over hill and vale in quest of her daughter. But none of the mortals she encountered could show her where her darling child was hidden. And then at last the Sun, who sees everything, revealed that Kori had been carried off to Hades. On hearing this terrifying news, the Mother of Harvest refused to let a single ear of corn grow, or a grain take seed. In vain the oxen toiled, in vain the harrows dug the seeds into the parched soil. Nothing grew; a burning sun devoured all the seeds, and the countryside was threatened with famine. The entire race of mortals would have perished had not Zeus taken pity on Man's distress and sent his messenger Iris to Demeter. But the bereaved mother gave free rein to her resentment and adamantly refused to let the harvest grow anew until she had found her daughter again. Zeus then mediated with Hades, the gloomy God of the Nether Regions, who allowed Kori to return to the light of day, bringing with her flowers, corn, and fruit. Mother-Earth, called Demeter, became Goddess of the corn that grows and ripens in the fields; her daughter Kori, that of the grain that disappears under the earth in wintertime but reappears with the coming of spring, in the form of new ears that ripen in summer, assuring an annual harvest of corn, dancing in the sun.

This Mystery of regenerated corn awoke an acute sensation of immortality in the Greek soul. The mere sight of an ear of ripe corn sufficed to teach the initiates of Eleusis that, whilst each plant contains a seed which makes it survive, each man possesses a spirit of life which renders him immortal. This certitude, acquired by analogy, gave the initiate the tranquil courage to live joyfully despite the trials in store, in anticipation of another happier destiny—dependent on his comportment in this life, just as a fine harvest depends on the sewer. "For initiates alone," Aristophanes exclaimed, "the sun shines in all its smiling radiance."

Pindar and Sophocles in turn declared: "Oh, thrice-blest are the mortals who depart to Hades after contemplating these Mysteries. They alone are capable of living there; for the others, there is nothing but suffering in store."

After carrying Kori off to the Underworld, Hades took her to wife. Under the name of Persephone, she reigned beside him over the people of the Dead who flowed unendingly into the eternal night of the Underworld. Everything death harvested on earth fell under Hades' sceptre, increased his wealth and became his prey. The bronze gateway to his empire was guarded by a three-headed monster, Cerberus; his keen dark fangs, his collar bristling with hissing vipers and his triple snarling jaws were enough to prevent anyone who crossed the threshold from retreating. After crossing the rivers and muddy swamps of this gloomy kingdom on a bark piloted by Charon, the souls presented themselves before the throne of Hades. There, beneath the eyes of the dread God whose memory conserves the minutest detail and whose mind penetrates the deepest thought, the souls were judged one after another. Three assessors, Minos, Aecus, and Rhadamanthus, helped him to pronounce a just verdict and make the punishment fit the crime. Those who had lived saintly lives were despatched to the Elysian Fields, a smiling plain, protected from the wintry cold and the torrid summer heat—a billowing plain steeped in kindness and serenity by a light even more transparent than that which still returns each summer to bathe the Attic countryside in a pure glow. Inhaling the perfume of myrtles and roses in the shadow of silvery poplar trees, joining in conversation with the sages of all the times gone by, hearing the poets sing their

Hermes Criophoros
(Museum of Fine Arts, Boston)

finest verses, they lived free from worry and care, sharing for ever the blissful joy that makes the Gods happy and content. As for those who had sullied themselves with crimes during their life on earth, the least guilty atoned for their sins pending their return on earth, where they would be

Sacrifice to Apollo (Louvre)

granted a new life and have the choice between mending their ways or completing their ruin; the most perverse and the incorrigible offenders were hurled into the depths of the Tartarus.

Whilst Kori was deified by the initiates of Eleusis, for the adepts of his stirring and consoling Mysteries Dionysos also symbolized rebirth and resurrection. Although the vine dies after the autumn grape-gathering, it comes to life again once spring floats back on the breeze. Moreover, in the poetic imagination of the Greeks, the very history of wine gave birth to a sacred drama. When the grapes produced by the earth are fat enough to be picked and cast into vats, the divine life that brought them to maturity does not die in the fruit that has been culled. The press crushes the grapes and converts them into a foamy liquid; the filled jars are buried in the earth as in a tomb. There the soul of Dionysos is preserved and intensified; by way of the wine it mingles with men's souls, helps them to unite with the God

78

and share all the thoughts and creations of his eternal drunkenness.

Zeus himself, the ancient Master of Daylight, came to be considered by the sages as the supreme God, the father of all the Gods, the king of mankind as a whole, the creator and organizer of the universe, and—by the fire of his thunderbolts—the relentless avenger of the inviolable order he had established according to equitable laws. Through his omnipotence, Zeus had created everything that existed since the beginning of time. The universe was filled with his magnificence; everything was governed by the omnipresence of his authority; everything was contained within the splendour of his infrangible unity, and all the benefits the Gods enjoyed were made available to us through his bounty.

THE LIFE OF THE GODS IN HOLY OLYMPUS—Zeus and all the other Divinities of Greece lived on the summit of Olympus, in a series of marvellous palaces surrounded by gardens. The winds never battered this blessed spot, and the gilded roofs of these immutable homes never heard the tempests dash against them. Pure, buoyant air enveloped them in serenity, and the limpid caress of ethereal light brought the sweet, transparent glow of eternal spring. Each God had his

Demeter of Cnidos (British Museum)

own palace there. The most glorious was that of Zeus. Each morning, when Aurora's rosy fingers opened the sky to unleash the Sun horses, all the great celestial Gods foregathered in Zeus' home. Seated on a·raised throne, their Sovereign Master received them in the most spacious hall in his beautiful dwelling. There they grouped round him like children seated round their father's hearth, revelling together in eternal bliss. And to illustrate their infinite joy, they were said to be seated at a perpetual banquet. The brilliant, golden-haired God Apollo charmed them with the strains of his ivory lyre. Clad in flowers and crowned with roses, the Charities dances on the lawns. The fair-complexioned Muses sang such melodious choruses and songs that all the Gods listened in rapt silence. As a restful change from song and dance, Hebe, a charming slender-limbed maiden, offered the guests ambrosia and

nectar in a cup of gold bringing them eternal youth and instilling in them the strength to watch untiringly over the government of the worlds and mankind. Such was the daily round of the Gods, who whiled away the hours in the family circle. Then, when night set fire to the stars, they returned to their respective homes, and mighty Olympus was steeped in sleep. The only light in the world that can still evoke the transparence and hue of the air suffusing the city of the Gods on Olympus, is the limpidity that wreathes Athens at sunset with a garland of

Herakles and Cerberus (Louvre)

violets, clothing the slopes of Hymettus and its outstretched rocky summit in a cloak of amethyst and dusky rose.

HERO-WORSHIP: HERAKLES—In Greek antiquity, hero-worship was not entirely dissimilar to the Christian cult of saints. Like the saints, the Heroes were the guardians of cities and of men, patrons of the fatherland, and foster-fathers of the soul of a race. They were also considered as man's intercessors in regard to the Gods, and their tombs and relics were venerated by the public. And, as if from the heights of a pagan Vatican, it was often the voice of the Oracle of Delphi that decreed whether such and such a Hero deserved to be worshipped, whether statues should be erected to him, and ceremonies performed in his honour, and whether the life and deeds of the person Apollo placed on the altars should be cited an example.

Apollo (Olympia Museum)

Encouraged by Delphi and extolled by the bards, Hero-worship spread throughout the land of Hellade. Each city and each district venerated its mighty dead. Each guild and corporation had its guardian, like the patron saints of today. The poets not only chose as tutors legendary Heroes such as Linos and Orpheus, but they also worshipped Pindar, Aeschylus, and Sophocles. The philosophic sects "heroized" the great philosophers who had founded them. Anaxagoras, Plato, Aristotle, and Epicurus himself became veritable objects of worship.

Of all the Heroes, the best-known and most admired was Herakles the great. Without over-denaturing the symbol of his legendary life, his adventures, and his numerous exploits, sages and moralists alike took it

81

upon themselves to derive a lesson of combative energy and material for moral instruction from his marvellous life and his twelve works. They glorified him as a benefactor of humanity, a righter of wrongs, an untiring lover of justice who never hesitated to place his courage and strength at the service of Right, to avenge offences swiftly, and to repress iniquity of any kind. "Herakles was wise," said Maxim of Tyre, "not for his own account, but in order that his wisdom should spread throughout the earth. Was he not the exterminator of monsters, the chastiser of tyrants, the liberator of slaves, the guide to independent spirits, the model of righteousness and truth?" As a symbol of the virtues portrayed in his life and legend, Herakles is to this day the dauntless example of generous, altruistic actions.

Thus do the Gods and Heroes continue to survive. They are still as vivid in Man's mind as they were beneath the bright sun which revealed them on Hellenic soil. Since ancient times, poets' songs and artists' dreams have prolonged their existence through all time. The Gods of Greece have become one with us; they ornament the gardens of Versailles, bring magic into the copses, joy into the meadows and vineyards sung of by the first poets. Through her intelligence, the goddess of Athens continues to teach reason, clearsightedness, and lucidity, and the gentle charm of Aphrodite never fails to inspire every living creature with the tenderness of love and the need to create, to reach the height of joy in renewing the youth of every race, the enchantment of souls, and the ineffable charm of corporal beauty.

Indeed, the Gods are not dead. . . .

THE ARTS

THE THREE ORDERS

DORIC

IONIC

CORINTHIAN

IN GREEK ART

Court Ladies (Candia)

AEGEAN ART

WHEN Sir Arthur Evans discovered the Palace of Knossos in about 1900, he literally danced for joy on the excavations. The importance of his discovery was, in fact, comparable to that of Schliemann on the site of Troy. Guided by intuition alone, these two poets of archaeology had braved the legends, the German challenging the Iliad, the Englishman affronting the Minotaur.

Little was known about the history of Aegean civilization, but it has bequeathed sufficient vestiges of its genius to be referred to as a prelude to the "Greek miracle". However, this miracle is confined to two centuries, whereas Aegean civilization endured over a thousand years. The ancient Minoan culture dates back to the beginning of the Third Millenary, and it was approximately between 2,000 and 1,400 B.C. that the Cretan world produced a wealth of palaces, frescoes, and works of art indicative of refined minds and a luxurious way of life. Then, after the decline of Cretan hegemony, the Dorian invasion carried the Aegean style as far as Mycenae.

Vestiges of primitive art found in the Cyclades show idols in the shape of violins, or oval masks with neither eyes nor mouth, topping comically misshapen bodies; two stylized figurines from Athens Museum, a piper and a flutist, would not be out of place in a museum of modern art. In Crete, on the other hand, one finds skilful potteries dating from the Neolithic Age, decorated with geometrical patterns that suggest kinship with Egypt and Babylon. Vases soon became works of art, assuming the form of an animal, or decorated with ornamental motifs in a wide variety of colours. Outstanding masterpieces are the Rython, or Bull's Head (steatite) found in Knossos, and the Herakleion, or Octopus Vase (Candia Museum). In sculpture and painting alike, the Cretan artists were amazing portraitists. They captured the very movements of the beast, wild and tame, and the figurines of startled chamois and heavy-jowled bulls found in Candia are as full of life as the blue monkey from Haghia Triada, lying in wait in the papyrus. The most charming motif of this kind is the wild goat suckling her kid, on a bas-relief in faience (Candia), and the most forceful is the wild bull hunt and the peaceful scene of tame bulls on the golden goblets of Vaphio, in Athens Museum.

There is no really monumental sculpture, but only small statues in alabaster or ivory, such as the ivory acrobat in Candia Museum, or vivid scenes such as the return of the harvesters, singing and chatting, depicted on steatite vases. The bronze figures are lithe and erect; one of the statuettes (in Berlin) was called the Dancing-girl.

The frescoes, too, impressed the discoverers by their modernity and when they brought to light the young Minoan with saucy eyes and mouth, in the manner of Toulouse-Lautrec, it was only natural they should name her *La Parisienne*. The palaces of Crete were more comfortably and hygienically equipped than Versailles under Louis

Vaphio Vase (Athens)

Prince with fleurs de lys (Candia)

Applied Ornament on Bronze Amphora (Athens)

XIV; the Cretan mode of life hints at a love of finery, wit, and easy living. Thanks to their wealth, they were able to ornament luxuriously the walls of the great halls and red and black porticos.

In Knossos there was a fresco 180 feet long depicting a procession of 500 people in double file. Candia Museum conserves fragments such as the vase-bearer, painted red on a yellow background; the wind-swept dancer; the court ladies in low-necked, blue-trimmed dresses bedecked with jewels and embroidery. The highlight of the collection is the bas-relief in painted stucco portraying an elegant prince surrounded by *fleurs de lys;* his long, agile legs seem to glide between the flowers. The fragment depicting the bullfight, in which three acrobats dance round a leaping bull, is of later date.

Little is known of Aegean rites, of which those fascinating bare-breasted goddesses, brandishing snakes, are an ominous presage—and even less of Mycenaean history, which has given way to legend. All we know is that it is a continuation of Cretan art. The dogs are blue, the trees red, but the resolute hand that traced the drawing on the fragment from a fresco found in Tiryns (Athens Museum) might well belong to a poster artist or decorator of today.

One of the golden masks with a fine moustache and half-closed eyes, discovered amongst the "treasures of Atreus" near the Lions' Gate in Mycenae, is said to represent Agamemnon. Another of these masks is a highly successful caricature.

The damaskeened daggers inlaid with gold or silver are decorated right to the tip with hunting scenes or wild cats chasing ducks (Athens Museum).

ARCHAIC PERIOD

IN the span of two centuries, the sculptured characters slowly come to life, gradually losing their stiffness, as if, from one statue to the next, the body were awakening in its chrysalis of stone. Marble muscles ripple, limbs become lithe, and a smile brushes the lips. The first examples from the 8th and 7th centuries B.C. present human blocks standing rigidly at attention; the style is as conventional as that of Egyptian statuary. One wonders if the idols, such as that of Artemis erected in a temple in Delos by a lady from Naxos, were not all copied from the same model, in the image of those stiff wooden figures known as *xoana* which have disappeared all but in name. In classifying what remains of archaic art, seeking trends and tracing co-ordinates between Dorian and Ionian style, Attic genius soon comes to the fore, as the flower of Greek genius.

The Cretans had already learnt the art of elongating bodies, and the sculptors of the Aegean Isles later followed suit. The gaunt lions of Delos evidently pleased the slender princes whose elegant silhouettes stray amidst the lilies and

Kori (Athens)

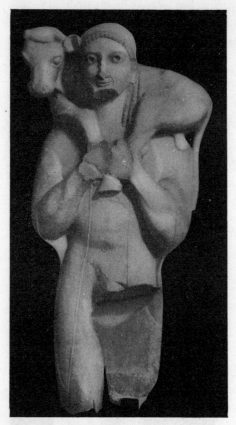

The Calf-Bearer (Athens)

irises in the frescoes of Knossos. But the "Dorian" current brought from Anatolia the fashion for squat, hefty forms. In achieving the synthesis of strength and elegance, Greek art became synonymous with harmony.

The islands, aloof from the bloodshed and quarrels but ideally placed to enrich themselves by trading, played an important role in transmitting oriental inspirations which, though difficult to define, sowed the first seeds of a vocation. In Paros and Naxos the most wonderful marble was available on the spot, and it was often used to make ordinary tiles. According to Pliny, the art of sculpturing marble was born in Chios. And it was also the Ionians who, in the 7th century B.C., originated the art of statuary in bronze, first in the form of individual parts fitted together, and later by pouring bronze round a clay kernel—a technique invented about 620 B.C. by Rhoecos and Theodoros, two artists from Samos.

In the 6th century B.C., numerous workshops were established in Thessaly and the Peloponnese. The artists used to travel from one region to another, as in Renaissance Italy, and it is often futile to classify them according to schools. In the earlier statues, the youth (*Kouros*) and the young girl (*Kori*) look somewhat embarrassed as if they did not know how to pose. But there is a smile on their faces, awkward though it may be. Excavations in Delphi brought to light statues of the twin athletes Cleobis and Bito, dropping from fatigue after bearing a heavy statue of the goddess Hera from Argos. Cleobis, in particular, expresses concentrated strength combined with supple elegance, and his face portrays that bantering gentleness seen in innumerable statues of Apollo, with slender lines and mocking lips.

The young girls are gracefully portrayed with plump cheeks and curly hair; and their veils are draped in coquettish folds above dresses of motley colours. The best conserved example of polychrome sculpture is "Kori 675" in Athens Museum, and the colourful traces of embroidered himation and green chiton conjure up vivid dreams. It is difficult to imagine the Gods of Olympus in the tawdry finery of Polynesian idols. In the classical age not only were the marbles patinated with vivid hues, but the embroideries and even the make-up of the faces sparkled with colourful high lights. Nudes were coated with a light glaze to bring out the warmth of the marble. In the Hellenistic era, gilt was generously used to give an appearance of wealth; under the Ptolemies the statues' marble skulls were adorned with skull-caps of gilded plaster. We might also mention that the bronze-founders had three types of patina—blue, dark-green, black—and the alloy most in demand was *hepatizon* (liver colour).

Two of the most graceful statues of the early groups are the *Moscophoros* (Calf-bearer), and the *Cavalier Rampin* whose head is in the Louvre, whilst his horse is in the Acropolis Museum. The shepherd and the young prince have the same smiling expression.

Theseus and Antiope (Chalkis)

91

Monumental sculpture was mainly confined to the frontons of temples; the triple-bearded Nereus in Hecatompedon (Acropolis Museum) is a typically meridional type of monster. The horrible Medusa prancing beside a panther (Corfu) reappears in Palermo Museum (metope from the temple of Selinus), massacred by Perseus. But let us linger in Delphi. Each town sent her best artists there to give voice to her glory. The Argives erected statues of their athletes, and Naxos a sphinx over six feet long with marble plumage and wings in the shape of a sickle. Sikyon built a votive "treasury" there, and Athens followed suit. As for the people of Siphnos, having just discovered gold mines in their island, they gave thanks to Apollo by erecting a Siphnian temple, surrounded by a heavily ornamented frieze supported by bantering caryatids. On the vestiges conserved in the museum the following episodes may still be traced: Herakles and Apollo quarrelling over a tripod whilst Athena acts as arbiter; Aphrodite fastening her necklace with a graceful movement of the shoulder whilst alighting from her chariot; Mercury guarding Athena's horses; the ladies in the Assembly of Gods, seated in a row as at the theatre, and huddling together to gossip; a homeric battle in which Hector and Menelaus come face to face over the body of a dead warrior; and another battle in which Gods and Giants come to grips. Throughout this lively strip, details are carefully balanced and clever "staging" links each scene to the next.

The fronton of Eretria depicts Theseus triumphantly abducting the Amazon Antiope; the maiden, dressed in a short tunic, is tightly clasped in his arms. Other fragments, especially those in Athens Museum, show how flexible sculptors had become by about 500 B.C., particularly in their treatment of faces: hence the rather pouting expression of the handsome, fair-haired Ephebe, and the mysterious smile on the youthful portraits of Kori.

The funerary steles preserved in Athens provide a series of snapshots of daily life, such as the portrait of the Hoplite Aristion, comfortably posed in his

Golden-haired Ephebe (Athens)

Exaltation of the Flower (Louvre)

starched uniform and brimming over with the joy of living, or that of the runner dancing an athletic ballet. The bas-reliefs of sporting scenes depicting a series of ball games, wrestlers, and hockey-players in action against a red background, were also painted to decorate a funerary stele. Another anecdotic scene shows two men playing with a cat and dog.

THE CLASSICAL AGE
5TH AND 4TH CENTURIES B.C.

WHAT is known as the classical age is restricted to the 5th and 4th centuries B.C., from the presentation of the first tragedies of Aeschylus to the death of Socrates in 399. It may be subdivided into three eras: the Dorian period (first half of the 5th century), corresponding to Spartan hegemony; Attic period (second half of the 5th century), under Phidias' influence; and finally the 4th century, the heyday of the great sculptors Scopas, Praxiteles, and Lysippus.

DORIAN PERIOD (500–450)—After the end of the Median wars the Peloponnese artists began to predominate. The temples of Aegina and Olympus and the sculptors in Argos and Sikyon introduced a cruder, more austere note into Greek art, in search of strength rather than grace. However, we should not be misled by dates, and a number of works attributed to about 500 B.C. (including the Koris in Athens Museum) are some of the most charming, closely related to that graceful "Ionian" style which never completely disappeared. The best example of this is the bas-relief in the Louvre entitled *Exaltation of the Flower*, in which two young girls, smiling at each other, intertwine their naked arms in a floral offering. Another exquisite bas-relief from the Prytanaea of Thasos shows Mercury, jovial and vigorous, in a winged cap, accompanied by a Charity.

On Ludovici's throne (Terme Museum, Rome), the central motif is the birth of Aphrodite, who emerges from her bath between two women who veil her from the waist down. The two "volets" of this triptych consist of the young veiled fiancée and the youthful naked flutist with crossed legs.

After the Battle of Marathon (490 B.C.), the Athenians erected their treasury in Delphi, decorated with a pediment relating the labours of Herakles. This can scarcely be described as archaism, but rather pre-classical style. The faces reflect a look of bliss, like the mysterious expression on Leonardo da Vinci's portraits.

On being discovered in 1812, the sculptures were bought by the Prince of Bavaria, and are now in Munich. The Western fronton, depicting a battle between Greeks and Trojans, outlines symmetrical groups

Procession of the Panathenaeans. Fragment of the Parthenon Frieze (Louvre)

round the hieratic statue of Athena: hoplites, archers, and two wounded warriors extending to the tips of the triangle. The eastern fronton is more damaged, but it still preserves magnificent fragments of the battle, such as the figure of Herakles, with one knee on the ground, drawing his bow. The marble was painted, and certain weapons (the arrows projecting from the wounds, for instance) were of gilded metal.

The mask-like faces often bear the rather disdainful "Aeginetan" smile.

The sculptors in Olympia between 468 and 456 B.C. also favoured a severer form of art in decorating the Temple of Zeus, which was to contain the ivory and gold colossus over thirty feet high, executed by Phidias. (It was abducted by Theodosius, and disappeared in the fire of Constantinople.) On the metopes (in the museum) outlining the labours of Herakles, the ardour with which the hero battles with the bull of Crete is disciplined yet full of violence, and some of the characters are as rigid as columns, as in the scene where Atlas offers the golden apples to Hesperides. The beauty

of the features is presumably due in great part to the search after expression undertaken by Polygnotus and the painters of the period centred round Athens.

Whilst the eastern fronton is peaceful in the extreme, representing rows of characters and objects grouped round Zeus at the betrothal of Pelops, the western fronton expresses the (rhythmic) fury of the battle between Centaurs and Lapithae. Apollo is raising his arm to put an end to the slaughter, and the snapshot shows us it was high time: the Centaurs' hands are already snatching at the naked bodies of the breathless maidens. The genial master who succeeded in stylizing these realistic scenes is certainly worthy to rank with Phidîas.

During this period, other sculptors from Argos and Sikyon gave voice

to a new style in which the search for form introduced greater simplification. The best example is the Charioteer of Delphi, with a body as stiff as a fluted column, and two fascinating silver eyes encrusted in smooth features. It is attributed to Pythagoras, whereas the impressive statue of Zeus (Athens), extending his left arm to hurl thunderbolts on the Titans, is ascribed to Ageladas. The latter work was found in the sea south of Euboea.

Myron of Eleutherios is better known. He studied the rhythm of the body in motion, and his *Discobolos* portrays the young athlete at the moment of supreme tension when the body is

MYRON—*Discobolos* (Vatican)

96

about to turn preparatory to releasing the discus. The impassiveness of the features concords with the rules of perfect mastery. Polycletus of Sikyon sought for the rhythm of ideal proportions in the human body, and he worked out a formula for the golden rule by which he could cast the complete athlete in bronze. His *Doryphoros* and *Diadumenos* are known only through replicas, but he is known to have triumphed over Phidias in the competition of Ephesus, the subject of which was a wounded Amazon.

Flutist from Ludovici's Throne (Terme Museum, Rome)

ATTIC PERIOD (450–400 B.C.)—After the peace treaty with Sparta (446 B.C.), Pericles decided to rebuild on the Acropolis all the shrines destroyed by the Persians; he entrusted the work to Phidias, who had already erected a statue of *Athena Promachos*. With extravagant liberality, Pericles decided to use the treasure of Delos to magnify Athens; all the marble and ebony were immediately heaped on the deserted plateau of the Acropolis, and workshops were established to fashion ivory, copper, and gold. In fifteen years the work was terminated in all its perfection, prompting Plutarch to exclaim: "The wonderful thing about Pericles' edifices is that, although terminated in so short a time, they were of such long duration. Hardly had the finishing touches been bestowed on each of his works, than its beauty imparted to it the character of an antique; and yet today they still bear the bloom and radiance of youth, so resplendent is the flower of novelty that guarantees them against the marks of time. It is as if they housed a spirit and a soul which rejuvenate them unceasingly and prevent them from growing old."

It was on the Parthenon, which has now become a symbol of harmony,

Abduction of a Lapith (Olympia)

that Phidias concentrated the main effort of the students working so homogeneously under his direction. The giant statue of *Athena Parthenos*, in marble, ivory, bronze, and gold, was displayed in the *cella*. Phidias had conceived a grandiose sculptural plan for this perfectly proportioned temple (in which the vanishing point is subtly distorted to enhance the visual pleasure), and its vestiges still form the most beautiful ensemble of classical art. All that remains of the exquisite embroidery is a tattered veil, and Lord Elgin stirred up a hornet's nest in 1810 when he carried off the largest strip, now the glory of the British Museum. But the Acropolis had already been sacked to such an extent throughout the centuries—not to mention the explosion of the powder-mill installed there by the Turks—that his act could well be deemed a precautionary measure to safeguard a threatened work of art. Of the 92 metopes, sixteen are in London and one in the Louvre. Forty remain in place, all lamentably mutilated. The fragments are too disconnected to give a clear idea of the scenes unfolded against a red and blue background, tracing the battle of Amazons and Centaurs. Here and there one can decipher an attitude, and discern the ripple of muscles. But the best testimonies to the vigour and style of the Attic studios are to be found in the monumental frontons and the frieze of the cella executed between 439 and 433 B.C. The subject of the eastern fronton was the birth of Athena, that of the western fronton, Athena's gift of the olive tree and Poseidon's offering of the salt spring. Although beheaded and scarred, the gods and goddesses surrounding the central motif on these two pediments are still highly moving. Ten of the forty have survived (in London). The statue of Dionysos, reclining, has preserved its head. And the bodies of the goddesses, indolently posed beneath their damp veils, are full of grace—especially the group comprising Demeter and Kori, and that known as the Three Fates.

Phidias' original idea was to have a series of pictures illustrating the ceremony of the Panathenaeans running all round the temple inside the peristyle, on a frieze over 500 feet long unfurling round the cella, rather than in broad daylight. The whole town was represented, in every class of society. It was, in fact, described as an ideal mirror, in which all the citizens of Athens could admire their own glorified reflection. Only the west section now remains in place. The rest is in the British Museum, apart from fragments in the Louvre and Athens Museum. These figures, over three feet high, follow the procession which carried the embroidered *peplos* from the Ceramicus Cemetery to Athens every four years. There is the *cortège* of maidens and ephebes, the foreigners (*metic*) bearing offerings on cushions, musicians playing the flute and the zither, chariots, soldiers, and last of all the horsemen cavalcading or preparing to take part in the procession.

Amongst the gods seated sedately like officials on their tribune, Athena, Hephaistus, Zeus, Apollo, and Artemis are to be seen.

Victory Fastening her Sandal (Athens)

99

Whether man or god, their bodies quiver with life. Never was marble more delicately hewn: one can sense the grain of the skin, the softness of the draped veils plucked here and there by a nonchalant hand, and the elusive grace of a half smile flickering across their faces.

The beauty of the Erechtheion lies in its caryatids (what could be more utilitarian than piles intended to support a tribune?—but the master-stroke is the introduction of slender maidens in the place of pillars). The little temple of Nike Athena also owes its grace to its maidens whose veils flutter gently in the breeze. The small statue of Victory fastening her sandal has lost its head, but none of the grace of her figure is lost beneath the skilful Ionian drapery.

Phidias' name is cited in connexion with numerous works scattered throughout the museums of Europe and America. But so little exact information is available that the head in Bologna Museum, now attributed to his *Athena Lemnia*, was long thought to be that of an ephebe. His influence has left its mark on funerary steles as a whole, such as the one reputedly from Hegeso (Ceramicus Cemetery in Athens), in which a young girl takes a last fond look at her favourite brooch before laying it in the jewel-case tendered to her by a little servant-girl, and on the relief showing *Demeter and Persephone* beside the youth Triptolemus (Athens Museum); or that of Orpheus and Eurydice, accompanied by Hermes (Louvre and Naples). The idealized bust of Pericles, one of the first authentic portraits, is attributed to Cresilas; but it was a Dorian, Paionos, who erected the impetuous statue of Victory with windswept veils, heralding the Victory of Samothrace.

PAINTING AND VASES—We shall have to resign ourselves to limiting our knowledge of Greek painting to the enthusiastic descriptions of poets, and scenes on vases. But it is rather like attempting to form an idea of the painting of Jean Fouquet and Chardin from the enamels of Limoges. There are,

Little Jockey (Athens)

Funerary Stele from Hegeso (Athens)

of course, the later paintings discovered in Pompeii. But they are simply a distant reflection from which it is impossible to obtain any details. Fortunately the value of Grecian ceramics is such that, after the geometric motifs of the Orientals, followed by mythological and warlike scenes, a history of civilization is outlined between the great Cretan *pithos* and the perfume urns of the effeminate Alexandrian princes. As early as the 8th century B.C., animal paintings heralded the naturalistic style. First Corinth and then Sikyon prepared the way for the impeccable Ionian vases of the 6th century B.C. Scenes of banquets and funeral ceremonies were soon added to the fabulous tales of the exploits of Herakles, Theseus, or Apollo. The studios of Corinth and Chalkis in Euboea are particularly famous for their vases with black figures against a yellow background. But at the end of the century, Attica boasted the best draftsmen. On the great "Francis Vase" in Florence, Clitias outlined a summary of mythology peopled by hundreds of figures: on the fringe of the procession of Gods at the wedding of Thetis and Peleus may be seen battles such as that of Cranes and Pygmies, or vivid scenes such as that of Achilles coming unaware on Troilus at the fountain. Exechias, who was an excellent animalist, also had a very sure sense of

composition, as seen in his picture of *Achilles and Ajax Playing Dice* or *Leda and Tyndar* (Vatican). But Athens innovated the technique of drawing in reserve, against a black background. These vases painted with red figures were not only an aesthetic improvement; the *hydries* (for water) and *oenochoes* (for wine) were reputed to preserve liquids more efficiently, and improve the flavour. From then on the workshops of Attica were to monopolize the innovation.

Apollo's Chariot with Athena, Mercury, and Herakles
(Bibliothèque Nationale, Paris)

Vases in the "severe", "free", and finally "floral" style, as they were classed in the 5th and 4th centuries B.C., represented subject pictures of horsemen and dancers, as drawn by Epilteos, or more skilful compositions such as the works of Euphronius, who detailed the psychological expression on the faces, and knew how to achieve an over-all effect as in *Theseus Receiving the Ring from Amphitrite* (vase in the Louvre). Hieron depicted courting scenes; Douris, who excelled in scenes of elegance, was also

Hoplite leaving for the War (Louvre)

capable of illustrating epics, as was Brygos, who set off the garments by introducing threads of gold. The art of the painter Polygnotus is reflected in the Penthelic goblet in Munich (*Achilles and the Amazon*), and in the *lecythoï* or small funerary urns with elongated white bellies, on which the defunct was glorified in scenes of his life or his funeral.

THE FOURTH CENTURY

D ESPITE the tribulations of Athens and her cession of political power to Thebes, she lost none of her radiance in the spheres of art and literature. Art—now divorced from the gods, in whom the people no longer believed—became more realistic. Mythology was transformed into a repertory of academic themes, and the artists no longer set themselves up as professors of morality. They preferred Eros to Ares, and at the beginning of the century Cephisodotus represented Wealth in the arms of Peace: *Irene Bearing the Infant Pluto*. It was at this time that theatres built of stone began to replace the old wooden tiers: the most perfect example is that of Epidaurus, built by Polycletus the younger. By introducing a romantic note in raised eyes and bodies arched in suffering or passion, Scopas of Paros heralded the tumultuous emotional effect of Hellenistic sculpture. He travelled widely, from the Peloponnese to Asia Minor. On the frontons of Tegaea he outlined the legend of the Boar of Calydon; impressive fragments of faces have been preserved in the museum in Piali nearby. Together with Bryaxis and Timotheus, at Halicarnassus he was commissioned to carve the tomb of Mausolus (whose portrait has survived in the form of a long-haired statue

PRAXITELES—*Aphrodite of Cnidos* (Louvre)

swathed in tremulous veils), and his *Battle of the Amazons* (British Museum) is both violent and accomplished. The unveiling of an Amazon recalls his finest work, the Maenad in Dresden, whose arched body bursts through tattered veils. His collaborator Timotheus worked on the temple of Asklepios in Epidaurus: the mutilated bodies of the Amazon and the Sea Nymph are full of ethereal grace.

In his statues Praxiteles sought perfection of the body in repose. The only work of Greek statuary on which a name-plate can be placed without

PRAXITELES—*Mercury (Olympia)*

query is his *Hermes of Olympus* bearing the infant Dionysos. The dreamy face beneath ruffled curls, and the rippling body of this "god of Seduction" denote the refined sensuality of an accomplished work of art. It might be styled "art for art's sake", but it is also the political symbol of an alliance between Elis and Arcadia, represented by the gods—a commissioned work. *The Infant Eubouleus* in Athens Museum is attributed to Praxiteles, and *Apollon Sauroctonos* (the lizard-hunter) in the Louvre and the young fawn reclining (in the Capitol) recall Hermes' nonchalant pose. His friendship with the fair Phyrne inspired him to create a new type of sculpture, Aphrodite in the nude. He was in fact the first artist who dared to present a model unveiled, and the way in which she shields her nakedness with her hand is more alluring than chaste.

The Aphrodite (known as Venus) in the Louvre, discovered on the Isle of Milo, and the *Demeter of Cnidos* in the British Museum have both remained anonymous. However, the *Belvedere Apollo* (Vatican) and *Artemis and the Doe* (Louvre) are attributed to Leochares.

Like Polycletus, Lysippus of Sikyon was primarily concerned with carefully thought out studies of the athlete at rest. The most perfect examples are his *Agias* in Delphi and *Apoxyomenes* (the wrestler scratching himself with a strigil) in the Vatican. Apart from studies of Herakles, he betrayed a marked preference for busts of ephebes. As a bronze emeritus, he became official portraitist to Alexander when the latter ascended the throne in 336. The Louvre and the British Museum possess remarkable effigies of this conqueror who opened the frontiers of Asia to Greek art. This Hellenistic era was heralded by the *Victory of Samothrace* (Louvre), depicting a prow-head facing the open sea with its wings outspread to the winds, probably to celebrate Demetrios' naval victory over Ptolemy at Cyprus.

Eros (Louvre)

PAINTING AND CERAMICS—
The finest terracotta figures, as found in Tanagra, Boeotia, and Myrina, near Lesbos in Asia Minor, date from the 4th century B.C. But the art originated in archaic times, and innumerable statuettes illustrating scenes of craftsmen (bakers beside their ovens, breadkneaders, washerwomen at the fountain, hairdressers, etc.) have been discovered in tombs. The careful finish applied to these works makes them minor masterpieces, and some of them still bear traces of a pink or blue patina bringing out high lights in the folds of the gowns and the conical hats of the young women,

Alexander (Louvre)

who are often arranged in charming groups. Led by Zeuxis and Apelles, the painters now turned to portraiture, whilst the urn decorators began to borrow themes from bacchic and theatrical scenes. The mosaic from Pompeii (in Naples Museum) depicting Alexander as a youth at the Battle of Arbeles, at the point where Darius was about to flee on his chariot, is said to be a reproduction of a painting by Philoxenos of Erethria. The fragments that remain are so perfect that it is by far the finest vestige of buried art.

HELLENISTIC ERA—In the wake of Alexander's conquests, in the 3rd century B.C. Greek art extended its sphere of influence as far as the shores of the Indus. The conqueror's prodigious advance left its traces even on the effigies of Asiatic gods, and one comes across disturbing examples of this Greco-Buddhist art, such as the sarcophagus said to be that of Alexander (Istanbul), and that of the Weepers. However, whilst trends inspired by Lysippus and

Antiochus III (Louvre)

Praxiteles are evident in the statues of gladiators and Aphrodites, · the realist trend widened the frontiers of sculpture far beyond the restrained art of the 4th-century masters. Daring, piquant, grotesque, or dramatic postures became the order of the day. As in the spicy literature of the times, eroticism inspired lascivious attitudes in statues of Dionysos and Eros. Scenes of drunkenness, decrepit old men and equivocal urchins were depicted. Some of these subject pictures were really charming, and studies of beautiful female figures became increasingly popular, such as *Crouching Aphrodite* (now in the Louvre).

The curious painted steles of Volo date from this period (3rd–2nd century B.C.). Greece sent her artists to all the new cities that were developing checkerboard fashion on all sides, and thus they became international. The great Pergamos altar from Asia Minor (reconstituted in Berlin) was the monument of an Attalide who wished to commemorate his victories over the Galatians. On a surface nearly 400 feet long and over 6 feet high, official sculptors represented a battle between Gods and Giants. Masters from the Rhodes School worked on the project, and the three authors of the *Laocoon* (Vatican) were also from Rhodes. The latter scene, which aroused immense enthusiasm when it was discovered in 1506, depicts an old man writhing with pain in the coils of Athena's serpent.

Some of the portraits are magnificent, such as the young man with a short beard in Delphi museum, or the energetic features of Antiochus III, long mistaken for Julius Caesar.

The Alexandrian school produced mighty works, like the symbolic

Crouching Aphrodite (Louvre)

Mosaic from Daphni

statue of the Nile (Vatican), and the statue of Ptolemy VI (1st century B.C.), crowned with the Pharaonic tiara, found in Aegina, and the harmonious lines of the peerless Aphrodite (Terme Museum, Rome), found at Cyrene on the African coast, are essentially Greek, even if the actual model was a fair Nubian. The Mediterranean had already become a Roman ocean.

BYZANTINE ART

WHEN the monk-illustrators of Mount Athos illuminated the psalters with miniature scenes representing Jesus against a background of gold, their minds would seem to have been preoccupied with Orpheus and Apollo, and Hellenistic motifs have been deciphered in the Byzantine mosaics. But the style of Phidias and Praxiteles became outmoded once Constantine invented the fig-leaf to clothe antique nudes, and decided to put an end to paganism by the edict of Milan in 313. Like that of Salonica, the Byzantine churches are on a circular plan, roofed with a dome. In Saint George's there are eight 5th-century mosaics of saints in prayer on architecture glittering with precious stones. In Saint David's, the Christ, depicted as a young god with a beardless face, preaches the law, surrounded by symbols of the Evangelists and Prophets. In the church of Saint Demetrius, two votive offerings saved from the 1917 fire include a portrait of a child presented by his parents.

After the Controversy over the Images (726–842), the iconographic arrangement was decided as follows: on the dome, Christos Pantokrator surrounded by angels and prophets; on the pendentives, the Evangelists; on the triumphal arch, the throne of Judgement; in the apse, the Virgin and the communion of the Apostles; on the walls, Christian feasts and full-length portraits of saints.

Kaisariani Fresco

Examples of 11th-century mural mosaics are to be found in Saint Luke's in Phocis, Chios (Nea Moni), Vatopedi, the monastery of Athos (Annunciation), and above all in the church of Daphni near Athens. Sixteen prophets unfurl their banderoles round Christ on high. On the walls the feasts are depicted: the Annunciation, Nativity, Adoration of the Three Kings, Resurrection of Lazarus, Doubting Thomas, Descent into Limbo. In the narthex may be seen the Childhood of the Virgin, and the Last Supper. The harmonious colouring and simplicity of line introduces a vigorous note unusual in Byzantine mosaics. Whilst the finest ancient icons are to be found in Mount Athos, at the beginning of the 14th century a school of fresco painters was founded in Mistra. In Peribleptos the new subject of the Divine Liturgy made its appearance: the angels bearing the instruments of Sacrifice to Christ who officiates at the ceremony; in Pantanassa, Lazarus rises from the dead in a tumultuous scene, amidst a colourful crowd. The walls of the convents on Mount Athos are covered with biblical scenes full of naïve fervour, and the Church of Kaisariani near Athens reveals an interesting collection of 16th-century frescoes. But the imperatives of the Byzantine liturgy are found in all the sumptuous arts; the Byzantine Museum

Fresco from the Vatopedi Convent (Mount Athos)

GREECE TODAY

Megarian Dancers

IN the 20th century the landscape of Greece is just as it was in the days of mythology. Although the forests are sparser than in those happy times when Endymion used to hunt the deer, and the rivers flow less vehemently than in the age when they were gods, the country's peculiar features have in no way changed. The mountains of Attica, the Peloponnese and Thessaly still exist, in the majesty of their bridled proportions and the harmony of their gentle lines; the islands are still there, dotting the blue sea like a shower of marble flowers; the upper regions of the soul still exist in the rocky acropoli dominating the ancient towns of Athens, Corinth, and Argos.

Immortalized by the fable of her gods and the genius of her people, throughout thirty centuries the country has miraculously preserved the same outward appearance as in the days of Homer, Euclid, or Aristotle. Climb the flowery slopes of Hymettus on a clear spring day, and you will find the asphodels and anemones that brush against your ankles are no different from the flowers that decked the paths where Demosthenes paced back and forth 2,300 years ago, meditating over his First Philippic. Land on the shores of the Isle of Myteline: nothing has changed since the days when Sappho composed her elegies and epithalamia there, or Longus chose it as a setting for his Daphnis and Chloe; the same olive trees still shelter those red anemones with which the shepherds used to weave garlands for the altars of the gods. Stroll through the countryside of Thebes in the sunshine of an Attic spring; listen to the song of the bees industriously gathering thyme, and remember that long ago in these regions they deposited on the lips of a child called Pindar the symbolic honey of lyric art, thus destining him to become one of the greatest poets of all time.

The tourist in Greece thus has the double pleasure of visiting one of the loveliest regions in Europe, and at the same time re-discovering the pictures evoked by his classical studies with a semblance of reality. I remember a certain excursion I made in the Mountains of the Meteora, in the company of several devotees of Ancient Greece; we had reached a bend in the pathway from which we dominated the valley of the Peneus, unfurled at the foot of the Pindus range. River though it may be in the eyes of contemporary geographers, the Peneus was once the father of Daphne, the charming

Popular Café in Athens

nymph of whom Apollo was enamoured and who, through her father's intercession, was transformed into a laurel in order to evade the god's advances. I showed one of my companions a cluster of the rosy shrub growing beside the river. "Look," I said to her, "Here is Daphne in person!" Peering through her field-glasses, she exclaimed: "How very moving!" Without the slightest doubt, she had seen the daughter of the river-god.

Port of Piraeus

The survival of historic spots that witnessed the birth of so many charming fables gives Greece an appeal not to be found elsewhere. Of course she has her place in the world of today, and fills a brilliant role in modern civilization; but for all that, wherever one goes in this wonderful country one cannot help seeking vestiges of her ancient physiognomy. And there is no lack of them, especially in scenes of everyday life.

The agora is still the agora. People come and go there, discussing trade, politics, business; the pros and cons cross swords there in tourneys of words in which voices are often raised to the pitch of anger; Maieutics, or Socratic

HOLIDAYS AND COSTUMES

The collection of costumes depicted here is not a set of museum pieces. It forms part of the vivid folklore that comes to the fore in every ceremony, religious and profane alike. This rich attire flutters to the rhythm of peasant dances and unfurls a garland of colour on every patriotic commemoration day and every occasion for rejoicing placed under the sign of Revival.

1–13 ATHENS: 25th March—National Holiday and military review (an Evzone of the Royal Guard).

2 MEGARA (Attica): Easter Tuesday holiday.

3 JANNINA (Epirus): Easter holiday.

4 ISLE OF SALAMIS (Coulouri): Easter Thursday holiday.

5 MENIDI (Acharnai-Attica): Good Friday.

6 GIDA (Macedonia): Easter holiday.

7 RHODES: flower festival.

8 ARACHOVA (Delphi): 23rd April—Saint George's Day.

8 DELPHI: June-July—festivals of folklore and performances of antique tragedies in the ancient theatre.

9 THEBES: 26th July—local holiday.

10 CORFU: 11th August and 12th December, festicals and processions in honour of Saint Spiridion.

11 ANOGIA: 23rd April, 15th and 22nd August —religious and folkloric festivals.

12 SALONICA (Thessaloniki): 6th to 28th September—international fair, festival of music and folkloric dances.

1-13 ATHENS: 28th October—National Holiday to commemorate the 1940 victories; review.

14 LARISSA (Thessaly): 24th November—religious procession.

doctrines, are still, unwittingly, the order of the day; the tradition of stirring up ideas is naturally perpetuated there —without it Greece would not be what she is: the very hub of individual thought.

There is nothing more pleasant than a random stroll amongst these barterers of ideas. You will recognize them as the public of one of Aristophanes' comedies: sharp-witted, subtle, and mischievous spectators whose critical minds relished in satires on customs or jokes at the expense of the powers-that-be; they are still there, all agog, to be sure not to miss a single deed or word of note from which some intellectual profit may be derived. They are avid for knowledge—not so much deep-seated learning as the game of observing the thousand and one details of human behaviour in the thousand and one contingencies of everyday life. Some of them sit for hours on a straw-seated chair outside a café, sipping a glass of water; with their arms spreadeagled across the backs of two nearby chairs, they watch life glide by, or wait for a friend with whom to run a commentary on the lesson of the passing moments.

There is not a country in the world where the little café or *kafeneion* in any town fills as important a role as it does in the tiniest village anywhere in Greece. These cafés supply very little liquor, an occasional coffee, and large quantities of water; Greeks are so fond of water that they appreciate the subtlest shade of flavour. In this country where fountains were deified, people have a definite preference for the water of this source or that, just as the French have a weakness for the wine of such and such a vintage.

You who are visiting Greece to relax and enjoy life in accordance with

Photographers in Front of the Temple of Zeus in Olympia

the precepts of Epicurus, never resist the temptation to linger on a café terrace whenever you need a rest from feasting your eyes on the beauty sights all around you. A few black olives, a glass of *raki* and cold water, a cigarette of refined tobacco from Thrace: there's food enough. In the land of the Seven Sages, food for the mind takes precedence over food for the body. The small cafés of Argolis, Boeotia, Attica, or Phocis, or those on the islands of the Archipelago, are all happy havens for everyone who savours the pleasure of living.

Needless to say, the leisureliness of the *kafeneion* was unknown to the Greeks of ancient times; for all that, they were far from ignoring the joys of drinking, and in fact they gave themselves up to it with an abandon one would be hard put to observe in their descendants. Without a thought of perverting taste, they invented the art of mixing the acrid flavour of pine

Monasteraki Square in Athens

resin with the fragrant juice of the vine, thus concocting *retsinato*, that resinated wine which still delights the distant descendants of the disciples of Dionysos. The origin of the mixture may be traced to the ancient Greek habit of pitching the inside of the goatskin bottles in which wine was preserved. Once the neophyte has overcome the nausea caused by the first sips, *retsinato* can be exquisite, especially if it accompanies a meal comprising rissoles of meat and rice wrapped in a vine-leaf, and goat cheese from the Peloponnese Mountains. Such is the joy of re-discovering Ancient Greece in the streets and squares of Hellenic provinces, and seeing her come to life again in the countryside and the islands where nothing has really changed with the passing years. The same shepherds still graze their flocks on the slopes of Taygetus, Helicon, or Parnassus, and the same skilful mariners defy the winds on the Aegean Sea.

Since time immemorial, the shepherds of Arcadia have been numbered amongst the blest .... Well may the traveller straight from the industrial cities of Europe or America envy the lot of these hermits who spend their lives in close communion with the mountains where the gods once dwelt. From morn till night they tread the grass the Nymphs and Satyrs used to tread; the air they breathe is scented with lavender, and the green leaves of squat holly oaks brighten the slopes where they lead their flocks. Are they really as happy as tradition would have us believe? They have an advantage over city folk in that they while away their days in the setting the gods and goddesses selected for their frolics; they live without a care on milk and cheese from their goats, fermented olives, and fruity oil. They carry a long crook—the original of the bishop's crozier—with which to hook the sheep by the leg. They hardly differ—at least in the life they lead—from the shepherd Acis who fell in love with the nymph Galataea, or the goatherd Daphnis dear to Chloe's heart; and they form a link with the days of the pastorals which, to all accounts, were one of the happiest moments in the history of mankind.

The seamen too bring the present face to face with the past. Sail on the violet-coloured sea that bathes the islands of the Archipelago; land on the shores of the Cyclades, mix with the fishermen busy mending their nets or caulking the hulls of their boats. The mariners of Naxos and of Mykonos have the same virtues as Ulysses' companions or the conquerors of Salamis; the sailors of Canaris are worthy to rank with those of Themistocles; the seamen on the coasts of Epirus or Thessaly are in the tradition of the mariners whose exploits filled the fabulous tales of Ancient Greece. And the gales that batter the boat in which you are bound for Delos descend from the winds over which Aeolus was wont to preside.

Greece is the land where everything recommences, and this is not the least of her charms. She takes care never to start from scratch or innovate in any way. She is ageless; ancient and modern are united within her in such perfect harmony that no one visiting her could escape from the one without at once being recaptured by the other. Besides, for the past 3,000 years without a break she has expressed her thoughts in the same basic language.

The Port of Aegina

Listen to the groups conversing in public squares: it is as if the Greece of Pericles were brought to life again in their speech. The inhabitants of the Eurotas Valley, Hymettus, or the Isles of Euboea and Skyros have command of a vocabulary which permits them to reason as in the days of Aristotle, and preserve the fluency of the language of Plato. The Spartans of the 20th century gossiping on the town *plateia* thus have a clarity of tone and an exactitude of expression hardly different from that which characterized the

Flower-sellers, on Queen's Day, in Athens

speeches of Pausanias; and laconicism still typifies the inhabitants of the *nomos* of Laconia.

However, during the 19th century a strange controversy arose amongst Greek writers, as to whether they should express themselves in archaic language, seeking inspiration in the ancient classics, or in the vernacular. Purists and popularists argued with each other. Should one write in the language of the streets or the language of Xenophon? There were authors who wrote alternately in both languages, according to the subject treated.

The first literary landmark in modern Greece is the *Hymn to Freedom* by Solomos. It dates from 1823, and the freedom of which he sang was that won from the Turks by the heroes of the War of Independence. Poetry made a worthy reappearance in the land of Hesiod and Pindar. Since then, it has continued to surpass prose. The Greek is as poetic as he is patriotic, in character and temperament alike. Costis Palamas is the finest personification of this. This great lyricist, comparable to the finest bards of ancient Greece, glorified his country in poems expressing the hopes of an entire people delving into the epics of her history. Sikelianos, another exalted poet, lauded his race, his soil and his faith in a long poem, *Prologue to Life*. Finally, to mention only the most outstanding names, Cavafis, a poet from Alexandria—where the Greek colony plays an important role—succeeded in expressing harmoniously the feelings of men of today, in the classical language spurned by the moderns, thus giving voice to the spirit of continuity of immortal Greece.

Faithful to tradition, the public throngs to see the ancient Greek tragedies performed on the selfsame sites where they were enacted in the past, in the theatres of Delphi, Epidaurus, or Athens. Sikelianos was the apostle of these productions, at some of which the public was swept away with enthusiasm, imagining itself back in the days of the gods and heroes. It is true that no other theatre in the world could offer a setting as resplendent as that of Delphi, for instance. When Sikelianos produced Aeschylus' *Prometheus Bound* there in 1927, the storm, which plays the part of a real life character in the drama, burst just at the right moment, not in imitation of thunder and lightning, but in the form of a real cataclysm: the public roared with applause.

Cavea Theatre of Dionysos in Athens

Apart from this, modern Greece no longer worships the Muses with the fervour of the Ancients. The Muses are encountered only in the guise of Greek ladies bearing the same names. Some of the latter are as far removed from art, literature, and science as a certain waitress in a café in Kalambaka (Thessaly) which I used to frequent; she went by the name of Terpsichore, and was short and plump; by no stretch of imagination could her gait evoke the Muse of the Dance, her hair was by no means crowned with flowers, and her hand was far from grasping the tray of glasses as if it were a lyre. And yet—such is the miracle of Greece—this Christian name which the clients echoed through the room endowed the good wench with an indescribable mythological quality to which I was not indifferent, and eventually I discovered in her a gracefulness of gesture not unlike the movements of a dance. Christian names such as Calliope, Clio, and Melpomene are common. Men go by names such as Hermes, Apollo, or Herakles; I have never encountered a Zeus, but if one looked hard enough one would be sure to find one. It is, then, true that Greece of yesterday and today forms one and the same country; customs alone have changed, and how could it be otherwise in a people who, after being the first in the world

Street-hawker in Athens

under Pericles and again under Constantine, fell under the Ottoman yoke for nearly four centuries? Although the Greeks strongly resisted, many characteristics of their customs can be traced back to the political influence of a Moslem power.

In remote country regions and villages, the women stay at home and hardly show their faces during public festivals. In village fêtes it is not unusual to see the men dance together for want of female partners. And even when in certain more liberal regions women are admitted to the dance, a handkerchief is held between the dancers' hands to prevent direct contact. Greek husbands are inclined to be jealous—hence their reluctance to see their wives in the arms of a dancer other than themselves. But in all choreographic themes akin to ancient tradition, the women are the first to demonstrate their graceful gait and rhythmic gestures in public in slow, harmonious processions accompanied by clarinets and sonorous drums. The nobility of the spectacle is exalting in the extreme. The songs sung on these ritual days are impregnated with the deep and melancholy beauty of oriental melodies, with occasional half-tones and quarter-tones that wring the heart.

But no description of traditional feasts would be complete without a word on the splendour of the Greek Easter festival: the feast of feasts, the rejoicing of an entire people, an occasion for gifts, vows, kisses, and carousal, when the streets stream with blood as each family slaughters the pascal sheep. In the early hours of the morning of Resurrection, the passers-by greet each other by announcing the great news: "Christ is risen from the dead; verily, Christ is risen." The public is given up to religious rejoicing, the churches overflow, the *pappas* officiate in their richest regalia, the air is filled with the splutter of candles, the smoke of incense, the glitter of gold, and songs of glory. And then the people eat. They eat the lamb roasted out-of-doors on an iron spit or a stake of hard wood. It is Easter-time, the feast of the Resurrection and the festival of spring. They say that the ninth month after Easter is the record month for births in Greece . . . .

Every traveller who has journeyed through the valleys of Attica and the Peloponnese, or set foot on the isles of the Ionian Sea, the Aegean Sea, and the Dodecanese, inevitably harbours in his innermost being memories of the customs and ways of life he has observed there. Through thirty centuries of history, they perpetuate the image of the wisest and most agreeable civilization of all time.

ATHENS

ATHENS

Interior of the Parthenon

ARRIVAL IN ATHENS

O F all the ways of arriving in Athens, the most striking is the famous approach Chateaubriand described in his *Itinerary from Paris to Jerusalem*.

Coming from the Peloponnese, he journeyed through Corinth and visited Eleusis. Then he entered a gorge, passed close by the monastery of Daphni, and wound his way round a little mountain planted right in the middle of the path as if to set off the scene to the best advantage. And suddenly through a gap in the landscape, he discovered the Acropolis resplendent in the morning sun. "My star", he wrote, "had led me along the right path to see Athens in all her glory."

On this side, things have hardly changed in appearance and the route which follows the ancient Sacred Way still affords a superb view of the citadel. It appears unexpectedly, with its buttresses standing out majestically

The Parthenon, East Façade

against the modern town and, monopolizing the landscape, it seems—as Chateaubriand noted—to lean on Mount Hymettus.

This, then, would be the ideal way of approaching Athens, if one could take one's time and respect tradition. And, in order to have a close-up of ancient times, one should first tour the Greek countryside, observe the mythological wonder inspired by a grove of centenarian olive trees, and receive the greetings of the old wives who sit on the village doorsteps spinning their distaffs.

But in our days who can afford the luxury of patience such as this, and who, indeed, would desire it? It is therefore more probable that the reader of this guide will relegate Chateaubriand's vision to the limbo of romance and arrive in Athens by sea or air.

The boat is not a bad solution. The crossing rids us of every care foreign to the journey, and opens up our minds. A sail on the Mediterranean is, in fact, the perfect introduction to a tour of Greek beauty spots. The Mediterranean is herself a landscape of Greece. By this I mean that Hellenic poets and prose-writers have described her time and again. They have discovered in her colours and epithets which dance so vividly in our memories that the dolphin frisking round the ship or the sea-green medusa floating between two waves assume the traits of legendary apparitions.

And then, the approach by sea brings us gradually into the zone of light in which Greece is so characteristically steeped. The brightness of the Grecian sky, above Attica in particular, is characterized both by its soft tones and the clarity it imparts to everything around. Without over-exaggerating the hues like the African sky, it produces a sort of internal glow, brings the countryside to life, awakens ideas. It is not so much a dash of colour as the wave of a wand.

But what does the wand conjure up before us the moment before we land, when all eyes are glued on the Acropolis?—a port which, in the image of all the large Mediterranean ports, is not particularly clean and not particularly tidy. Though we did not expect a vision of marble, we were at least hoping to see the elements of noble architecture; yet all that Piraeus offers is a series of shabby façades.

I know that over the past few years an effort has been made to embellish the port. Demolition and rebuilding have been bordered with flowers. No matter! I am afraid this vestibule to Athens will always be a disappointment to the pilgrim. No one will ever mistake Piraeus for a god!

Another popular way of travelling to Greece is by aeroplane. The first time I flew there I was loth to forgo the

The Parthenon,
seen from the Propylaea

pleasure of daydreaming on an ocean crossing. However, the journey from Paris to Athens by air is in itself a revelation. The porthole unfolds an astonishing film: first we descend the Rhone Valley, where most of the villages still trace the outline of the Roman oppidum, then we graze the sky above the summits of the Alps, cross the Esterel, look down on scenes of Tuscany, the holy roads of Umbria, and finally Rome, a quarry of monuments which has been exploited for the past 2,000 years.

And then the landscape changes, becoming a kaleidoscope of colour. Every hue of blue and green shimmers on the Adriatic Sea, according to the

depth of the water and the shadow cast by the clouds. The Ionian archipelago resembles a herd of wild beasts lying sluggishly in the sun in a shifting pasture. Soon the soil of Greece looms up, reddish and parched like the islands, but more jagged, less accessible—a world apart, a wild headland worthy of the gods and heroes she has engendered.

At Missolonghi we look for a luminous furrow on the surface of the sea. We pass south of Delphi, where a storm is eternally brewing. We fly over Corinth, surmounted by a battlemented wall where Byzantines, Franks, Venetians, and Turks stood watch, gazing down on the oldest temple in Greece.

The aeroplane thus hurtles us through time as well as space. And shortly after, the goal of the journey appears. On a steep, solitary rock the Propylaea and the Parthenon loom up, making everything seem flat and effacing the modern city round them. We realize in a twinkling that this little colonnade is the materialization of beauty. And whilst the aircraft is circling round to land, this hour of suspense weighs heavily, retarding the moment when we can at last lay our hands on "the ideal crystallized in Pentelic marble."

The Acropolis seen from the Hill of the Muses

THE ACROPOLIS

ATHENS is, in fact, the Acropolis.

If the visitor seeks to discover in his innermost heart the echo of Athenian civilization, he should make a daily trip to the Acropolis. There is nothing monotonous, nothing fatiguing about these repeated visits. Every changing hour brings a change of light and a new wonder to admire. This rocky platform, crowned with marble, becomes a springboard from which the mind leaps out towards sublime ideas which never fail to move the spectator. A summit where our loftiest reflections encounter our most exhilarating feelings—that is what it represents to me each time I return there.

Why? First because on the Acropolis, whichever way one turns, there is an impression of perfect harmony: harmony between the crest of the hills and their contours, harmony in the architectural blocks, harmony in the alignment of columns. Everything indicates that the people who selected this spot to consecrate it to their art were truly inspired. A feeling for nature, a boldness of conception, a love of grandeur tempered by knowledge of human capacity, and lastly an exquisite choice of materials— their genius lacked nothing.

Evening is the witching hour for this divine concert. In the dazzling light of noon the rock has neither that storm-blue hue nor the turbid relief which lend it

The Propylaea

so secret an aspect. And the gradations of the surrounding hills are no longer distinguishable. Hymettus, in particular, is an evening flower which blooms only at dusk.

The Propylaea is the first building on the Acropolis to greet the traveller. With what architectural type should it be identified, and to what end? None, and that is why it is unique. Mnesicles, who designed it in the days of Pericles, undertook to erect neither a temple dedicated to a divinity, nor a monument celebrating a victory. On complicated foundations he built a simple passage, or vestibule, framed by porticos on a grandiose scale. Another outstanding feature is the absence of sculptures on the frontons. It was a thing of beauty, whose sole aim, beauty, for beauty's sake, was achieved by the choice of medium and the architectural layout.

The medium is a marble with a grain like white, unctuous flesh. This peculiar property is attributed to the fact that not having been polished to excess, the marble has retained an impalpable dust of crystals which catch the light.

What knowledge and skill it would require to speak with authority on the marbles of Greece. The place of origin is not everything. One would imagine that each monument had its individual nature and reacted differently to the passage of time. The stone of the Propylaea and that of the Parthenon both come from the same quarry. Yet one is white, intact, luminous; the other has russet-tints, and at nightfall in the setting sun it resembles a lionskin.

The Propylaea, which rise up like an outpost looking out to sea, and command a wonderful view of Salamis, were seriously mutilated long before the other monuments of the Acropolis. In the Middle Ages Frankish barons disfigured the building by surmounting the south wing with a tall square tower. It still existed a hundred years ago and was demolished only on the intervention of the archaeologist Schliemann. During his journey through Greece, the French writer Maurice Barrès feigned to be interested only in vestiges of the Frankish invasion, and carried the paradox to the point of shedding a tear over the disappearance of this clumsy casemate.

Even though it is a figment of imagination, I prefer the rapture expressed by his contemporary Charles Maurras in his work entitled *Anthinéa*: "From this column, the first to appear in the choir of youthful Propylaea, I opened wide my arms to clasp all the space I could hold and, bending my head, I embraced it like a sweetheart ...."

The shifting sands of fortune have also left their traces on the small temple of Athena Nike known as Wingless Victory, which used to jut out—rather recklessly—to the right of the Propylaea. This delightful monument, no larger than a room four yards square—and yet as exquisite in line and as ornate as a precious casket—was demolished in the 17th century to make room for a Turkish bastion. It was rebuilt—not without difficulty—and left standing until it was realized that its location on the edge of the Acropolis—and on a spur—was not without danger. A few years ago it was again dismounted, stone by stone this time, to be rebuilt more staunchly. A strange destiny indeed befell this monument to Victory which the Athenians named *Apteros* (wingless) so that it might never again abandon their town, and which on the contrary flew from one spot to the next.

But rest assured, the loveliest gems from this temple have been preserved in the Museum. They are the marble bas-reliefs which decorated the outer balustrade, representing figures of Victory in various poses: presiding over sacrifices, leading heifers to the altar, holding up trophies. The most famous figure in this round of goddesses is that of a Nike lifting her tunic and fastening her sandal.

As one advances towards the Acropolis, the Parthenon seems to grow bigger. And yet there is nothing overwhelming about its majestic mass, thanks to the impression of flexibility emanating from its lines. Shall I describe the archaeologists' explanation of this prodigy? I summarized it as follows in my book *Le Demi-dieu*:

"In this model of rigour and rectitude, there is apparently not a single truly plane surface. The shaft of each column is swollen, whilst the entire colonnade and the walls have entasis—that is to say, they are not perpendicular but lean a little toward the interior—and lastly, there is not a single horizontal arris that is not slightly convex." I include this rather technical quotation to reveal the secret grace of the Parthenon and—if I may say so—analyse the emotions of those who observe it. But this emotion can be enjoyed to the full without recourse to science. And hardly has one set foot on the steps or entered the colonnade than these fundamental theories are forgotten, or almost. It is the quality of the medium that stands out, and the unexpected splendour of the countryside that enchants the onlooker. The marble has a patina of dull, dark gold which, as already mentioned, imparts a lionskin hue. This unusual shade is attributed to a lichen which covered the stone. But from close to, this imperceptible substance looks like an iridescent powder incorporated in the marble.

And now, through this forest of gilded trunks let us look towards the hills and plain of Athens. The modern town is one long stretch of flat roofs which in no way arrests attention. The cynosure is the unbroken line of mountains—Hymettus, Parnassus, Pentelicus, and Aegaleos.

Oh! What would we give to be able to express the plenitude of feelings experienced simply by contemplating those columns and that landscape .... How we would like to convey all that passes through our minds when this simple cry escapes us: "How beautiful it is."

Yes, I know .... You are about to maintain that we are approaching the Acropolis and

Temple of Athena Nike

its monuments with preconceived admiration substantiated by all the legends of our school days. But this is untrue! Never have I experienced the physical sensation of the beauty of the world as much as when I saw the marble of the Propylaea or the columns of the Parthenon. Never have I felt that urge—nay, need—to devote a major place in our lives to all that is beautiful. A unique combination of circumstances achieved a miraculous accord between mind and matter. And the revelation endures to this day.

The third monument which still exists on the Acropolis is the Erechtheion. It is thirty years earlier than the Parthenon, and so different in style, arrangement, and decoration that it is difficult to believe a single generation separates the two styles of architecture. There is as much divergence between the two buildings as between a Romanesque façade and a Renaissance portico.

Caryatids on the Erechtheion

The Parthenon was Doric, the columns of the Erechtheion are Ionic. The Erechtheion aims at slenderness rather than strength, grace rather than majesty. It is adorned with roses, palmettes, and pearls. Moreover, the columns are replaced by statues of women.

This last originality is worthy of note, since, for the first time in the history of art, it brings us face to face with a family which has since produced a long and often redoubtable line of descendants—the caryatids. But the six caryatids of the Erechtheion are not degenerate creatures, that is to say, frozen in allegoric poses. Their bodies are robust, their faces determined, whilst the supple, upright back, and the tense limb advancing beneath the gown are full of expression. The coiffure and the anatomy of these statues are dictated by the laws of architecture, but, like all the creations of the great Athenian artists, they are not studio models: they are full of life and spirit.

GREEK STATUARY

THE spirit of life is in fact the dominant trait characterizing the art of great Greek sculpture.

First there was the archaic period, with its frontons and groups in painted tuff that ornamented the first Acropolis, dating from the 7th century B.C. They were found in the excavations round the citadel, and were placed long ago in a small museum scooped out of the very plateau on which the Acropolis stands.

The National Museum is not completely reopened at the time of writing. I am therefore not sure where that forceful statue of Herakles wielding his club to crush the head of the Hydra rising above its coils may now be admired. Another fragment of the fronton represents Herakles wrestling with a monster with three bodies. They are primitive, disorderly works, born of a fabulous imagination, revealing an art still in its childhood, under the trance of legend. Readers who are familiar with other regions of Greece should not attempt to compare these frontons with those in the museum at Olympia, particularly the magnificent battle of Centaurs and Lapidae which Apollo arrests by raising his arm. This is not a work in stone, but in marble from Paris, with a hint of nascent majesty and disciplined might. It is, in fact, much later, dating from the 5th century B.C. But how can one fail to be moved at sight of these first gropings of the Athenian artist? How can one help admiring the amazing metamorphosis which was to

transform these monsters into models of perfection and lead sculpture from general types to individual figures, from gods to human examples?

The figures are already discernible, half-goddess, half-woman; the pose is still inclined to be set, but the expression of inward warmth and the daintiness of attire endear them to us immediately. They were called the *Korai*, and no one could ever forget their haughty or pouting smiles, or their eyes narrow with mockery but sparkling with covetousness. The marble still preserves traces of the original colour. Both type and treatment bear the stamp of Asia Minor's influence, and yet there are signs

The Acropolis seen from the Theseion

that the purely Hellenic artist has passed this way. The statues are infused with a soul, and the realism of the costumes foreshadows the inimitable draperies of the school of Phidias which were later to outline the bodies of Athenai and Victories. The Korai are not flowers in bloom, but roses in bud.

The Couroi gallery, also in the National Museum, contains a collection of great statues of men from the archaic era on, illustrating the development of Attic statuary. Study them closely: they represent the March of Man.

The most ancient specimens, obviously inspired by Egyptian art, are merely expressionless idols. And then the faces gradually light up in a smile, identical throughout like that of the Korai. At last, after one or two clumsy efforts, the limbs give a hint of movement and the bust begins to flex. The artist is clearly attempting to progress. Having ceased to imitate, he strives after personal creation. And he has become conscious of his aim: the union of realism and beauty.

Next come the great works of the 5th century, reaping the benefit of technical progress, the materials close at hand, and the surge of intelligence which intoxicated Athens in the reign of Pericles.

All the statues, bas-reliefs, and friezes representing Athena, Nike, processions of virgins, Apollo, Hermes, and Ephebes perpetuate the peerless flower that blossomed in Attica.

Can one trace the principle of a school, discover a common character?—No doubt. I shall attempt to define it as a mixture of sobriety and realism, the marriage of thought with movement taken from life.

If I may venture to make such a comparison, I would describe it as a dialogue in

Hadrian's Arch

144

Temple of Olympian Zeus

stone reminiscent of Plato, representing a subtle collusion between the game
of abstract reasoning and that of human forms.

Athens' genius in statuary consisted first of refining and idealizing the
forms bequeathed to her by the Barbarians, and then seeking balance
between inner life and mobility.

Look at the famous bas-relief from Eleusis, in which Demeter hands an
ear of corn to the youth Triptolemus. The scene has all the nobility of an
initiation, and yet it is as simple as a pastoral landscape.

Pause in front of the stele known as *Athena Melancholica*, which Clemen-
ceau had copied for his tomb. The helmeted goddess, holding a lance and
clad in a tunic which falls in stiff folds, seems to be delivering a funeral
oration.

Besides, without surrendering to mental impressions (always a dangerous
practice as far as art is concerned), one might say that most of these funereal
steles of Attica—the beautiful ones, at least—show signs of spirituality
resembling Christianity. All these dreamy expressions, presentiments, and
farewell scenes are more akin to the Christian Middle Ages than to pagan
times. And this is probably the reason why Rodin advised us to study the

Greeks in order to have a better understanding of our 13th-century statuary.

But the best way to understand the Greeks is by observing the Greeks themselves. Their unrivalled mastery and amazing inventiveness prompts us to exclaim "How true to life!" whenever we admire their works.

Hackneyed though it may be, the classical example of this twofold enthusiasm is without doubt the Parthenon frieze.

As we know, it may best be admired in the British Museum, London, since Lord Elgin had the major part of it transported there. Is this loyal servant of his country to be condemned or absolved? I am inclined to forgive him. Imagine the condition of the Acropolis at the

The Zappeion

beginning of the 19th century, under Turkish domination. Everything was falling into ruins, and no attempt was being made to safeguard the treasures. And, as a Frenchman, have I the right to criticize? We have only to read Monsieur de Marcellus' account of the abduction of the Venus of Milo. There is no doubt that the French sailors wrested her by force from the population of the island. And she may well have suffered in the process!

As I mentioned elsewhere, the beauty of the Parthenon frieze comes not only from the relief and the effect of loftiness, but from the breath of life that animates the bodies, or rather, the relief and loftiness derive from this breath. The torso of one of the youths, or the neck and withers of a horse, form a scene by themselves. For the first time, the figures quiver with life. And yet there is no sign of stress, no trace of lyricism.

Observe the disciplined impetuosity in the elbows glued to the thighs: in every detail the artist is master of his subject.

In this cavalcade of ephebes, each gesture is simple in the extreme. Greek sculptors, accustomed to scrupulous modelling of nudes, and admiring distended limbs and tense muscles, have succeeded in expressing in marble all the presentiments of the flesh.

Linger, then, in the Museum, in front of one of those specimens transported from Epidaurus, representing a battle of Amazons. That bold drapery revealing a thigh, and the bust thrust fiercely forward, send shivers down one's spine.

TREASURES FROM THE MUSEUMS OF ATHENS

SEVERAL towns in Greece boast museums of major importance: Delphi, Olympia, Epidaurus, Volo, Candia, and Athens. And as the provincial towns have limited their collections to local excavations, it goes

Gateway of Athena Archegetis

Odeon of Herodes Atticus

without saying that Athens Museum is the richest of them all, having drawn on the country as a whole.

Whilst the marbles in Athens illustrate the evolution of Greek sculpture, visitors should by no means overlook Olympia where, in addition to the fronton described above, they may also see Praxiteles' Hermes and Paeonios' magnificent Victory—and Delphi, where the Charioteer is displayed.

Until recent years the Charioteer, in his long pleated gown, was considered the finest bronze in Greece. The question as to whether he has been dethroned by the treasures discovered in the sea near the Isle of Euboea some twenty-five years ago will be frequently raised throughout the journey, since the Greeks of today never stop cavilling whenever their artistic patrimony is at stake. Just as the gods used to vie with each other, each statue now has its partisans and forms its own little clan.

A huge Zeus or Poseidon, retrieved from a watery grave after 2,000 years, is now the pride of the gallery of bronzes in Athens Museum. This amazing vision represents a man no longer young, but in the prime of life, bursting with energy. The face radiates joy, the arms are held out to embrace. His brow is not severe like that of a god, and he looks more like a legendary character—a triumphant Ulysses. It is quite understandable that the Greeks admire him as the arch-type of the founder of a race.

Beside him are his shipwrecked companions—for this miraculous catch was obviously retrieved from the jetsam of a ship transporting the works of art. It includes an infant cavalier—called "the jockey" on account of his pose—doubtless from a later period, although the treatment, more developed though it may be, is lighthanded and free from mannerism.

What an exalted idea these galleries in Athens Museum convey of the need for beauty in the Hellenic world! What fertile imagination, and what deftness of hand! We of the West were still living in darkness whilst they were amassing exquisite images and forging precious objects.

In the gallery of Mycenaean antiquities, look at the wealth of jewels, royal weapons, and vessels found in tombs, and above all those strange gold masks resembling the sun, buried with each defunct king. The exquisite motifs and sumptuous materials—crystal, horn, alabaster, not to mention the precious metals—can match everything modern art and luxury can create.

And the list does not stop at funerary offerings and votive objects. The bronzes in another gallery—statuettes, engraved plaques, mirrors, vases, and lamps—clearly portray the accustomed setting of a civilization for which beauty and refinement were indispensable companions throughout life.

The Grecian urns in the Museum alone merit detailed study. The variety of forms is a clear indication of the potter's searchings and his fun in creating. The amphora has two handles; the lecythos, which is more elongated, has only one; the mixing-bowl is the commonest type; the cantheros, a goblet with upswept handles, has all the grace of a piece of English plate.

As for the decoration of these urns, it forms a universe of patterns—geometrical, fabu-

Byzantine Chapel at the Foot of the Ramparts of the Acropolis

The Theseion

lous, or symbolic, familiar or picturesque—as whimsical as a tapestry and as stimulating as a folkloric scene. Some of the compositions are thought to illustrate certain of Homer's tales, or other eclogues.

And now, imagine these urns in an ancient Greek house: a plain fabric—white or purple —is draped to one side; objects in bronze and statuettes of clay are scattered here and there. A mat of woven straw carpets the floor; olives glisten in a goblet. Why does this imaginary setting remind me of a poem—a short yet perfect poem expressing essentials in a few words?

It is impossible to describe in these pages the riches accumulated in long galleries devoted to ceramics, or to dally over the diverse origins of these urns. Curiosity, surprise, and personal preference in turn slacken the visitor's steps. Speaking for myself, I was particularly arrested by the urns of the Mycenaean period, decorated in reddish brown on a pale yellow background, depicting sea flora or fauna, or horizontal bands resembling the stripes on shellfish. The Ionian period is remarkable too, with its ornate decoration in which a specialist of the East such as René Grousset would undoubtedly have discovered purely oriental themes.

Having summarily described an ancient dwelling, I should now like to draw attention to a museum which attempts to reconstitute modern Greece. Anyone who spends a few days in Athens should be sure to visit the Benaki Museum of history, painting, and costumes. This treasure-house of Hellenic folklore, full of evocative images and vestiges of original works, was created and directed by one of those Greeks whose love for his country is as consuming as a vocation. The collection grows richer each year, and the friends of Greece are entitled to a showcase there. Byron is well represented by a manuscript.

THE SECONDARY MONUMENTS

HARDLY have I written this adjective than it strikes me as detrimental to the monument I am about to describe. Is secondary the word for the Theseion, a temple built very little later than the Parthenon, in almost identical style, and the best preserved of all Greek temples? Is it, then, only the fetishism of the ruins that draws me there?

No, but it is, in addition to its architectural purity, the triumphal setting, the call of greatness, and an indescribable, sublime seductiveness rarely experienced elsewhere.

Travellers have long been inclined to compare Italy with Greece, ascribing to the one colourfulness, voluptuous contours and, in short, charm, and to the other the austere beauty of a diagram devoid of emotional appeal.

To my mind, the hallmark of Greece—her landscapes, her buildings, the scenes she evokes —is the way in which she stirs our enthusiasm without a trace of vulgarity. As for the colours, what of the reddish-brown hue of her soil, the deep green of the cypress, or the silvery-grey olive trees? The shades neither mix nor merge, they stand out in crude patches. Compare them with the subtle shades of the sea and the light reverberating on the marbles. Throughout Greece one experiences voluptuous sights and intoxicating impressions without ever being nauseated. If you favour blandness, this is no place for

Pamphile and Demetria
(Ceramicus Cemetery)

151

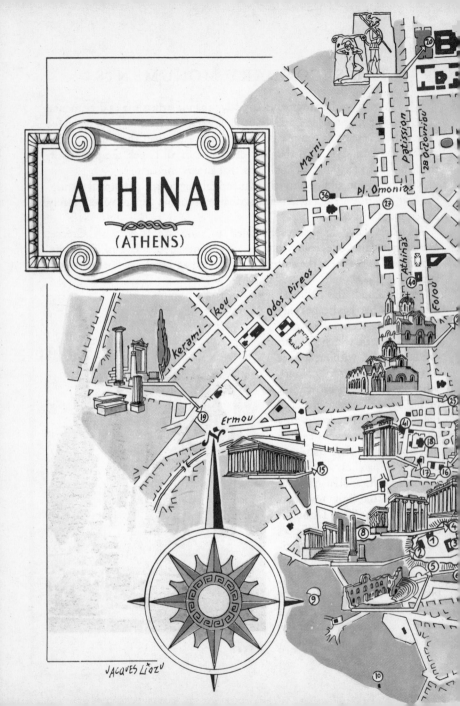

1–Acropolis
2–Propylaea
3–Parthenon
4–Erechtheion
5–Odeon of Herodes Atticus
6–Portico of Eumenes
7–Theatre of Dionysos
8–Areopagus
9–Pnyx
10–Monument to Philopappos
11–Olympeion
12–Hadrian's Arch
13–Monument to Lysicrates
14–Stadium
15–Theseion
16–Tower of the Winds
17–Roman Agora
18–Hadrian's Library
19–Ceramicus Cemetery
20–Archaeological Monument
21–Monuments of the
    Acropolis
22–Byzantine Monument
23–Benaki Museum
24–Ancient Mitropolis
25–Kapnikarea
26–Aghioi Theodoroi
27–Omonia Station
28–Academy of Athens
29–University
30–National Library
31–National Tourist Office
32–Institut Archéol. Français
33–American Archaeological
    Institute
34–British Archaeological
    Institute
35–Old Palace
36–Royal Theatre
37–Zappeion Park
38–Lycabettus
39–National Garden
40–Post Office
41–Monasteraki Station
42–Unknown Warrior's Tomb

you. Above all, there is moderation in these pleasures. It is the mind that stores up remembrances. However, these stones should not be looked upon as classroom models transplanted into modern life. They require solitude; they suffer at this separation from their gods; they demand space.

The Theseion must be seen and admired. Its unbroken silhouette and harmonious proportions proclaim the genius of Greek architecture. But they proclaim it in the manner of an Academy of Art, where elegance lacking in warmth and obedience to established principles are the order of the day. What architect, painter, or writer could fail to appreciate this rebuke! After observing, studying, or reading, every artist should create in his own inspired moment of enthusiasm. Diligence may well be impassioned: it will never be more than a virtue.

Do not let these digressions astonish you. The enchantment of Greece is the way in which she provides a digression at every step.

Thus, on descending from the Acropolis and catching sight of the two theatres—that of Dionysos, the elder of the two, and the Odeon of Herodes Atticus dating from Roman times—how can one fail to think of Greek dramatic art and her great tragedians? It is the melting-pot of tragedy as we know it: our contemporaries are still seeking inspiration therein.

In Greece, there is a certain relationship between the evolution of dramatic art and the evolution of architecture.

The drama of Aeschylus is like a Doric column, made of blocks of stone unadorned. Planted flush with the earth, it seems to rise as if unaware of its own strength, and at times one has the impression that it is weighted down by the roof of the temple.

There is something primitive, brutish, and fatalistic about the art of Aeschylus. When designated by the chorus, or brought face to face with each other, his characters remind one of colossal boulders with gnarled faces, evocative of imprisoned souls.

Ceramicus Cemetery

Doric then succeeds Ionic. The column becomes more svelte and asserts itself by the very strength of its outline allied to an independent quality which its predecessor lacked.

Such is the art of Sophocles. His tragedies are richer and better constructed than those of Aeschylus. From the technical standpoint, they introduce a sense of composition which is novel. From the moral standpoint, they take account both of Man himself, and his character.

Aeschylus set us trembling by showing us what was dangling above our heads. Sophocles moves us by bringing us face to face with our conscience.

Corinthian is then superimposed on Ionic. It is as if the elongated capital, decorated with ornaments as tantalizing as a casket of jewels, added a feminine touch to Greek architecture, hitherto so strict and sober.

Beauty, which we sense is skin deep, and an expression by no means lacking in strength, though capricious and changing, now pervade the whole building and modify its appearance.

And it is by a similar process that Euripides, the last of the three great tragedians, adds the realism of passions to the presentiment of fatality and the penetration of conscience, the apanage of his forerunners.

"The Doric, Ionic, and Corinthian styles form a ladder running from sobriety to delicacy," said Vitruvius, the great historian of art.

By interpreting "delicacy" as a portrayal of pathos, you will realize this is a brilliant parallel with the movement of Greek tragedy.

In the span of barely a century, she invented all we now know. Born of simple dances and Dionysian festivals, she grew up, created her own setting, her own laws, and introduced to the stage all the resources of human conflicts and the colour of drama in all its forms.

The Theatre of Dionysos is the most interesting to visit. Its sculptures and bas-reliefs, the state of preservation of the stage, tiers, and seats reserved for great dignitaries, all help to evoke the plays of old.

However, the Odeon of Herodes Atticus, with its high two-storeyed wall, is more practical nowadays, especially at night. A few years ago, by the light of the moon which blanched the entire Acropolis —a sight I shall never forget— I saw a magnificent production of Aeschylus' *Agamemnon*.

The rest of ancient Athens can well be visited in the course of random strolls through the town. In mentioning the famous spots, I shall content myself with indicating the most propitious time for a visit.

The light of morning is kindliest to the ruins of the Olympeion. It was once a large temple, terminated by Hadrian; of the hundred columns on

Monument to Lysicrates

The Tower of the Winds

which it rested, only sixteen remain standing. They are tall and graceful, decked with acanthus in Corinthian style against the blue backcloth of the sky, set in a landscape embracing the slopes of the Acropolis, Mount Hymettus, the sea, and the islands.

On the other hand, evening is my favourite time for visiting the rocky terrace of the Pnyx, now deserted but once the noisy centre of popular assemblies. The Agora and the Pnyx were the two cradles of democracy. "In Athens," said Fénelon, "everything depended on the people, and the people depended on the spoken word."

Evening also lends itself to reverie in the Ceramicus Graveyard, the finest steles from which have, incidentally, been transferred to the Museum. Evening, too, is the best time to tour the neighbouring hills of the Acropolis, Mouseion, Areopagus, and the Nymphs' Hill, and muse over the Parthenon.

It sinks slowly into the darkness, like the sun when it has ceased to blaze but still beams over the landscape.

Finally, your footsteps will lead you to pause in front of two exquisite little monuments. One is a votive rotunda in Pentelic marble, in honour of Lysicratus the choragus and the tribe that triumphed in the choruses of the ephebes. It dates from the 4th century. The other, which is later, is Andro-kinos' Clock, or the Tower of the Winds. Each side of this octagonal tower is ornamented with a winged figure naïvely representing the winds that blow round Athens, with their symbols.

THE ENVIRONS OF ATHENS

CRUISES round Greece have their good points. Far be it from me to disparage them, since on several occasions they have permitted me to call at spots—certain islands in particular—which would be difficult to visit other than in a conducted tour.

But there is no getting away from the fact that the aim of such tours is quantity rather than quality, and sauntering is out of the question. For anyone who really wants to know Greece, a cruise is a quick way of forming an opinion and selecting future halting places.

One will then find time to discover the environs of Athens later, on one's own, and at leisure.

However, two particular excursions can easily be made, even if one spends only a few days in Athens. The first is the ascent of Lycabettus, that wooded hill in the form of a mitre immediately dominating the town.

Morning is the time to go, if you want to avoid the heat and excessive reverberation. It takes a good hour on foot to reach the little chapel on the summit. The stiff climb is

Athens seen from Lycabettus

158

rewarded by a panoramic view extending from the mountains of Corinth to those of Argolis, from the Isles of Salamis and Aegina to Pentelicus. Below, the Acropolis stands out as the centre of this natural rosette. And yet one does not feel the same fervour as between the columns of the Parthenon, and the habit of air travel may perhaps have made us indifferent to unending vistas such as this.

Frankly speaking, the ascent of Lycabettus, once so dear to tourists, seems to me to be a little out of date these days. It is the Rigi of Athens.

But I hope you will be able to watch the procession that comes down from the chapel

Byzantine Church of Kapnikarea

on the night of Good Friday. From below one can see the little lights of candles or lanterns dancing on the hillside, vanishing, and winding round again. This procession, which then marches through the streets, and in which all the persons of rank take part, is one of the most famous festivals of modern Athens.

Another easier excursion, on the main road from Athens to Eleusis, is a visit to the ancient convent of Daphni.

As mentioned above, it was by way of the Daphni Pass that Chateaubriand made his way to Athens. In his haste, he hardly mentioned the church, and apparently completely overlooked the mosaics inside.

And yet it is a sublimely poetic spot, naturally dedicated to mystic transformation and evocative of daydreams. At first it was devoted to a temple to Apollo, surrounded by laurels—hence the name—then an early Christian monastery, the fortifications of which may still be seen.

After being abandoned or sacked by the Crusaders, the buildings were

Mosaic in Daphni Church

taken over by the Cistercians who added Gothic to Byzantine and, offering this hallowed earth as a sepulture, made their convent the last resting-place of the Dukes of Athens.

Ravaged by the Turks, the Catholic convent became Orthodox in the 16th century. The remains of the second cloisters date from this period. After that, building came to a standstill, and everything gradually collapsed into another type of silence—the stillness of ruins. Nowadays Daphni has the appearance of a little rustic dwelling-place crowned by a dome. Shrubs grow up on all sides, dominated here and there by a cypress tree. The monastic spirit has buried itself in the rural surrounds, since the guardian of this once hallowed spot has converted it into a small farm. Matins are now sung by the cock, and the pigeons play the role of angels. The cult of the gods has given way to domestic pantheism.

But let us not be content with this vague poetic fascination, and venture inside to see for ourselves.

Although frequently restored throughout the course of the centuries, the interior of the church is a very curious model of Byzantine architecture.

From the exterior the dome might be mistaken for a dove-cot, but the interior is adorned with wonderful mosaics on a golden background representing Christos Pantokrator and his Prophets. There is something Slav about this Byzantine Christ which, to western eyes, inspires fear rather than love.

Other excursions round Athens should not be overlooked, but they depend on the amount of time available and the season in which one goes there. One spring, I remember meeting a friend who had already been in Athens a week. When I exclaimed: "But I haven't seen you anywhere!" he explained to me that he had spent his time exploring the hills of Athens on horseback. Not the delightful, shady retreat of Kephissia where Athenian society repairs on summer evenings; not Tatoi, the lovely royal residence, unhappily damaged during the civil war; but Hymettus, Pentelicus, and Parnassus. In the company of a guide, he used to set off early in the morning along almost imperceptible paths. It was the season of flowers. They are short-lived in Greece, but whilst they last the wild anemones weave a thick carpet of brilliant colours in the fields.

He confessed that the ascent of Hymettus is rather disappointing. Trees are sparse, and the soil arid. But the route runs past Kaisariani, once a monastery like Delphi, half-hidden amongst the leaves. Nowadays it is a farm, and the landscape is completed by a spring—an uncommon sight in Attica.

He spoke of Pentelicus in more glowing terms: although longer, the ascent is far more beautiful. There is a magnificent view across the plain, and in places the mountain looks as if it had gutted itself to spew its marble on Athens. His first

Church and Monastery of Daphni

Omonia Square in Athens

halt was the convent of Pendeli, or the strange, unfinished castle of the Duchesse de Plaisance, an enigmatic 19th-century character. I have seen the dwelling: all that remains is a half-burnt façade in the middle of a forest; it reminded me of one of Gérard de Nervals' poetic evocations.

In short, he lived in the midst of romantic pastoral scenes, enchanted by vivid colours and fragrant air. He assured me that the scenery and sensations brought him as close to ancient Greece as all the museum pieces. I can well believe him. On my very first voyage I too fell under the spell of the land and its extraordinary power of evocation.

Antiquity may be reached by travelling along the road of History and visiting Marathon, 25 miles from the capital. But one should go well armed with a stock of schoolroom memories, for the battlefield is now no more than a vineyard.

No monument has been erected there. On the other hand, you will be taken to see a huge mamelon, which is apparently a burial mound. And—as excavations have testified—in this giant molehill the heroism of Miltiades and his hoplites slumbers amidst fragments of lecythes and calcined remains.

THE MODERN TOWN

Is the active seed of this past greatness, this artistic genius which I have attempted to summarize—or rather sketch—in these few pages still to be seen in Athenian life as it appears to the present-day traveller? The question is naïve, and best ignored. The richest civilizations might well be described as little patches of mildew appearing on certain spots of the globe at given moments, thanks to a favourable exposure. This precocious maturity and relative superiority confront them in every sphere with tasks which later diminish and pass into the hands of other executants. And the "Greek miracle" is perhaps simply this.

But Athens, who rose to such great heights and accomplished her task so well, has not degenerated, as proven by her history—that of the 19th century and the present century alike.

Although a gay town nowadays, she has more self-respect than many another Mediterranean city, linking lightheartedness with a sense of tradition.

The University

The people in the street are friendly and interested in everything that goes on, but neither obsequious nor servile.

Where can this best be observed? I was about to suggest an itinerary and talk about shops and market-places, but a scruple held me back. I should succeed only in shortening the time that should be devoted to the sublime, unique sights. Athens, I repeat, is the Acropolis, and that unforgettable sight of the Parthenon seen from the hills opposite. Ornamental borders should not be scrawled round the bottom of a picture such as this.

I shall therefore content myself with saying that Stadium Street is the liveliest, whilst Hermes Street, intersected by a delightful Byzantine church, is the small traders' quarter. In Venizelos Street and Academy Street (now F. D. Roosevelt Street) there are some beautiful façades. That of the former Royal Palace (now the Chamber of Deputies), on the other hand, is broad, cumbersome, and military in aspect; its sole virtue is that it dominates Constitution Square, the centre of the town.

The square is never empty, and it is amusing to see how late the Athenians linger there, either strolling about gesticulating wildly, or sitting quietly in front of a glass of iced water.

Shoeblacks

CENTRAL
GREECE

Isle of Corfu

THE IONIAN ISLES

THE ship transporting us from Italy to Greece makes a brief call in the port of Santi-Karanta, for which the only justification is, perhaps, a certain fondness for colour. We should scarcely notice the difference between the blue of Italy and that of Greece, were it not for the happy intervention of the yellow Albanian coast. Once we have crossed this saffron curtain, our eyes are attuned to discover the endless azure expanse stretching from Corfu to the Dardanelles. Coming from Brindisi, as soon as we encounter the first Ionian island all that we loved about the Tyrrhenian and the Adriatic begins to pale. The images of yesterday become confused, dim, and heavy compared with the dazzling reality before us. Corfu resembles a luxurious basket of flowers and foliage set on the dazzling platter formed by the sea, as a token of welcome. Soon we shall enter the port of the same name, through roads dominated by a double summit of pointed cypress and the battlemented ramparts of a citadel built by the Venetians.

CENTRAL GREECE

0 ——— km ——— 50

23° 24° 40° JACQUES LIOZU

39°

AGHEON

AEGEAN

LAMIA
Stylis
Agriovotani
Istiea
Orei
Aidipsos
THERMOPILAI
KALLI-
DROMON
Kalmena Vouria
Limni
Kymi
Atalanti
Dirfis
Kiphissos
Orchomenos
EUBOEA
PARNASSOS
2457
Chero
Kar-
ditsa
CHALKIS
DELPHI
neia
Itea Arachova
LEVADIA
Kyriaki
HELIKON
Thivai
(THEBES)
Tanagra
OCHI
Karyst
Erythrai
PARNIS
Tatoi
Marathon
KITHAERON
Korinthiakos
ELEFSIS
Kiphisia
Dafni
ATHINAI
Loutraki MEGARA
Salamis
PIREEFS
(PIRAEUS)
SALAMIS
(SALAMINE)
Vouliag-
meni
Lavrion
Saronikos
Soinion
EGINA
MATROUNISOS
23° 24°

CORFU—The name Corfu is not, as one might imagine, derived from that of Kerkyra, as the Corinthians called the colony they founded on the route to Sicily in the 8th century B.C. The conquerors—who were Liburnians—settled on a promontory flanked by two ports; Kerkyra soon rose to power, divorced herself from Corinth, and founded her own colonies in Epirus. When Athens backed her against Corinth and Sparta, she served as a pretext for the Peloponnesian War. She was restored to the Empire of the Orient in 336, only to fall under the domination of the Angevins of Naples in 1267, and that of Venice in about 1386. At that time the Byzantine town was called Stous Korphous, or city of summits, because the ancient citadel was built on the hilltops—hence Corfu. The fall of Venice in 1797 and the treaty of Campo-Formio put an end to Corfu's destiny as an individual power, and her history became confused with that of the Ionian Isles (Corfu, Paxos, Leucadia, Ithaca, Cephalonia, Zante, and Cerigo—the Isle of Cythera south of the Peloponnese). The Republic of the Ionian Isles became in turn a protectorate of the French, the Russians, the Turks, the French again, and then the English (from 1815 on), and was incorporated in the Hellenic kingdom only in 1864, in the reign of George I.

These motley influences make the Ionian archipelago quite distinct in character from Greece proper. Whilst there are no signs of the Ottoman yoke, there is still a hint of Venetian alacrity in the air. But it is time to land in Corfu. Ploughing our way through a bustle of light boats covered with blue and white striped awnings, we reach the Customs wharf. In honour of some local festival—Saint Spiridion's Day, for instance—the whole town is decked in the two colours that characterize both the Greek flag and the landscape. How gay are the steep streets of Corfu at eight o'clock in the morning with their chaos of paving-stones, stalls, housewives dressed in black like Corsicans or Catalans, young donkeys laden with baskets bulging with vegetables, white-clad sailors, old men in pleated kilts and red tasselled boots! We reach the Esplanade, a military zone between the town and the former citadel, and direct our steps towards the Royal Palace, formerly residence of the English governors, and now the home of the Archaeological Museum.

The 6th-century marble fronton brought from the Temple of Artemis in Palaeopolis is in itself worth a visit. The central figure is a mighty Gorgon who protrudes her tongue as she tramples her enemies. But the major charm lies in the contrast between this terrifying sculpture and the frivolous parlour, furnished in the style of George IV, where it is exhibited. The Archaeological Museum thus gives a foretaste of the style of pleasure in store for us in Corfu. The style is "composite". If, leaving Corfu by way of the Canoni Promenade, we make our way towards the antique city of Kerkyra a few miles south of the town, we shall pass by the tomb of Menecrates, the English gardens of Villa Monrepos, the convent of Saint Theodoras, the insignificant ruins of the Temple of Artemis where the Gorgon used to figure—all contained within the Palaeopolis Peninsula, where Kerkyra was built long ago between the Bay of Kastrades and the Kalikipoulo Lagoon. In their day the Venetians defended the entry to the lagoon by a cannon—whence the name of the promenade.

From the emplacement of the cannon, one should look down on the landscape formed by the islets of Vlakherna (where a little convent shelters half-a-dozen nuns beneath its sloping roofs) and Pondikonisi, the summit of the Corfiote composite, since its cypress-clad rock evokes memories of Ulysses, reputed to have been washed ashore there by the tempest; Empress Elizabeth of Austria who came to consult a hermit on the island; Boecklin who painted it in his *Isle of the Dead*, and Salvador Dalí who enhanced Boecklin's picture with surrealist deformations.

Isle of Corfu

I describe Pondikonisi as the "summit of the composite" since this island is the perfect base for excursions in quest of Corfu's former charms. The longest expedition lies along the wild west coast where, on the Haghios Nikolaos headland near Paleokastritsa, Victor Bérard places the town of Ulysses' host, Alkinoos, King of the Phaeacians. The famous gardens sung of in the Odyssey reputedly lay at the foot of the cliffs of Lacones, and there is no denying that the setting might well have inspired Homer. We are quite prepared to believe Bérard, especially when we reach the gracefully curving Bay of Ermones by way of a road that winds beside the rushing river. Yes, this must surely be the spot where Ulysses was cast up by the sea, to be welcomed ashore by fair Nausicaa and her gay companions.

Wherever one goes in Corfu, there is no escape from legend. Whilst the Fable of Homer becomes reality on the shores of Ermones, the real-life character Elizabeth of Austria now leads a fabulous posthumous existence there since her tragic end inspired so many writers. With its pseudo-Greek peristyle, pompous frescoes and statues, contrasting with the gardens planted with palm and lemon trees and the delightful terrace, the Villa Achilleion—built for Elizabeth in 1890—disconcerts the too-unbending visitor. But, to judge it in the right perspective, one should first invoke the genie who lived there—that "Empress of Solitude" who, according to Barrès, sought in those mediocre paintings and that clumsy luxurious reconstruction a mere "background to her dreams".

To take leave of Corfu, let us climb up to her Old Fort. From the lighthouse lantern we bid farewell to the town and her churches, the Venetian forts, the hilltops, ancient Kerkyra, the islets, the gardens, and the distant mountains of Epirus.

LEUCADIA AND ITHACA—Leucadia, which is not so much an island as a peninsula—also known as Santa Maura—is of little interest except to partisans of the German archaeologist Doerpfeld. He situated Ithaca there, regarding the remains of Mycenaean buildings on the plain clad in olive groves between the sea and Mount Elatus, as the home of Ulysses himself. Doerpfeld actually chose to be buried on the other shore of the bay of Vlikho, at the tip of Cape Haghia Kyriaki. Being inclined to agree with Victor Bérard that Leucadia is "too much of a peninsula" ever to have been considered as ancient Ithaca, we prefer to look up from the sea at the tall white cliffs of Cape Doukato, and dream of the Leucadian Leap—the ancient

Paleokastritsa

Greek cure for lovesickness. Countless paintings and sculptures have extolled the death of Sappho, who reputedly hurled herself from this cliff into the sea. For the Pythagoreans, the Leucadian Leap symbolized the ascent of the human soul to immortality.

The earthquake in the summer of 1953, which wrought havoc in the Island of Ithaca (which we, like Bérard, regard as Ulysses' true homeland) and her neighbours Zante and Cephalonia, plunged Greece—and indeed the whole world—into mourning. Not only did we sympathize wholeheartedly with a people who has never failed to set an example of courage and nobility in the face of misfortune, but we dreaded the complete disappearance of a portion of the cultural patrimony of humanity. This supreme peril seems to have been averted. Whilst the toll of human disaster is beyond computation, neither Ithaca nor Zante disappeared beneath the waves. After mourning their dead, the Greeks are already attempting to make life blossom anew there. As Jean Cocteau put it, Greece is the only land which is at one and the same time a reality and an idea. Therefore the least I can do is to give you an idea of this island of Ithaca,

Nidri, in the Isle of Leucadia

the cradle of Homer's Ulysses, which is temporarily out of bounds.

The most remarkable feature about this rocky island—barely 15 miles long and 4 miles wide, separated into two mountain ranges by an isthmus dominated by Mount Aeto—is that, on approaching it at sunset, without the slightest doubt it resembled that brief description from the *Odyssey*: "Ithaca, which one perceives from afar ...." To the north, the tallest summit, Mount Anoi, is surely Homer's Neriton; Mount Exoi, further to the right, was long mistaken for the Neion of the *Odyssey* (according to E. Seillière), but the latter is now identified with Mount Karaveikon in the south. The coast is high above the sea—"abrupt, unfit for horses, good for goats" says the *Odyssey*—and the entrance to the port of Vathi is narrow. Vathi is, by the way, the modern phonetic spelling of the word *Bathus*, meaning "deep".

There are few settings as evocative of the Homeric era, and as poignant to my way of thinking, as this circular bay hemmed by steep hills. Sparse cypress and clumps of olive trees punctuate the clay-coloured soil with black and silver dots.

"At the tip of the port of Phorkys (Port Vathi) is a long-leafed olive tree, and close by, a delightful dusky grotto dedicated to the nymphs known as Naiads. Within it there are urns and amphorae of stone where the bees deposit their honey. There are also large stone looms on which the nymphs weave purple veils .... This grotto has two doors: one, facing Boreas, is accessible to mortals; the other, which is divine, opens on to the Notus; no man can cross the threshold: it is the passage of the gods." This Odyssean description of the Nymphs' Grotto is surprisingly accurate. The grotto could be entered with difficulty by way of the northern opening. The southern door was simply a slit, quite inaccessible to anyone but a spirit. As for the "marvellous works the nymphs wove on their stone looms", the stalactites formed by the water that seeped through the chalk rocks corresponded precisely.

Vineyards and olive groves, a wealth of foliage almost concealing rare vestiges of steps, a view embracing the mountains of Leucadia, the distant rocks of Acarnania, the nearby Neriton—such was the landscape in which the farm and orchard of Laertes, the father of Ulysses, were set.

To the south, "a day's journey from the capital" (*Odyssey*), rose the high plateau of Marathia where the flocks of Eumaeus used to graze. At the foot of the Raven's Rock, the water of Arethusa's fountain flowed into two natural basins. Before descending through a narrow gorge into the calm, deserted Bay of Porto-Andri where

Ulysses disguised as a Beggar, confronting Penelope

Missolonghi

Telemachus disembarked, from the summit of Marathia—Ithaca's greatest blessing—one looked down on one of the loveliest expanses in the world, and one of the richest in memories. Nearby, to the west, lay the next port of call, Cephalonia; to the north, Leucadia; to the right, in front of Preveza, stretched the waters of Actium; beyond, the purple slopes of Acarnania and the summit of the Pindus; farther south, Missolonghi; straight ahead, the rocks of the Echinades, site of the Battle of Lepanto; and then, the Gulf of Corinth. Beyond spread the sandy shores of Pylos Bay where the Battle of Navarino was settled; and on the distant horizon, to the south, the summits of Mount Taygetus concealed Sparta and Mistra.

With respect to Cephalonia and Zante, the other Ionian victims, I will not repeat the detailed description I have devoted to Ithaca, since archaeology and legend played a less important role than Mother Nature and human labour. Nature expressed herself in the beauty of the trees (the fir trees of Cephalonia were of a special variety, the *Abies Cephalonica*), labour in the form of ports, and remarkable crops (the town of Zakynthos alone merited the epithet "Flower of the Levant" which the Venetians applied to the Isle of Zante as a whole). In Ithaca, the spirit of Homer defies ruin. Cephalonia and Zante suffered total disaster. It would be too painful to raise the veil of mourning that shrouds them.

ACARNANIA

THE REGION ROUND LEPANTO—Homer described Acarnania as the "dark continent". We land in Kryoneri, the port of Missolonghi, where Byron met his death. The town is imprisoned by fever-infested marshes, between the two torrential deltas of the Phidaris and Achelous. The desolate landscape adds a touch of melancholic nobility to the outline of the sanctuary of Artemis in Calydon, and the more remarkable ruins of the New Pleuron with its well-preserved walls and vestiges of stairways winding round its towers. It also befits the sanctuary of Aetoliko, built in the Middle Ages on an islet linked to the mainland by two stone bridges. Close by, the Trikardo Kastro mountains shelter the ruins of Oeniadae—curious vestiges of a port with buttressed piers, a basin hewn out of the living rock, and a great doorway of arch-stones leading to the Acropolis. But Nature is gradually coming into her own again.

Since our excursion in Epirus terminates at Preveza, whence we shall

Lagoon of Missolonghi

The Venetian Citadel in Lepanto

proceed non-stop to Delphi, before returning to Actium I suggest we make a rapid trip across Aetolia as far as Natpaktos or, in other words, Lepanto. How moving this little port appears, nestling in a circular basin protected by two fortified headlands from the illustrious gulf of the same name! The clamour of history and the mighty din of the naval battle of 1571, in which the Venetians, led by Don Juan of Austria, destroyed the Turkish fleet, and in which Cervantes lost an arm, in no way ruffles the silence of the empty city, crested by a citadel and girdled by Venetian walls. Night is falling. There is not a ripple on the water. At the far end of the gulf, the Peloponnese grows dim. A star appears on the summit of Mount Panakhaiton.

Human industry and force leave their imprint on the earth. But in the sea they dissolve without leaving a trace. The naval battles of Lepanto and Actium changed the destiny of the West, yet when we visit the sites where they took place, deserted shores and tranquil waters assess for us the vanity of our undertakings and Nature's indifference to our striving.

In the little port of Lepanto, we dreamt of the Crucifix and the Crescent. Actium, where Octavius defied Antony, is the last stage on our trip across the "dark continent".

THE ENVIRONS OF ACTIUM—We then reach Agrinion, a modern town rebuilt after the 1887 earthquake; her sole charm lies in the lovely lakes of Apokouro and Aghelo-Kastro nearby. From there we shall visit the ruins of the ancient capital of Acarnania, Stratos. In crossing the Achelous by way of an iron bridge, we recollect that in his *Iliad* Homer referred to it as a river "with which no other can compare". Poetic licence, maybe, but for all that it is a difficult river to ford.

The origins of Stratos are extremely ancient. The French School has found pre-Hellenic foundations there. The walls date back to the 5th century, and the great Temple of Zeus was built in 338 B.C. It comprised six columns on the façade and eleven on each side, but all that remains is the base. The long wall of the battlements encircles several hills. Other hills, rising beyond the plain of Lake Rivios which we shall visit next, accentuate the ruggedness of the setting. Our route opens on to Fort Karavassaras, where we should have landed if we wished to reach the mainland from Leucadia. Karavassaras would be without interest, were it not dominated by the ruins of a high-perched town containing a curious basilica and linked to the gulf by two walls.

Mount Panakhaiton, seen from Acarnania

Little Fruit-vendors on the Aitolikon Bridge

Some thirty miles beyond we reach Arta—formerly Ambracia, the capital elected by Pyrrhus, King of Epirus, whose name is familiar to us through Racine's works. Ambracia commanded the entrance to the river Arachtos. The great bridge spanning the river is breathtakingly beautiful. Legend would have us believe that the construction of this masterpiece was linked with human sacrifice, since it could only be terminated thanks to the devotion of a young woman who was walled alive in one of the piles. This cruel ransom in no wise detracts from the serenity of the arches whose reflection in the Arachtos completes a series of perfect circles.

Arta boasts other wonders—her Byzantine churches built in the 13th century on the plan of the ancient basilicas. The Metropolis of Panaghia Parigoritissa, the church of the Epirote despots, is roofed with domes. The pendentives are unique: they rest on a series of columns jutting one above the other, supported by other horizontal columns which pierce the wall and project on the other side. The mosaics on the dome are Byzantine, but the sculptures are in Italian style.

Bas-reliefs of varnished terracotta decorate the church of Haghios Vassilios. The builders of Haghia Theodora respected the basilical plan. The lesson in Byzantine architecture taught by Arta could be completed by a visit to the surrounding convents founded by Michael II in the 13th century—Kato-Panaghia, and the monastery of Blachernes where the monarch is buried. But we prefer to reach the tiny port of Kopraena without further delay. A coaster takes us across the gulf and speeds us to Preveza, our last port of call in Epirus.

The memory of that same Pyrrhus who chose Arta as capital also welcomes us there. In his days, Preveza was called Berenicia, in homage to Berenice, mother-in-law to the King of Epirus, and the wife of Ptolemy, King of Egypt.

But the real-life character Pyrrhus—heir to Achilles' mythical son and victor over the Romans at Heraclea and Asculum, who was killed in 272 B.C. by a tile which an old woman hurled at his head during the capture of Argos—is of far less interest to us than

Byzantine Church in Arta

181

the trio Octavius, Antony, and Cleopatra, of whom we come to dream on the shores of Actium.

Facing Preveza there is a spit of land called Acte. Beyond it are the remains of a temple to Apollon Actios, which Augustus erected to commemorate his victory.

Beyond that again, the chapel of the Holy Apostles juts out over a marshy lagoon which was once the port of Actium. It was beside the future Temple of Apollo that Antony pitched his tents when he sped from Patras after the first victorious offences of Octavius' army. His naval base was located near the chapel. After his cavalry had met with further setbacks not far from the River Louros, and marsh fever was decimating his army whilst Lemas fell to Agrippa, Antony again struck camp at Actium, with thoughts of retreat. Ranging his fleet along the channel, he hoped to entice the enemy's heavy vessels and then surround them with his lighter boats. But Agrippa scented the stratagem and took to the open sea. Antony ventured after him, only to be overwhelmed by Octavius' nimbler vessels.

Bridge of Arta

At the height of battle, the galley of Cleopatra took flight; Antony followed in her wake, abandoning his squadrons to disaster.

In Actium (or, to be precise, north of Preveza), human pride triumphed over nature's indifference to our acts which impressed us in Lepanto. Octavius—or rather Augustus, as he was known—was not content with building the Temple of Apollo in Actium. To commemorate his victory he required an entire town, no less—Nikopolis.

In a setting almost

Menidi, on the edge of the Gulf of Arta

as bleak as the one Louis XIV selected for Versailles, a Roman town grew up, supplied with spring water by an aqueduct (of which a few arches survive to this day, higher up in the Valley of the Louros). Augustus depopulated neighbouring cities in her favour, including even Ambracia. The monotonous plain where black and white sheep graze is still dominated by tall arches and a stage wall rising above the ruins of the Grand Theatre of Nikopolis.

The theatre marks the end of our expedition across Homer's "dark continent". The ship which is to whisk us non-stop to Delphi's port, Itea, is awaiting us.

DELPHI

THE Grecian landscape resembles a fake setting invented by the wiliest of the gods. The genius of the people who conceived the style to which the West as a whole owes its inspiration is not just a matchless model of plastic inventiveness: it is a grossly undervalued example of obedience, not blind but farsighted, to the laws of nature and the oracles of the Immortals.

Guided by the dual moral imperative—"Know thyself" and "Nothing superfluous", the Greek architect was content to stress in a perfect drawing a pattern which already existed in the landscape in an obscure form. Delphi, the supreme pilgrimage towards which we are making our way across the sea, could well be referred to as "Trismegistus", or thrice great, like the god Hermes. She is great in her natural outline, great in her history and the masterpieces with which the Greeks enriched her, great in the example of archaeological science—the pride of the French School—which she offers to modern visitors.

The Theatre of Delphi

Day has scarcely broken when, after hugging an unbroken coast, our boat at last discovers a flaw and penetrates into the Bay of Itea. In both colour and form the bay itself resembles the blade of a sword thrust into the flanks of the tawny Locris, dotted like a panther with scattered spots of green. Itea, the ancient port of Chaleion, is lacking in character. Since the Middle

BEUVILLE

Ages it has supplanted the antique port of Kirrha, built in the 6th century
B.C., slightly south-east. Until Roman times ships laden with marble from
the isles and "Peloponnesian poros" for the sanctuaries of Delphi used to
put in at Kirrha. The latter port was built on the site of far older cities,
anterior to the arrival of the Achaeans in Greece (the oldest dates back to

the second millenary B.C.). Close by was the capital of the country of Kirrha or Kissa, to which Delphi was rigorously subjected until 590, when a coalition of Greek states destroyed her in order to "liberate" the oracle.

This "land of Krissa", the wooded plain and lower valley of the tiny river Pleistos, is the overture (in the musical sense of the word) to the fabulous opera of the mountain of Delphi, whose rosy soil and silvery glades captivate us as soon as we land there. Naïve Westerners as we are, at first we mistake the magnificent trees that intertwine their stout branches above our heads for oaks; they are in reality millenary olive trees. In the 5th century B.C. a strip of this dense forest was cleared to make way for the Hippodrome. The young charioteer whose statue (of which a replica exists in the Louvre) awaits us at the summit, competed there in his day. Beyond the giant olive trees a last surprise is reserved for us at the inter-section of the routes to Amphissa and Delphi: a stately caravan of camels approaches, as if from the dim, distant past. As regular as clockwork, unperturbed by the trials of war or the bustle of modern mechanical inventions, it assures a shuttle service between Itea and the bazaar of Amphissa. This strange encountèr incites us to make a slight detour and interrupt, by an Ottoman interlude, our pilgrimage through antiquity: Amphissa (or Salona), a picturesque city rising in tiers at the foot of a Franco-Catalan castle. With its battlements built on the ruins of an acropolis, the castle itself, or Kastro,—the lair of the barons of Salona—has a Frankish accent; let us confess that we prefer the delightful arcaded fountain, whose oriental grace is an unaccustomed but refreshing sight.

But, after this exotic halt, there is no delaying the physical and mental transformation every traveller undergoes as he climbs from slope to slope towards Delphi, a veritable eagles' nest perched on the edge of the terrible Phocian wall. It is impossible to resist the magic power of a setting such as this. The cliffs and the double summit of Parnassus imprison the city of oracles on three sides. Standing at the foot, one has to throw back one's head, as in the depths of a well, in order to see the sky. The fourth side gives the opposite type of vertigo: Delphi ceases to stifle us and becomes the rim of another gulf foaming with a cataract of sacred olive trees which swarm across the Pleistos gorges between Parnassus and Kirphi as far as the Bay of Itea, shining like a round flat coin hurled into the abyss.

In describing Delphi as an eagles' nest, we were expressing not a word picture, but reality. It is a daily sight: each morning the birds emerge from

Sunrise near Delphi

the wild rosy mouths of the Phaedriade rocks and soar into the air like ships setting sail. They cleave the icy transparent mass and then, supported by the span of their wings, glide above the ruins, the trees, and the foaming torrent, ready to swoop on their prey.

HISTORY OF THE DELPHIC ORACLE—The site of Delphi is branded by an immemorial predestination to prophecy, which strikes all who arrive there even before they visit the sanctuaries which testify so nobly to the use the Greeks made of this quarry of the Supernatural.

Pierre de la Coste-Messelière—who, continuing the work of the pioneers of the French School, Théophile Homolle and Emile Bourguet, devoted to Delphi the best part of his life as an archaeologist and his talent as a writer—wrote: "All the resonances of the universe converge there; everything around is a sign or an omen: the earth, the air, waters, and fire all secrete the prophetic revelation. Before attempting to interpret it, the first task was to cull it. Several gods aspired in turn to do so." Their conflicts and concord form the history of the Delphic Oracle.

The Earth was the first to speak. Through the boughs of a bay tree and the bubbling of a spring, she propagated the orders of the Chthonian divinities. Themis, her daughter, and Poseidon the Achaean joined forces with her, spreading prophetic readings to the flame dance, the entrails of victims, and the flight of birds, in this spot guarded by a fabulous being, the Python. Then, Apollon Delphinios, the island god worshipped in the form of a dolphin by Cretan mariners, journeyed from the land of Krissa as far as the Chthonian fief, defied the Python, and wrested away the tripod and the fetish stone of Omphalos, "the navel of the world". The conquered land ceased to be called Phthô, and adopted the name Delphi. Apollo's victory was followed by a troubled period. A compromise had to be made with the former divinities, allowing Poseidon to resume the use of his divinatory secrets (on a secondary plane), conceding "lots" to Hermes,

and wrestling with the Dorian Heracles who, were it not for the intervention of Athena, would have carried off the sacred tripod.

On this tripod Apollo, the master of the locality, placed a woman—Pythia. Seated beside the Omphalos in a low room called the adyton, she drank water drawn from the fountain of Kastalia, chewed bay leaves, and entered into trances. The obscure words that spouted from her mouth were written down and transcribed by the priests (prophets). This first "translation" was submitted to consultants, who asked the exegetes for a clearer or more fully expounded ex-

Delphi

Mount Parnassus

planation. Apollo's triumph modified the severity of the Oracle, hitherto inexorable. According to Pierre de la Coste-Messelière, "he lightened the yoke of fatality, tempered with pity the chill rigour of the old laws, teaching men to despair no longer." Other gods—Athena Pronaia, and more particularly Dionysos, the beloved brother of the god of light—soon joined Apollo.

Alas, this moderation of the Oracle was a failure in the political sphere. There is no need to enter into details of Greek history itself, although it is closely linked with that of the Oracle which dictated its destinies. From the 7th to the 4th century B.C., Delphi was the centre of the largest amphictyony, a religious confederation of several States which met there each spring; but it was also the pretext for four "holy wars" in which the

Hellenes flew at each others' throats. The sanctuary was coveted by the great States, who fought as fanatically for possession of the Oracle—even at the cost of reducing it to ashes—as for the honour of restoring it to its splendour. Time and again throughout the centuries fire, earthquakes, and pillage destroyed the temple. After each catastrophe, offerings flowed in from all sides; the sovereigns of each country (from Amasis of Egypt to Croesus of Libya) contributed sums of money for reconstruction, and dedicated their treasures to the Oracle.

But its decadence began with the Thracian invasion in 88 B.C., pillage by Sylla in 86, and Nero's abduction of 500 statues. Hadrian, Herodes

Atticus, and the Antonines attempted to restore the splendour of Delphi; Plutarch piously officiated there as priest from 105 to 126 A.D. But Pausanias in his day visited the temple not as a pilgrim but as a historian. The Christian Emperors Constantine and Theodosius carried away its treasures to Constantinople. In the 4th century A.D., the taboo on paganism fell on barren ground. The Earth, first goddess of the spot, came into her own again, burying the last vestiges beneath her. Daphni lost even her name, becoming the hamlet of Kastri,

Delphi

inhabited by the mountain folk of Parnassus.

The resurrection of Delphi dates from 1892. It was achieved by the French School of Athens, the very first foreign scientific institution in Greece, founded in 1846. Prior investigations had paved the way, such as the explorations of Jacques Spon from Lyons in the 17th century, Laurent in 1838, and O. Müller in 1840. The French parliament voted a budget for the expropriation of Kastri, and the village was transported to the west of the excavation site.

Tholos of Marmaria in Delphi

From 1893 to the present-day, discoveries and restorations continue to enrich the patrimony of the civilized world.

THE SANCTUARY—For our visit—not to say perusal—of the ruins of Delphi we shall follow the same itinerary as Pausanias. By way of preamble, on a terrace lined with olive trees the easternmost spot, Marmaria, presents the Temenos of *Athena Pronaia* (the sacred precincts of Athena, the Guardian or Providence). The main buildings comprise: the Doric temple of alluvial stone which, at the end of the 6th century, replaced an older and smaller building, some of the capitals of which have been used again as "padding"; a Doric shrine, and one known as "Aeolic", built in about 530 by the Greeks of Marseilles, in Ionian style similar to that of Siphnos, but purer; on the façade, two columns with palm-shaped capitals took the place of caryatids. The most dazzling monument, to our way of thinking, is the Tholos. No one knows the purpose of this rotunda in Attic style, of white Pentelic marble, with a plain moulding of blue limestone from Eleusis (370–360 B.C.). The columns, re-erected in 1938, are remarkably free in treatment, contrasting with the other austerely classical elements. Further west, a limestone temple survives on a site less menaced by collapse than that of the temple of alluvial stone, constructed in about 360 B.C. The same material was used for the Theban shrine. The Doric order holds sway in all its severity.

We leave Marmaria by way of the west. A pathway shaded by olive trees leads us to the Gymnasium, rebuilt in the 4th century, and converted by the Romans. It occupies two terraces, one above the other. The upper terrace comprised a portico of roofed colonnades—the *xyst*—standing against the mountain. In front was the paradromis, an open air racing-track. The

lower terrace contained a palaestra and the thermal baths. The spot was reserved not only for the athletes' physical exercises: mental sports took place in the portico of the xyst, where a class in astronomy was also given.

We follow the road down to Arakhova and, returning towards the centre of Delphi, halt at the mouth of the huge rift which cleaves the Phaedriade rocks. Trickles of water murmur in the depths of the crevice and gather in a basin hewn out of the rock, to form the Castalian Spring.

This is one of the most renowned and perhaps the most delightful resorts in the

Sacred Spring in Delphi

pilgrimage to Delphi. During our stay we shall frequently return to sit at the wooden tables of the humble café sheltered from the sun by two venerable plane trees. In the classical era, the Greeks used to purify themselves at the famous spring, whose silvery waters were later said to inspire so many poets. To-day there is only an old man seated on the rim, piercing the morning air with the sharp notes of his pipes. How beautiful a landscape! To our right are the huge Phaedriade rocks concealing the summits of Parnassus from Delphi. The one on the left is named "the Rose" (*Rhodini*); the other, "Flamboyant" (*Phlemboukos*). From the second boulder, which dominates the countryside, the impious were hurled. In those days it was called *Hyampéia*. To our left, on the other side of the road olive groves extend to Pleistos and Itea below. Beyond rise the

Apollon Pythios in the Ravine of the Phaedriades

wild slopes of Kirphi. On this side Delphi sheds her vertiginous appearance. Moved by the tender rosy hue of the earth which shows through the glistening foam of olive trees, we relax in pastoral peace.

Still following the pilgrims' way, we proceed to the Temenos of Apollon

193

Treasure of the Athenians in Delphi

Pythios. These hallowed precincts loom up before us in two parts; the lower section is a steady slope, the upper one a series of terraces. The surrounding walls and the breast-walls are either regular (5th century B.C.), or rubblework (6th century). The great Sacred Way winds from one to the other, bordered with votive chapels known as Treasures, offered by rival cities. Along the slippery streaked marble paving-stones, we review one after another the votive offerings of the Spartans, the Arcadians, Argos, the Aetolians, the Athenians, the Epigoni, the Tarentinians, most of which have been reduced to substructure. The Treasure of the Sikyonians was built of Doric tuff at the end of the 6th century B.C.; the metopes preserved in the museum are excellent models of this graphic, animated style. The Treasure of the Siphnians was built of the produce of their island's gold mines in 526 B.C., and decorated with two caryatids in the skilful, flowing Ionian manner (now in the museum). Higher up, the magnificently situated Treasure of the Athenians dominates the turning in the Sacred Way. It was probably constructed in 490 B.C.; in Doric marble from Paros, and re-erected in 1903 with scrupulous care. The inscriptions on the walls include two hymns to Apollo with musical notations.

Near this distinctive monument, a circle of crags marks the position of the most ancient Oracle in Delphi, that of the Earth, or Ge-Themis, which used to be guarded by the Python and is still preserved in its natural state. The rock, fissured and broken into steps, is said to be that of the Sibyl. Another rock to the rear indicates the site where the Great Naxian Sphinx was built in 560 B.C. (now in the museum). Raised on a column, it used to dominate the spot where Apollo killed the Python.

In front of the Polygonal Wall, the Portico of the Athenians rears its slender Ionic columns of Paros marble, as delicate as ivory flutes proffering themselves to the rosy lips of daybreak.

The Polygonal Wall (547 B.C.) supports the long terrace which extends at the foot of the temple, forming the first of the three landings on the Median Sector of the Temenos. This masterpiece of bonding with curvilinear joints has survived twenty-four-and-a-half centuries, unscathed. Its limestone from Parnassus is gilded by the sun. Throughout three centuries it served as Record Office for the Delphinians. We have already related the successive destructions and reconstructions of the Temple of Apollo through the course of time. (The present vestiges in grey-blue limestone date from the 4th century.) Reduced as it is to a mere skeleton by a series of destructions and pillages, in studying it in an abstract way, so to speak, by wandering along the lines of stones, one is overwhelmed with melancholic emotion. This immense debris resembles a ship wrecked against the mountain—the jetsam of some supernatural disaster. We have still to mount another step and discover the profound, haughty, sonorous shell of the Theatre, hidden by the stage wall. To venture a pun—a favourite Greek pastime, after all—it is by far the most "dramatic" sight in Delphi. And here it is permissible to silence the voice of scholarship. Reverting, then, to the shell: set in the mountainside, dominating the entire countryside, the theatre reaches that degree of perfection where human effort vanishes. Our admiring eyes light on a giant ammonite, abandoned by the retreating waters. In olden times, a tide of poetry washed these spires, making the clamour of tragedy resound through this hollow. The stentorian voice of wounded Prometheus rent the air, accompanied by the murmured lamentations of the Oceanids. But what need is there of tragedy and protagonists? Beyond the stage wall and the deserted orchestra stalls, an eagle hovers; foam soars up from Itea; thunder roars from the jowl of the rocks. Without human music or voices, the theatre of Delphi produces its own spectacle.

Leaving the highest tiers of this lofty spot, we climb still higher, slightly north-west, to visit the stadium scooped out of a bank—the culminating point of the town. The present condition of the stadium is due to the liberality of Herodes Atticus. Before it was rebuilt of limestone from Parnassus in the 2nd century, the spectators used to sit on tiers of earth, as in Olympia. From the presidential tribune, or proedria, the jury of honour used to award wreathes to the best athletes. Greek genius has made it possible for these ephemeral victors to conquer time. The Museum contains a number of masterpieces; one of its rooms is a kind of annex to the stadium. Thanks to the sculptor Lysippus, the wrestler Agias and the runner Agelaos, his younger brother, defy the centuries within its walls.

BOEOTIA

FROM DELPHI TO THERMOPYLAE—In leaving Delphi for Thebes, we pick the most audacious and most recently constructed road. Before descending towards the wide flat expanses of Boeotia, it rises as far as the Arakhova saddle, leaving behind it the ruins of Marmaria where our Delphic pilgrimage began.

Arakhova is precariously balanced on the edge of the rocky spur dominating the Pleistos Gorge. But as we wind round Parnassus, its massive proximity is more vertiginous still. No words could express the overwhelming sensation inspired by those vertical cliffs, the stark nakedness of their flanks, the solitude of their crest. By nature this mountain is reserved for the

View of Arakhova

gods—Apollo and his brother Dionysos—and their mysterious retinue. One of the secrets of the Greek landscape is the realistic way in which mythology and legend assert their presence. After the gods of Parnassus comes our first encounter with Oedipus, at the crossroads of Megas, where the three routes leading from Delphi to Thebes, Daulis, and Ambryssos (Distomo) used to intersect. Oedipus was marching towards Thebes, his true homeland. A stranger riding on a chariot threatened him with a whip. Oedipus killed him, without realizing that it

Leivadia

was his father, King Laius, since he had been raised abroad in Corinth after being abandoned by his parents. Like the destiny of Oedipus, the Megas crossroads is steeped in tragedy.

By way of Distomo—after visiting the Hosios Loukas monastery where the big 11th-century church harbours a dazzling treasure-chest of remarkably well conserved Byzantine mosaics—we reach Leivadia, whose Frankish castle and balconies overlook the Hercyna Gorge. This picturesque spot provides a delightful rest after exhausting days amidst the ruins and the lofty settings of Delphi. The torrent dashes between spinning and fulling-mills where cotton cultivated on the dried-up lake of Copais is treated. Rich in Frankish ruins and memories of the Turks who made her the second town in Greece after Athens, Leivadia looks out on to the summits of Helicon and Parnassus. Springs gush on all sides, cold and hot, salt and fresh alike, whilst

Cheronea: Kerata Pass

ancient legend poetically adds its contribution to this wealth of motley charms. The "Krya" spring is perhaps the famous Mnemosyne or spring of Memory. It is dominated by votive niches hollowed out of the rock, and below, imprisoned in a cave, seethes its antidote—the Lethe, or spring of Oblivion.

We shall take advantage of our stay in Leivadia to visit the nearby ruins of one of the oldest cities of Heroic Greece: Orchomenus. For those who delight in journeying into the past, Orchomenus is a gold-mine. Archaeologists have found there remains of superimposed structures going back to the stone age, pre-archaic and archaic "Mycenaean" vestiges, as well as a Macedonian tomb and town. The inhabitants of Orchomenus venerated Apollo's son Asklepios, the healer, and those charming people the Charities, now known as Graces.

From the games and the graces of Orchomenus it is but a step to the Campus Martius of Cheronea .... A great battle in which Greece, divided, lost her independence, in which Philip of Macedonia asserted his might, crushing his foes after a feigned retreat, and the youth Alexander made his debut by annihilating the sacred battalion of the Thebans—all this is symbolized by the great lion of Cheronea, in white marble, set on a pedestal in a peaceful countryside green with cypress trees. Another battlefield, Thermopylae, is set against a background of mountains and marshes. In ancient times this pass, which owes its name to thermal springs, was situated between Mount Callidrome and the sea. But the river deposits from the Sperchios gradually made the waters retreat. One would require a translation of Herodotus and a great deal of patience to retrace in this melancholy setting the position of the Gates, the main passage, and the fortresses that existed in the days when Leonidas and his Spartans heroically resisted the armies of Xerxes. The latter would, of course, not have ventured past the ramparts behind which 7,000 Greeks were fighting, were it not for the assistance of a Malian, Ephialtes, who showed him a path via Mount Plinkion. Attacked from the front and the rear, Leonidas dismissed the Greeks, retaining only 300 Spartans, 700 Thespians, and 300 Theban hostages.

O Stranger, go, tell the Lacedemonians
We are fallen here, obeying their commands.

(HERODOTUS)

As in Cheronea, a lion was erected in Thermopylae, but it no longer exists. The road narrows, identifying itself with the ancient route; mills, the sulphurous springs whose waters seethe in little whitish basins, and a rust-coloured brook which is perhaps the Phoenix, accompany us as far as the entrance to Lamia. This delightful, rather Turkish-looking little town marks the northern-most point of our travels. The walls of her Franco-Catalan citadel afford a fine view of the wooded summit of Mount

The Lion of Cheronea

Oeta. Herakles built his stake there. The firs on the mountainside resemble those of Cephalonia, but the species is less rare.

After reconnoitring as far as the frontiers of Thessaly, we retrace our steps. We seem to be moving back in time as well as space, since the vast, tawny Theban plain is ageless. This "land of old Cadmus" is, indeed, the ideal setting for the tragic legend of Oedipus. There is nothing specific to contradict our imaginings. With infallible foreknowledge, we situate Oedipus' encounter with the Sphinx (the singing dog with a woman's head)—fabulous though it was—at that ill-fated spot designated as Sphinx on maps and on the sign-boards of a tiny station. And yet it is no more than a scarcely perceptible nook in the desert. A marsh and a puny knoll which casts a dubious shadow at sundown suffice to inspire reverie and terror.

Until the plague and misfortunes befell the royal family, Thebes was the ancient city of elegance, and on her deathbed Antigone lamented her "handsome harnesses". In all her rural modesty, modern Thebes has maintained this tradition. The horse-fair and exhibition of saddlers' wares held there regularly form a lively, colourful scene, as ageless and noble as the site itself. The Fair of Thebes not only resembles the one held on the same spot 2,500 years ago: it is, besides, the most faithful European replica of the markets of Arizona or New Mexico.

After commenting on Thebes' "intemporal" character, we can hardly be disappointed by the mediocrity of the remains found there. Aside from the museum, whose collections of Boeotian funerary steles are remarkable, there is little more than a list of glorious names: the tomb of Amphion (who built the town to the music of his lyre), the Oedipian spring (where Oedipus washed off his father's blood), the Cadmean field (where Cadmus sowed the Dragon's teeth), and the presumed site of the palace of Amphitryon and Alcmen. Last but not least, the great tower of Saint-Omar, a vestige of the castle of Cadmus built by the Franks in the 13th century when Thebes was the capital of the duchy of Athens, is a particularly moving sight.

That same topographical curiosity incites us to leave Thebes and visit the battlefields of Leuctra, where Epaminondas triumphed in 371 B.C., and Plataea, where the Greeks defied the Persian army in 479 B.C. The town of Plataea was enlarged several times, and the ruins of her widespread fortifications enclose vestiges of Byzantine chapels and the substructure of a temple. But Boeotia is not only a tragic setting befitting to battles and to the misfortunes of Oedipus, she abounds in springs, and her myriad waterways

Gipsies in Euboea

are collected in a series of aqueducts. The vast Lake Copais, once the heart, has now been drained in order to plant cotton. The Isle of Gia, which dominated the basin to the north-east, shelters the ruins of a palace comparable to Tiryns and Mycenae—a Pelasgian enceinte, with doors opening on to oblique corridors, flanked by towers.

After tragic Thebes and feudal Gia, it is a relief to evoke the inspired slopes of Helicon, the Valley of the Muses, and the Hippocrene spring. But alas, this relief is merely a memory . . . . Pillage of the sanctuaries dedicated to the graceful goddesses of Poetry, and deforestation, have disfigured the landscape.

EUBOEA

I F we are really in search of rustic calm (and relief from archaeology and legend, if only for a while, in order to enjoy them all the better for an interlude), we must leave Boeotia and the Greek mainland, cross the Euripus Channel, and discover Euboea. I say "discover", since this island, a little more than ten miles long and thirty miles wide—the largest after

Crete—so un-insular in contour and climate, is shunned by cruises and tourists in general. This is a pity. Euboea, which the Venetians christened Negroponte when they occupied the island in the 14th century, enchants visitors by her agricultural wealth, and in particular her variety of forests, where chestnuts give way to silvery lime trees which in turn, 2,600 feet above sea-level, surrender to magnificent fir trees such as those we admired in Cephalonia. The Atalanta Canal separates Euboea from the mainland, and the main ports lie on this western coast. The east coast, on the Aegean Sea, is sheer, with the exception of Kimi where one can embark for Skyros.

The history of Euboea is that of the Thessalian, Thracian, Ionian, and Dorian colonists who settled there, inclining alternately to Athens and Boeotia, to suit the interests of the moment. As a result of the Crusaders' conquest in the 13th century, the tertiary baronies of Chalkis, Karystos, and Oreo were occupied by the Dalle Carceri family of Verona. In the 14th century the Venetians occupied the entire island, which passed into the hands of the Turks in 1470.

After crossing the Euripus, we land in Chalkis, which is not unlike Patras but on a much smaller scale. Her somewhat melancholy charm derives from the mingling of Venetian and Turkish influences. It was a great mistake to demolish the Venetian ramparts, but the former Government Palace—now the prison—and vestiges of the aqueduct have survived. An ancient mosque, a pretty fountain, and above all the way of displaying wares in the little shops recall the passage of the Turks. The curious church of Haghia Paraskevi completes the motley effect, blending 6th-century Byzantine style with 14th-century Champagne style which the Crusades superimposed on the original basilica. But I promised to have done with archaeology and history in Euboea!—a promise difficult to keep in any part of Greece. However, leaving Chalkis by the north of the island, we may if we wish relax in Achmaet Aga, in the rich valley of the Kereus, at Histiaia or Xirokhori, girt by wooded mountains, or at Skala of Oreo, the

Fortress of Eleutherios on the Road from Eleusis to Thebes

delightful port of the old colony of Oreo, vaguely reminiscent of Natpaktos on the Gulf of Lepanto.

In the centre, mountaineering enthusiasts will want to climb the Dirfis, beneath the shade of the giant chestnuts and lime trees mentioned above. The small summer resort of Kimi is also surrounded by beautiful trees, with a fine view across the Aegean Sea and the Isle of Skyros.

To the south, archaeology catches up with us on the way to another holiday resort, Karystos, since we pass by Eretria, a highly important Ionian colony. The ruins, which should not be overlooked, include the Temple of Apollon Daphnophoros, the fronton of which was decorated by that wonderful archaic sculpture of Theseus abducting Antiope, preserved in Chalkis; the Temple of Dionysos; the Theatre, with its network of passages for the coming and going of the actors; the Pelasgian walls of the Acropolis which commands a beautiful view of the pink and white Pentelicus, the ochre-coloured Citheron, and Parnassus, blue in the distance. The charming summer resort of Karystos, at the foot of Mount Ochi, with her rocky belvedere of Kastro and her picturesque suburbs, represents the last stage in our Euboean wanderings.

ATTICA

FROM CITHERON TO MEGARA—There is a choice of roads from Boeotia to Attica, and we select the route via Eleusis. A halt in this hallowed spot, where the Greeks used to be initiated in the mysteries of life and death, will provide a meditative prelude to our entrance into the town that could well be called "The City of Light", or again "The Eternal City", yet proudly contents herself with the name Athens. But before leaving Boeotia, we cast a friendly farewell glance at the lakes, Euboea, Helicon, and the Dryos Kephalae Pass. And we recollect once more the unhappy fate of Oedipus, since it was on the nearby summit of Mount Citheron that the future victor of the Sphinx was exposed by his father, King Laius, warned by an Oracle that his son would kill him. Forestalling the wolves, shepherds liberated the infant who had been fastened by the feet, head downwards. They bore him to the King of Corinth, who brought him up in princely fashion. Citheron is the first scene of the terrible Theban adventure of a hero who only found freedom from care (in Corinth) and appeasement (in Colona) far from his homeland.

Natives of Megara

In the Citheron range again, on emerging from the Kaza Pass the impressive, well-preserved ruins of the fortress of Eleutherios crest a spur rising up between two ravines. The city, which was originally Boeotian, surrendered to Athens in the 6th century. At that time, in honour of their union the ancient wooden statue of Dionysos Boeotian was transported to the foot of the Acropolis in Athens, and venerated in a temple which was soon surrounded by theatres. The first drama was presented there in 534 by Thespis. The Eleutherian origin of Dionysiac tragedy is perhaps more moving than the battlements and the towers of the 4th-century fortress.

On going down towards the plain of Eleusis, we make a slight detour in order to visit Megara, a delightful spot spread across two hills, from which her whitewashed houses reign over vineyards. It was a capital idea to come here at the time of a local festival. In the wide square, which must have been

Edy Legrand

the agora of ancient Megara, we are suddenly confronted with a vision of Greece as depicted by Byron, Chateaubriand, and the orientalist painters. Instead of mantillas, the dancing girls wear long white scarves with lace trimmings covering the brow, and fringes of crude silk interwoven with gold thread. Their red smocks, embroidered at the seams and on the sleeves —as Delacroix painted them—frame necklaces of multicoloured glass beads. The severity of their dark skirts with wide pleats is relieved by vivid pink, green, or yellow aprons. The embroidered flounces of their white petticoats flutter round their ankles in time with the rounds (danced to an ancient rhythm similar to that of Catalan *sardanas* from which they are probably derived). The Megarians are celebrated for their beauty; as to the country's traditional gaiety, it too has its titles to fame. If Dionysian tragedy was born in Boeotia, Megara gave birth to comedy. In fact the Latins termed a certain way of enjoying oneself: *megarensis risus*.

Harvest in the Region of Megara

The ancient town, above which the modern one was built, has left a confusion of remains. It boasted two acropoli, Karia and Alkathoos. The former is now crested with windmills, the latter with towers and medieval chapels. From these gentle heights we survey the whirl of dust raised by the rounds in a cloud spangled with flashes of embroidery and jewellery.

Leaving Megara in the opposite direction from Eleusis, we proceed to the tip of the Isthmus of Corinth. It is impossible to resist the charm of a short walk along the road to Loutraki, beside the beautiful Saronic Gulf. The road is rugged, running below the threatening Skironian Rocks from which Skiron used to hurl travellers until the day he was himself slain by Theseus. In contrast with the wonderful but entirely different luminosity of the Greek mainland, the limpid blue of the gulf is a delight to the eyes. Leaving the Corinth Canal on our left, we conclude our excursion with a really modern evening in the watering-town of Loutraki, one of the Athenians' favourite outings. Like a lighthouse shining from afar across the deserted countryside, her casino attracts gamblers and dancers from Athens.

We scarcely have time to share their pleasures, for, after a night's rest, we plan to awaken very early and see the sun rise over Eleusis and the Bay of Salamis. Present-day Greeks are fond of night life. It is fashionable to go from Athens to the casino in Loutraki after dinner, and return home at dawn by way of the wonderful road we shall take after a good night's sleep. Strangers such as ourselves should have wide open eyes and clear minds, in order not to miss the minutest detail of the daily miracle of daybreak over Attica. When Homer described it as "rosy-fingered dawn", he was not employing some vague, flowing expression, but depicting the subject in its true colours. The indescribable hue of which he speaks gently brushes the tips of the pine trees of Daphni and spreads across the bay, flat and glistening like a sword.

Suddenly, the bare outlines of the landscape clad themselves in a lilac cloak, and our car heads towards Eleusis through an ephemeral springtime.

ELEUSIS—Eleusis means Arrival. Historically, or rather legendarily, the name designates the spot where Demeter, in her quest for her daughter Kori (Persephone) who had been abducted by Hades (Pluto), was welcomed by King Kelebs. In recognition of his hospitality, the goddess reputedly donated the first ear of corn to the King's son, Triptolemus. To perpetuate the memory of this boon, the king-priest Eumolpos (the just) founded the Mysteries, at Demeter's command. Eleusis, the seat of a sacerdotal State, was annexed by Athens in the 7th century B.C. The cult of the great goddesses Demeter and Kori was practised for over 15 centuries, until the edict of Theodosius II prohibited the Mysteries. All the citizens of Athens had to be initiated, whilst Greeks of every nationality could celebrate the Mysteries and undergo the ordeals of initiation on the occasion of the great Eleusinian Mysteries, which lasted ten days, from the 13th to the 23rd boedromion (September to October).

It is not my province to expound the famous Mysteries. I shall content myself with quoting two texts of Aristides the Rhetor, which, in my opinion, respectively give the best definition of the type of play performed in the Sanctuary, and the spiritual benefit man derived from initiation.

Eleusis

The first is as follows:

"Eleusis is the common *Temenos* of the Earth; of all the divine graces accorded to man, it is the most terrible, and the most marvellous. Can one name a spot where more wonderful recitals of the myths have been sung, or dramas of greater import gripped the mind? And where, to match these recitals, has one seen finer spectacles than these, performed in the midst of indescribable apparitions, before countless generations of blissful men and women?"

And the second:

"The advantage of panegyric is that it brings one pleasanter hopes as to the end of life, and makes one look forward to better conditions, instead of wallowing in darkness and *borboros*, the fate that awaits the uninitiated."

The state of the site, devastated by Alaric in 355 A.D., does not, alas, provide the visitor with any irrefutable information on the Eleusinian rites. A big, ivory-coloured Pandora's box without a lid, broken open and abandoned on the shores—such is Eleusis. No matter! Those humble remains piously outlined on the ground, gleaming white and girt with blue, form a sort of marble walk that lends itself to reverie. Let us, then, wander there, dreaming of the happy days of the sanctuary of the Great Goddess, prohibited to the uninitiated, surrounded by a doubly fortified wall, flanked by towers, built in the days of Pericles and Lycurgus. Above the wall all that could be seen was the summit of the buildings. Six months after initiation to the minor Mysteries, after sacrificing a pig washed in sea-water the postulants penetrated into the sanctuary—as we are now doing —by way of the Greater Propylaea, rebuilt under Antoninus Pius. In imitation of Athens, they comprised a basement containing a vestibule flanked by two Doric porticos, inside and out. The Greater Propylaea intersected the outer wall and opened on to a court between the two enceintes. The Mystae assembled in this court to reply to a questionnaire; then they passed under the Lesser Propylaea, the entrance to the inner wall. Beyond, the Sacred Way, paved in Roman times with white marble and Eleusian stone, led to Pluto's sanctuary, the Plutonion. It was composed of two grottoes in the cliff, and in front of the larger of the two was a small megaron. By way of this grotto, Pluto abducted Kori.

What remains of the Sacred Way terminates in the Telesterion, the most important building in Eleusis, reserved for the initiation ceremony. It was not a temple but a pillared hall 160 feet square. The ceiling was supported by six rows of seven columns each; the hall, seating 3,000 people, was girt by eight rows of tiers, partly hewn out of the living rock, partly of stone, broken only by doorways. The architects cited by Plutarch were Coroebos,

The Coast between Salamis and the Corinth Canal

Metagenes, and Xenocles. The south-east side opened on to the wide Portico of Philo, named after its designer. An upper floor contained the sacred objects (*hiera*), which were revealed to the *Mystae* at the conclusion of the ordeals and symbolic plays.

To form a general idea of these plays, we should imagine a combination of the mystic atmosphere of Lourdes and the aesthetic background of

Bayreuth as a setting for this drama, opera, or film representing Demeter's Passion after the abduction of Kori, followed by the reappearance of the young goddess. As for the Mystae's torchlight "voyage" right round the initiation hall, it was not unlike the Christian rite representing the "stations of the cross".

Above the Telesterion, the Temple of Demeter once crested the summit of the rocky spur. All that remains are Roman vestiges, partly covered over by a chapel of the Panaghia. The little bell-tower and the blue and white striped walls of this humble chapel project a Christian shadow on the excavation site. From this altitude there is a wonderful view across the bay, the coasts of Attica, and the Isle of Salamis. Lower down, on the north-west corner of the sanctuary, is the Museum, containing several Eleusinian bas-reliefs. Near the entry, a marble bench flanked by rose-laurel provides a pleasant rest. The vista embraces the arsenal of Salamis; modern warships, painted grey-blue, recall the fact that on this spot, at the instigation of Themistocles, the Athenian fleet attacked and vanquished the squadrons of Xerxes. Below, on the Attic coast at the foot of Mount Aegaleos, from a golden throne the Persian king followed the phases of the battle. When his vessels were destroyed, he returned to Asia by land with his defeated army.

But the blaze of this remembered glory quickly dies in our mind and drops like a rocket into the sea. There remains that gentle Eleusinian phosphorescence which accompanies us as far as the exit to the sanctuary. We now know that the famous "Greek serenity" so clumsily extolled by disciples of Renan and Anatole France is the contrary of impassibility and indifference to the end of all things. It is faith in the immortality of the soul —and it was in Eleusis that the Greeks learnt the secret.

DAPHNI—The road followed by the procession coming from Athens to be indoctrinated was much the same as the one we are about to take, in the opposite direction. It is still called the Sacred Way, and here and there are dotted substructures and cavities from the votive chapels and altars which bordered it. Everything around is hallowed: the plain, the two lakes, previously reserved for the priests, still teeming with fish, and dedicated to Demeter and Kori; the pass traversing the Aegaleos Mountains—the continuation of Parnassus, separating the plain of Athens from the bay of Eleusis. Let us linger here a moment. The sandy shore is dotted with iron chairs and tables, beneath a murmuring roof of reeds resting on four stakes of wood painted pink and white like a barber's pole. Sipping *ouzo*—a beverage made of aniseed and drunk in all the Mediterranean countries under different labels such as *raki* and *anisette*—we contemplate the dazzling sea, the hazy blue contours of Salamis, distant Megara and Eleusis whose cliffs and ruins loom up like white lumps of sugar. To the right, beneath the blazing sun, the hillside glitters like mica. Behind us, the fir trees of Daphni, outlined against the light, dance in the breeze.

If, despite our apparent nonchalance, we were not rather hurried travellers, and above all if nearby Athens were not tempting us on, we would dally beneath this roof of rushes, waiting for night to fall, as in the days of the Great Procession. And then, our deserted blinding sand would become as Sophocles described it in his *Oedipus Colonus*:

"A shore ablaze with torches where—for mortals whose tongue has been touched by the golden key of the Eumolpidae priests—those august guardians, the Goddesses, watch over the holy mysteries."

But, regretting the songs and dances performed by torchlight by the ancient Mystae, it is time for us to move on towards the convent of Daphni. And, beneath the pines surrounding the monastery, in broad daylight a

Port of Koulouri in the Isle of Salamis

Daphni

Christian festival perpetuates the ancient rite. Coming from Attica on donkeys, peasants dance rounds to the sound of the sound of the flute, backed by a mighty orchestra of storks. The sweet-sounding name Daphni, meaning laurel, recalls that the Mystic Procession took place in veneration of Apollo. We shall not visit the exquisite Byzantine church consecrated to the Dormition of the Virgin, which replaced the temple dedicated to the God of Day. A guide better qualified than I will take you there from Athens.

COLONUS—On approaching Athens, there is no bridling our rapture. Climbing up the gentle slopes of the Haghios Ilias, we at last set eyes on the ethereal city, set like an offering of gold and ivory on the huge lionskin formed by the Attic plain. It was from this very spot that Chateaubriand hailed her in his inimitable way. Let us leave this French nightingale to his song and proceed to the suburbs of Colonus where, in the branches of the olive groves in the ancient Academy, Greek nightingales sing.

"It was to the land of handsome horses that you came, stranger—to dazzling Colonus, the loveliest of countrysides, where the limpid notes of a thousand nightingales ring out more beautifully than anywhere else in the world ...."

The olive grove of Colonus stemmed from a cutting from Erechtheion. Akademos was the legendary proprietor. "There is a tree which, so I understand, has never taken seed either in Asian soil or in the great Dorian isle of Pelops—the silver-leafed olive—an invincible tree which regerminates from its own seed beneath the relentless stare of Zeus and the glaucous eyes of Athena." (Sophocles).

Here, blind and persecuted, Oedipus enjoyed the protection of Theseus and the sweetness of a merciful death. Here, in his domain consecrated to the Muses, Plato taught his disciples. Here the misanthrope Timon shunned mankind in his tower. And here the only science which unites men instead of dividing them—archaeology—is honoured. On the limestone hillock where Colonus used to rise, two fraternal steles have been erected: one marks the tomb of the German Otfried Müller, the other indicates that of the Frenchman Charles Lenormant.

MODERN ATHENS—If I were reasonable, here again I should leave you to enter the promised city on your own. Some illustrious elder—an Academician—should take up the torch and lead you on a tour of the age-old wonders that never fail to dazzle newcomers and faithful pilgrims alike. To be precise, the passing of the torch should take place in the gardens of Akademos! But I prefer to cheat and accompany you into Modern Athens myself. I adore this youthful capital (only 120 years old); like the ancient city, she has grown up round the Acropolis which dominates her on all sides, and the Byzantine kernel. The colouring is miraculous. When I said above that Attica resembled a lionskin, that was an understatement. Attica is light itself taking shape to produce Athens—with her simplified houses, her "Neo-Greek monuments", her Royal Palace constructed in 1834, her University built in 1837, her Academy erected in 1860 to the plans of a Viennese architect, Constitution Square planted with eucalyptus and palm trees, bordered with charming cafés and luxury hotels—Athens with her marble pavements musky with pepper-plants quivering like bunches of feathers. Athens is the outcome of some mysterious alchemy, thanks to which the sunlight, transformed by invisible bees, is hardened into a kind of appetizing honey cake.

Her straight avenues and regularly divided districts form the honeycombs. But this golden city, constantly exposed to the heat of the sun, boasts an oasis—the royal garden, a haven of 480 acres, created by Queen Amelia. It is planted with all kinds of trees and bright with flowers, the loveliest of which are as blue as the eyes of Pallas. Adjoining the garden, beneath a different kind of shade, the Zappeion quarter displays its open-air restaurants and cabarets. There one can become acquainted with Greek cooking—

Mediterranean in savour, but lighter than Turkish and less crude than Spanish cooking—famed for its red mullet, leg of lamb with marjoram, and lamb grilled over a wood fire. The wines of Attica, Demestiko, Dekelia and far-off Tegaea are exquisite; the Greeks drink them resinated, but we prefer them natural. This golden, ethereal city throngs with the liveliest, bravest, and pleasantest of people, hurling another challenge of buoyancy and balance at the heavy laws the stranger—ever a barbarian—trails in his wake. Listen to the chatter of the Athenians who are eating ice-cream at the next table. The lightning way in which they shape the Logos is the only form of human speech to fend the air with wings. Volatility is, in fact, the main preoccupation of the race. Look at the soldiers guarding the war memorial, or the entrance to governmental buildings: this is almost the only army in the world to progress and yet still go into battle with flying kilts! On holidays in particular, the *evzones* assemble and file past with red boleros, white woollen tights that mould their legs like statues, and skirts pleated like fluted columns. But there is nothing ridiculous in the sight. All those dancing flounces and the big pompoms sticking up on their pumps (*Tsarouchia*) like the prow of a felucca, perpetuate Achilles' lightness of gait, or young Sophocles' manly dance on learning of the Victory of Salamis.

PIRAEUS—A wide autostrada leads us to the beaches of Old Phaleron (still scarred by the war). The seaside café bears no trace of human luxury, but sand scooped into natural partitions separates the clients' tables with the ageless elegance of sand-castles. And from there, after a swim in water so transparent that the tiniest ripple on the surface sends a shadow dancing across the sand below, I shall take you to Piraeus. There we stroll through the colourful port, past the covered market with its piles of oranges and water-melons, its vendors of lottery-tickets, and its little shoeshine boys, and along the quays beside green waters iridescent with petrol in the big dock of Kantheros. From the other side of the Akte peninsula, we proceed as far as the deeper basins of Zea and Mounouchie.

AEGINA—Anyone who takes a pleasant stroll along the quays of a port as lively as Piraeus is immediately tempted to make a trip on the ocean. In Marseilles, for instance, the obvious excuse is a visit to the Château d'If. In Greece, needless to say, the most inconsequent excursion is inspired by nobler motives. We embark on the little tourist steamer which speeds us to the port of Haghia Marina, on the east coast of the Isle of Aegina. There, cabs are waiting to take us on a trip to the Temple of Aphaia. The thirty-

Gulf of Salamis

minute journey across a bleak countryside is accompanied by the old-fashioned rhythm of trotting hoofs. The mare, wearing a canvas petasus on her head, goes by the name of a Muse (ours was called Erato!). The Aeginetans, who are fine seamen, vying with the Athenians (Pericles referred to Aegina as a speck in Piraeus' eye), distinguished themselves at the Battle of Salamis in 480. Immediately after that glorious date, the beautiful temple we have come to visit was erected on an artificial terrace. Aphaia was a very old native god, akin to the Cretan Artemis. A primitive shrine had been dedicated to him on the same site. Leaving our equipage, we proceed on foot to climb the wooded hillside dominated by the remaining columns of the temple. There are 22 of them: 20 in the peristyle, 2 *in antis* of the pronaos. The temple, built of local limestone, is a Doric peripteral, hexastile (6 columns in front, 12 on each side), resting on a substructure approached by three steps. The columns, many of which are monolithic, measure over 17 feet, including the capital. As in the Parthenon, the cella was divided into 3 naves by a double colonnade of superimposed orders. It opened to the east and west on to a pronaos and an opisthodomos with two columns *in antis*. Like the roof, the frontons were of Pentelic marble. Their wonderful sculptures in "heroic style", re-discovered in 1811, were purchased by Louis I of Bavaria, for the Munich Museum of Sculpture. If we had more time, we should leave this magnificent belvedere in the Temple of Aphaia —which seems to hurl a challenge across the sea at her nearby rival Athens—and cross the island from east to west to visit Aegina, the main town. Her museum, containing vestiges of the ancient ports, dominated by the terrace and the unique, 26-foot column from the Temple of Aphrodite, would suffice to enchant us. And what

Athens: Plato's Olive Tree

Antiquarian's District in Athens

of the old monastery of Panaghia .... and the beautiful, unscathed frescoes in the Omorphi Ecclissia basilica?—But it is time to return to Athens, since tomorrow we have to make a last excursion together, in the region of Hymettus and Cape Sounion.

Before leaving that peerless city, which I shall not re-enter with you, I want you to discover the most unusual and moving luxury of modern Athens. We return to Constitution Square, almost deserted at this hot hour. In the middle, beneath a clump of trees which is denser than we imagined, we stumble unexpectedly upon a cool green lawn. A gardener is specially appointed to tend those few yards of common grass, which in this latitude is as rare as an oriental carpet in London or Paris. On seeing this "personal gardener", one is inevitably reminded of the "immortal" soldier Xerxes detailed to protect a handsome tree that lay on the path of victory. And this is the supreme lesson Athens has to teach us—that of courtesy. Athens honours this valueless lawn at its true worth: as a stranger. And this is the way she acts towards us all—the secret of her unforgettable welcome.

Evzones in front of the Monument to the Unknown Soldier

KEPHISSIA AND MOUNT PENTELICUS—The heat of noon is so intense in Athens that, on our way to Kephissia, we feel akin to the true Athenians who seize the slightest excuse to leave their town and take refuge beneath the cool shade of the plane trees and poplars in this charming village. Although less than 900 feet above sea-level, one has the impression of being in the mountains. Modern villas have taken the place of the favourite domain of Herodes Atticus. I doubt whether the small talk of present-day holiday-makers has the flowery grace of Aulu-Gelle's speeches, extolling the charm of *Attic Nights*. In his days people erroneously thought that the principal spring of the Cephissus took its rise there—hence the name Kephissia. In recommending Greek wines just now, I should have mentioned another rival drink: water. Its unique coolness is the secret of the Athenians. The smoothest comes from a spring near Kephissia, and bears a name as fluid as its waters—Amaroussi. Having quenched our thirst and taken a light meal, we are ready to set off in search of another source—a sacred one this time. To her Athens owes the eternal youth of her monuments—the source of Beauty and Endurance concealed in the flanks of the Pentelicus. It is the source of virgin marble which descended from its mountain home in the 5th century B.C., to be transformed into temples. In the deep veins of its ancient quarry, this wonderful substance is dazzling white as milk or snow; but once it is exposed to the air, oxidation of its iron elements turns it amber or gold. We are 2,275 feet above sea-level, dominated by the crystalline fronton of the highest peak of Pentelicus, on the very altar of the sublime Material. Amidst the ineffable watered effects that shimmer on the foamy contours of the quarry (somewhat like a pyre of jasmine and periwinkles), in the welter of rocky profiles, in our minds we hew a whole future of columns and gods—a future which is, in the end, no more than a memory.

Another time, without me, you will go from Athens, by way of Marathon —renowned for her battle and her dam—to the distant latitudes of Rhamnonte, one of the remotest spots in Northern Attica. On a terrace looking out across the sea, with a view of the gulf of Euripus and the tall powerful summits of Euboea, you will visit the ruins of the Temples of Nemesis

Landscape in the Environs of Athens

Battlefield of Marathon

and Themis. The first is a Doric peripteral, hexastile, of which the sub-structure and a few pillar sections may still be seen; it dates from the 5th century, and was never completed. The second, smaller, temple is Doric *in antis*, and dates back to the 6th century.

FROM HYMETTUS TO CAPE SOUNION—Today, on leaving the fief of Marble, we only have time to border on the "domain of Fire". In contrast to the Pentelicus group to which she is geologically akin, at sunset the saffron slopes of Mount Hymettus glow purple in the heat, like a treasure-trove of fiery gems glittering above Athens, who herself shimmers in the twilight. Apart from the wild gorges where myrtle, pine, and cypress grow, the mountain's barren flanks are clad only in a mantle of sweet-smelling plants. These provide the famous Hymettus honey which—so the legend runs—

was deposited by the bees on the lips of the babe Pindar. But we leave this mellow atmosphere behind us on entering the Laurion Mountains, by way of the bleak, rugged, and somewhat disquieting Pan Pass, with the summits of Mount Pani to the right, and Mereda to the left. Down an abrupt slope, along a dangerously winding road we reach the mining city and port of Laurion. Lead, silver, zinc, and manganese form the wealth of this strange town, whose gloomy appearance, chimney-stacks, air laden with foul-smelling fumes, and melancholy buildings suddenly transport us to the desolate setting of our own distressed areas. Leaving Laurion by way of a brighter but deserted heath, we imagine we are escaping from this industrial inferno, to rediscover Attic serenity on the "sublime promontory" of Cape Sounion, as the Greco-French poet Jean Moréas described it. Sublime is the word, but not serene. One has only to approach this furthermost tip of Attica, spotted like a panther and crested with twelve columns of marble

paler than smoke, to see classical pessimism in its true colours.

To what should we attribute this delightful yet poignant sensation of sadness? To the pallor of her ruins, the materials of which were not brought from Pentelicus but from the neighbouring quarries of Agizila and, washed by so many storms, have never bronzed like the Parthenon? To the haughty outline of the cape which dizzily projects above the shimmering flatness of the Saronic Gulf? To the pyramid-shaped Isle of Patrocles which rises up opposite the cape, like a funeral monument to the hero whose name she bears? To the skeleton-like appearance of the Temple of Poseidon (an austere

Temple of Aphaia

Temple to Poseidon on Cape Sounion

Doric edifice, built in the 5th century by Pericles), due to the fact that the flutes on its columns are reduced from 20 to 16, and their lack of entasis accentuates the slenderness of the building?

It is doubtless inspired by the bleak effect of general desolation. It is not in the least surprising that Byron's romantic cult of solitude and despair found a perfect pedestal in Sounion. On the drum of a column we are shown the poet's signature, engraved in such large letters that it must have taken him months to inscribe it.

The setting sun accentuates the ghostly character of Sounion. This is not Greece, but her spectre—a musical spectre, such as Gautier's and Weber's *Rose*, which seems to curl up in spirals above slumbering Attica, like smoke or perfume. At twilight, a kind of invisible frost begins to coat the cape, the sea, and the islands. The sun, which has almost disappeared, melts, quivering like that of the Hyperborean nights. And we suddenly recollect that, according to a legend of Delos, Lohengrin came there from the North, riding on a swan. No indeed, palpable as it is, the Temple of Sounion is too much like a memory, a mere idea.

Let us return to Athens, where life courses through the illustrious veins of the temples of the Acropolis and where, in speaking of the Greek miracle, one can use only one tense—the Present!

NORTHERN
GREECE

NORTHERN GREECE

KNOWING Greece is not just a question of rhapsodizing over the Acropolis, dreaming in the moonlight at Olympia, admiring the impressive setting of Delphi, running the risk of sunstroke in the ruins of Mycenae or Delos, strolling in the Cyclades and Crete, and enumerating all the treasures of the museums of Hellas.

Knowing Greece is also listening to the sibylline murmur of the oaks of Dodona on the slopes of Tomaros, traversing the beech forests of Pindus, visiting the monasteries of the Meteora, climbing Olympus, crunching golden apples in the garden of the Hesperides, savouring the cool glades of the Vale of Tempe, venturing into the virgin forests of Lower Olympus dear to the Orphic muses, wandering through Macedonia as far as Mount Athos, and in Thrace as far as the Turkish frontier.

Northern Greece is undoubtedly less rich in vestiges of the past than Attica or the Peloponnese, but the countryside alone is so beautiful that it would merit a visit solely on that score, not to mention the fact that customs and traditions have remained unchanged for tens of centuries. But however assiduously one consults the programmes of cruises in Greece, one never discovers a visit to the North. At most, one occasionally finds a reference to the Meteora or Mount Athos.

OLYMPUS

AND yet surely the most wondrous name in the whole of Greece is that of Olympus, the sacred mountain, the home of Zeus and the other gods of Greek mythology? At the beginning of the 19th century, the mountain served as a lair for the *Klephtai* or snipers in the rising against the Turks; it was also rife with fearsome bandits known as *Listai*, who calmly used to ransom ill-fated travellers. The frontier then separating Greece from Turkey intersected the Olympus range so that, in time of danger, the brigands were always sure to find a hiding-place on one side of the frontier or the other. They were thus able to drag tourists who fell into their hands from one lair to another, until they had been paid the ransom.

Mountain Betrothal

But since the Greek Army vanquished the Turks in 1912, Olympus as a whole is in Greek territory. In 1913 the Hellenic Army systematically began to purge the region and rid it completely of terrorists.

But even then tourists did not begin to flock there. It is true that for a long time the journey was a regular expedition entailing the most outlandish equipment: tents, camp-beds, cooking utensils .... and even a cook—not to mention mules to transport this cumbersome kit, agoyatai to lead the precious steeds and take care of them, and an English-speaking guide!

Although camping material is still indispensable, travelling conditions have greatly improved, especially now the railway runs through Litochoron and Katerini. In September 1927, to celebrate the foundation of the Greek Alpine Club in Athens, a party of 25 tourists—including half-a-score of girls—successfully attempted the first group ascent to the summit of Olympus (9,850 feet). Since then, mountaineering has become popular in Greece, and the shelter built at over 6,500 feet above sea-level is in constant use. The guides have even taken to lulling tourists to sleep by singing the chant of the Klephtai—which no longer succeeds in striking a note of terror.

I must confess that personally I have never ventured to sully the whiteness of the eternal snows of the "Throne of Zeus" with my footsteps. Mountaineering has always seemed to me to be dangerous and horribly fatiguing. But I admit that, over a few glasses of ouzo, I always enjoy hearing my Greek friends tell me of their sporting exploits on the sacred mountain.

Heracles Joannides always extolled to me the unique view from the summit, embracing the Aegean Sea, the archipelago of the Sporades, the Cyclades, the mainland of Greece, Macedonia, and Mount Athos. On a clear day, he assured me, one could even see the Dardanelles and the coast of Asia—but that was probably a friendly quip.

What enchanted him most was that curious population of Olympus composed of groups of nomadic shepherds, the *Sarakatsani*. They form veritable republics of a patriarchal type, in which the older women alone enjoy certain privileges. Sarakatsani dances are extremely odd, and the shepherds play the *floyiera*—a kind of small flute made of boxwood or reeds—with amazing virtuosity.

Happy is the inspired tourist who arrives at the appropriate moment to attend a wedding. The official ceremony, which always takes place on a

Troops of Horses on the Plain of Thessaly

229

Sunday, is preceded by six days of rejoicing (from Monday to Saturday), when everyone dances, sings, and makes merry. Then it is time for the wedding. The entry of the young couple into their home is saluted by volleys of rifle fire. And the next day, amidst general applause, one of the bride's brothers rides through the village on horseback, carrying a perch decorated with flowers, to which a napkin—symbolizing Hymen—is attached. A final feast, in which the bride and groom do not take part, concludes the ceremony.

In certain regions of Olympus the rite is even stranger: the young girl, riding a beribboned horse, is led complete with trousseau to her fiancé's home. The entire family follows her on horseback or mule. The procession is preceded by musicians, playing gay melodies. But, just before they cross the fiancé's threshold, they halt for a moment, whilst the musicians play a funeral air to recall the vanity of existence and the presence of grief in everyone's life. The people stand meditating, and then a voice suddenly proclaims: "The earth we are trampling beneath our feet will receive us! To punish it, let us beat the earth which is going to devour us." And everyone stamps his feet. Then the musicians resume their gay and lively melodies. The procession enters the house, and the feast begins. . . .

Mount Olympus

On the eastern slopes of Lower Olympus where inextricable forests overrun the mountain as far as the sea, at the foot of giant trees one may find fresh, clear brooks (teeming with huge, savoury crayfish) which form delightful little lakes in the vales. And in the forests clinging to the mountainside, the enchanted murmur of tiny waterfalls echoes on all sides. There is nothing terrifying about this wild spot—quite the contrary: it is a peaceful haven for dreamers.

THESSALY

THESSALY extends from the Othrys mountains (in the south) as far as Olympus (in the north), and from the Pindus chain (in the west) to the sea. The verdant capital, Larissa, was severely damaged by German and Italian troops in the last war. Her wounds have now been bandaged, and the town is more enchanting than ever.

The train journey there, by the Delphi-Lianokladi line, is a wonderful

revelation. The railway plunges through gorges in the magnificent mountains of Phthiotis, one of the loveliest of which, Oeta, dominates the Valley of the Sperchios. On the way through, we recollect that on the summit of Oeta Herakles lit a pyre on which he flung himself, to put an end to the intolerable suffering caused by the tunic of Nessus which his naïve, jealous wife, Dejanira, had sent him by a slave, when the hero was captive to the charms of Iola in Euboea. The legend adds that immediately the bonfire was lit, the thunder struck Herakles and consumed him instantaneously, purifying everything that was mortal about him. Zeus then bore him into the heavens, and accorded him a place amongst the demi-gods.

Evocations of History follow fast on the heels of Mythology, as, on the way to Volo, we visit the Bridge of the Paleopharsala where Caesar vanquished Pompey in the battle of Pharsala. The train actually crosses the battlefield where Pompey lost about a third of his army—1,500 men—and Caesar only 200 legionaries.

But reminiscences of schooldays should not be allowed to prevent us from admiring that wonderful plain of Thessaly, the granary of Greece which stands out so vividly in contrast with the bold mountains, abrupt rocks, torrents and gorges of Phthiotis. An enchanting road runs from Volo to Larissa, by way of the quaint town of Velestino nestling in the ravine of the Macro-Vouni, in the midst of gardens where fountains murmur. This is the native soil of the bard of Greek independence, Righas Pheraeos, who was delivered to the Turks by the Austrians, and executed in 1798. This entire region, thickly clad in woods, is abundantly irrigated by a series of little canals which link the various lakes—of which there are many in this fertile region.

In the immense gardens surrounding Velestino, the trees are laden with superb fruit. The harvest is despatched all over Greece by way of the port of Volo, which is quite as beautiful as Naples. During the season, the very air is fragrant with fruit, and the medley of perfumes seems to impart an overtone of gaiety to all the 40,000 inhabitants.

This delightful town, situated in the sweep of the Gulf of Pagassitikos, prides herself on her fine cathedral of pink stone which rises up beside the sea.

Near Volo, at Pagassai, the most curious funerary steles have been discovered. They are decorated with so-called "encaustic" paint (the colours being thinned with molten wax), adding a bright touch to the sombre marble background. These steles are worth seeing if one wants to have an idea of Greek painting in its heyday. At present they constitute the principal ornament in the Museum of Volo.

In the Volo region again, one can visit the domed Mycenaean tombs of Diminio, and the remains of a great prehistoric palace at Sesklo, which is probably the ancient city of Lolkós from which the Argonauts set forth to conquer the Golden Fleece.

Further south, at the entrance to the Gulf of Pagassitikos, the strange city of Trikeri is perched like an eagle's nest, with houses dotted amongst the crags. The interiors are surprisingly rich in decorative and household objects brought back from the four corners of the earth by the local mariners, famed throughout Greece for their expert seamanship. Their wives are extremely proud of them, and this probably explains the women's noble gait and the rather theatrical poise they adopt when, for instance,

Peasants on their way to Market in Larissa

they go to the fountain, carrying an ancient amphora on their shoulders. A less picturesque aspect of the village is its penitentiary colony for women.

To return from Trikeri to Volo, one has to cross that veritable garden of Hesperides situated between Mileai and Lekhonia. The finest fruit in the world is cultivated there, including a species of peach known as *Mastos Aphroditis* (Venus' breast) because it has a pointed tip, shaped like a nipple. These delicious, firm peaches are quite devoid of down, and their rosy-amber tinted skin tempts the eye. They are highly appreciated all over Greece, especially in Athens where they overrun the fruit stalls, vying with melons, grapes, apples, apricots, and pears from the same region.

Nearby, the Aghria promontory produces the finest apples in the whole of Greece, known as *firikia*. They are extremely sweet and fragrant, and at blossomtime the landscape assumes the most delightful appearance, decked in huge bunches of tiny flowers, dazzling white, mirrored in the sea below.

The whole coastline is broken by a series of little bays and huge boulders of craggy rock. The beaches—such as Khorefto, which is girt by a magnificent beech forest—are both lovely to look at and pleasant to stay in.

Larissa

Bay of Volo

On leaving the peninsula of Magnesia, you should be sure to visit Mouressi. It is a quaint little village where rivulets run through narrow streets, beneath flowery arbours. The perron of St John's Church is so wide that the villagers dance there on holidays. You should also stop in Tsangarada, a veritable garden-city of isolated houses roosting amidst the verdure, white churches decorated with rose-windows of brightly coloured Rhodes faience, and centenary cypress trees. Further on there is a pretty summer resort known as Portaria, the hive of ceramic craftsmen. I almost overlooked Makrynitsa, who prides herself on her 18th-century houses and little squares where lovely marble fountains hide under secular plane trees, and that other delightful holiday resort, Zagora, nestling beneath chestnut and olive trees.

On entering the wonderful beech and chestnut forests of Pelion where brooklets ripple and enchanting waterfalls sing, remember that this is the home of the Centaurs where Saturn, transformed into a horse, fell in love with the ocean nymph Philyra, who gave birth to Chiron. At the foot of Mount Pelion you may see the huge cavern of the Centaur, who numbered amongst his disciples Aesculapius, Theseus, Hippolytus, Jason, and above all Achilles. The grotto recalls the strange destiny of the centaur Chiron, who taught medicine, music, and justice to Herakles, and met his death in the war his pupil waged against the Centaurs. One of Herakles' arrows, steeped in the blood of the hydra of Lerna, misfired and stuck Chiron in the knee. Herakles despairingly tried to find a remedy, but the wound was incurable, and writhing with pain, Chiron begged Zeus to put an end to his suffering. As the son of Kronos, the Centaur counted amongst the immortal, and Zeus answered his prayer by transferring his immortality to Prometheus, and placing Chiron in the Zodiac, where he formed the constellation of Sagittarius.

But it is time to cross the Peneus and make our way towards the loveliest valley in Greece—if not in the whole world—the Vale of Tempe, extolled by poets of all time.

On the way lies Tyrnavos, a small industrial town of little importance, beyond the fact that it is the capital of the cotton and silk industries. The brandy distilled there is held in high repute; it has a strong bouquet and, being 40° proof, burns the throat and brings tears to the eyes. But if you watch the local people, you will observe that they drink it all day long whilst nibbling lamb offal roasted on the spit. Imitate the natives, and you will find that Tyrnavos brandy has by no means usurped its reputation.

The cool Vale of Tempe, a wild yet idyllic transverse valley extending for about six miles between Olympus and Ossa, is clad in secular plane trees whose trunks emerge from the waters of the Peneus. Turpentine, and mastic-trees, rose-laurel and Abraham's balm, grow there in profusion, beside Apollo's cherished shrub, the myrtle. In the past, on the right bank of the Peneus there was a sanctuary to Apollo, who purified himself in the waters of the river after slaying the Python.

It was also to this pleasant smiling setting on the banks of the Peneus, which flows slowly by beneath an immense leafy vault echoing with the song of countless birds, that the *theoria* of Delphi, or holy procession, came every eight years to gather the laurel required by the Oracle.

But the most agreeable spot in this valley is the Nymphs' Spring. Beside it, nestling in the greenery, is a pleasant, arboured café where one can sip *ouzo* or *masticha* in a setting unique in the world.

A few hundred yards further on, the Peneus hurls itself into the sea. Opposite is the Chalcicum Peninsula and Mount Athos—but first we shall visit the Meteora. It would be pleasant to make our way there by returning

Volo

upstream along the Peneus as far as Kalambaka. However, as this is not yet possible, let us go by ròad, or better still by rail: the line runs to Trikkala, and there is an extension to Kalambaka.

But first we shall make a detour to the delightful summer resort of Ambelakia, perched on the Ossa nearly 2,300 feet above sea-level. This small town used to number 6,000 inhabitants. It was very prosperous in the 17th and 18th centuries, and in fact still is, since cotton and silk continue to be manufactured there. From 1788 to 1811, a kind of cooperative was established there, in which rich and poor, adults and children alike participated. After deduction of a tax to cover communal expenditure on schools, churches, social works, organization of leisure hours, and upkeep of the town, everyone was paid according to his capacity. But Ali Pasha, who frowned on this cooperative, decided to dissolve it, and nowadays it is no more than a memory.

THE METEORA

T HE name, meaning "hovering between heaven and earth", admirably befits the convents built in the 14th century during the war between the Emperor of Byzantium and the Emperor of Serbia, who then resided in Trikkala. War has always favoured brigandage, and it was probably to protect themselves from pillagers that the monks built their monasteries on those giant rocks hewn into needles or pilasters. The most ancient convent is that of Panaghia Doupiani. Then, in 1367, the cathigoumenos (monastic superior) Kyr Nilos decided to have four other convents built on neighbouring rocks. Between 1356 and 1372, the coenobite Athanasios had the convent of the Meteoron built on the summit of the Great Rock, and retired there with seven other monks, who accepted the severest rules. Not a single woman was ever admitted to the convent, and the monks were even forbidden to give a crumb of food to a woman. Thanks to the patronage of the hermit-king Joasaph and the generosity of his family, the Meteoron rapidly became the most important convent in the region.

In the 17th century, there were twenty-five convents in the Meteora. But their superiors began to quarrel, and the convents fell into decay.

Nowadays, only five convents remain, two of which—the Meteoron and the Varlaam—are closed to women. The rest are half ruined and uninhabited.

The Meteoron was pillaged by brigands

Vendors of Onions in Trikkala

in 1831, but it still merits a visit if only to admire the church of the Transfiguration, the Crucifixion, and the Resurrection. The primitive chapel contains a curious picture which represents the founder in the costume of a western monk.

As for the Varlaam, its outstanding feature is a collection of excellent frescoes in the church, painted by the Theban Frangos Castellanos in 1565.

A Convent in the Meteora

The passing traveller can spend the night in the convent guest-room, which is particularly beautiful.

These two monasteries are inhabited by only a dozen monks, although they could accommodate over a hundred.

The most remarkable convent of all—open to both men and women visitors this time—is Saint Stephen's (Haghios Stephanos). The half-score of monks living there always welcome visitors in accordance with the rites of Greek hospitality: first a glass of *masticka* with Turkish delight and a glass of water, or a glass of *ouzo* with a dish of jam, a cup of Turkish coffee, and a glass of cold water. One can take a meal with the monks, and there are rooms for tourists. The convent's wine is celebrated throughout Greece.

St Stephen's convent is by far the most beautiful and comfortable in the Meteora. It boasts the finest view across the Pindus chain and the Vale of Tempe, and is the pleasantest spot in which to spend a few days before crossing the mountains separating Thessaly from Epirus.

EPIRUS

B y way of the Metsovo Gap, let us cross the Pindus chain and venture into the former domain of Achilles' son, King Pyrrhus who, according to Racine, took his virtuous captive Andromache there. It is undoubtedly the wildest region in Greece, and the least well known, probably

because tourists long ran the risk of being waylaid and abominably ransomed. But nowadays Epirus is as safe as any other region in Greece. For all that, it is not often visited, perhaps because it is poor in ruins.

There is, of course, Dodona, site of the oldest Oracle in Greece—even older than Delphi. In Homer's *Iliad*, Achilles speaks of this Oracle consecrated to Zeus, whose voice used to echo in the sacred oak wood on the slopes of Tomaros. The sacred wood exists to this day; the wind still howls in the branches of its ancient oaks, but the warnings of Zeus are no longer discerned in the rustling of the leaves.

This delightful excursion is enhanced by the fact that, coming from Jannina, we first cross the pass separating the Tcharacovista Valley from that of Jannina, and on the way we admire the little chapel of Saint Nicholas, commanding a wonderful view over the Pindus chain and Lake Jannina. The ruins of Dodona are only half-an-hour's walk away. The theatre is bigger than that of Epidaurus, and fairly well preserved, but most of the treasures unearthed in the course of various excavations have been transported to Athens Museum. Rather than loitering here, let us return to Jannina, the capital of Epirus, built on the shores of Lake Jannina which teems with eel and crayfish. The town itself is

The Meteora

of little interest to archaeologists, since it boasts no outstanding monuments. Daydreamers may care to wander through the Bazaar, although this too is not particularly ancient, having been destroyed by fire in 1869 and entirely rebuilt shortly after.

To the west of the town rises the Aslan Aga Mosque, where a terrible drama was enacted a century and a half ago. The story—which inspired a fine poem by Valaoritis, as well as a number of popular songs—is that of Kyra Phrossini, the lovely wife of a rich Greek merchant who was obliged to travel frequently on business. One day when her husband was in Venice, Kyra lent a complaisant ear to Mouktar Pasha's declarations of love, and became his favourite. But Mouktar's father, Ali Pasha, also fell in love with her. Whilst his son was away waging war against the Pasha of Andrinoples, Ali attempted to steal Kyra's heart. When she scorned all his entreaties, he had her arrested, together with the sixteen Greek maidens forming her suite. The unfortunate victims were led to the foot of the Mosque, and drowned in the lake. According to another version, they were drowned at Perama, on the island. The exact location of this stupid crime is a minor detail; what is more important, it brought

The Pindus Chain

Metsovo Costumes

tears to the eyes of generations of Greeks, who cursed the name of the tyrant Ali Pasha.

By way of consolation, we should visit the picturesque island of fishermen where we shall find the 11th-century monastery of St Nicholas Dilios, St Nicholas Spanos dating from the 13th century, and St Pantaleimon where, taking refuge from the Turks in January 1822, Ali Pasha was eventually discovered and beheaded.

Wandering through Jannina, one is impressed by the atmosphere of wealth pervading this mercantile city. But trade is not the sole preoccupation of her 22,000 inhabitants: Jannina is one of the most ancient cultural centres in Greece since the fall of Byzantium. Her schools are renowned—especially the one founded in 1282 by Michael Philanthropinos, which was unfortunately destroyed when, besieged by Ismaïl, Ali Pasha set fire to the city in 1820.

The region is extremely fertile in cereals and fruit. Her grapes produce that amazing Zitsa wine which gladdens every tourist's heart.

But Jannina is not Epirus, and we should also visit Arta, Parga, and Preveza. The roads are not very good, but the countryside is magnificent.

There is a particularly beautiful road from Jannina to Arta, which runs beside the river and crosses handsome forests of plane trees.

On reaching Parga, if you have the energy, climb up to the ruins of Souli, 3,280 feet above sea-level. The town, renowned in the past for its endless struggle against the Turks, was difficult to reach. The houses were built like forts, perched on enormous rocks. In the 16th century it was a confederation formed by four Greek villages in an attempt to throw off the Turkish yoke. They adopted a democratic regime of a patriarchal nature, comprising an assembly of heads of clans in which the people participated. In the 18th century, the Souliots succeeded in liberating 66 villages from the domination of the Turks, but in 1803 they were obliged to surrender to Ali Pasha, who had pledged himself to send them into exile. All the Souliots abandoned their village, marching in three columns. One of these, led by a bishop, was attacked by Ali Pasha's soldiers. The Souliots took refuge in a fortress, which they blew up, killing their attackers in the same fell swoop. As for the Souliot women, rather than fall into the hands of the Turks, they flung themselves over the precipices of the Acheron with their children in their arms, singing: "A fish can live only in water, and a Souliot woman in a free land."

Heroism, alas, does not pay, and the ruins of the Souliot villages are an inexpressibly desolate sight. On the other hand, it was to Ali Pasha's sinister victory that France owed General Bourbaki, since his father went into exile there and was married in Pau. When visiting Epirus it is useful to know that Bourbaki was of Souliot origin.

Lake of Jannina

Mosques in Jannina

Before leaving the region, you should take a glimpse at the banks of the Achelous. This river, said to be the oldest in Greece, separates ancient Aetolia from Acarnania. Legend has it that the first men settled in these parts. They lived on acorns from the forest of Dodona, and quenched their thirst in the fresh water of the Achelous. The legendary origin of the river is not very precise. Some say Achelous was born of the Ocean and Tethys, others the Sun and the Earth. At all events, he fought Herakles for love of Deianira. The first time he was defeated, he took the form of a snake, and the second time that of a bull. But Herakles seized him by the horns, overthrew him, wrenched off a horn, and drove him into hiding in the river Thoas, which has since been known as the Achelous. The Naiads retrieved the horn, filled it with flowers, and transformed it into the Horn of Abundance.

Legends also avers that Achelous seduced the muse Calliope and became father of the Sirens. He was, moreover, extremely susceptible, as illustrated by the following adventure that befell the five daughters of the Echinus, the nymphs. In inviting the gods to a feast to celebrate the sacrifice of ten bulls, they overlooked Achelous. The river was so hurt that he flooded his banks, sweeping the nymphs out to sea. But Neptune intervened and changed them into islands, the Echinades, which may be seen at the mouth of the river.

MACEDONIA

MACEDONIA, the largest province in Greece, was alternately conquered, liberated, and martyred by all the races to the North, East, and West who coveted the territory. Since the mass transfer of population which took place round about 1925, Greece at last seems to

Lake of Jannina

have consolidated her position there. Over 500,000 Greeks from Asia Minor settled in the region, simultaneously with the departure of 350,000 Moslems. The newcomers rebuilt the villages, restoring their former names preceded by *Nea*, or "new".

Macedonia prides herself on having witnessed the birth of two of the most illustrious men of all time: Aristotle of Stagira in the Chalkidiki peninsula, founder of the Peripatetic School, and his pupil and friend, Alexander the Great. She was, besides, the first European country in which St Paul preached Christianity, at Philippi, in the year 52.

Her titles to glory are thus beyond dispute. But Macedonia is also recommended to tourists for the beauty of her thickly wooded countryside, her magnificent lakes, lovely mountains, and wide verdant plains watered by grey-green rivers where buffalo with enormous horns come down to drink. How far removed this all is from Greece's traditionally arid soil! Drought is unknown in this region where rivers flow on all sides. Once Macedonia is better equipped and exploited to the full, she will be able to feed the entire country.

On our way back from Epirus, let us first make a halt in the charming town of Kastoria, once an important city in the Byzantine autocracy of Epirus, rising up on a headland beside a lake girt by forests. Nowadays she numbers barely 10,000 inhabitants; however, she continues to prosper thanks to a Jewish colony which settled there over a century ago and established a profitable trade in weasel and marten fur.

Whilst in Kastoria, be sure to visit some of the beautiful 18th-century houses: they have been classed as historical monuments on account of their magnificent carved woodwork and frescoes. At least two of the seventy-two churches in the town also deserve a visit: the Taxiarchis church, containing some fine frescoes, and Haghios Stephanos, which boasts a curious archaic fresco of the Crucifixion.

The best way from Kastoria to Naoussa is via Florina and Edessa, although—apart from her fruit, which is the finest in Greece—the only attractions in Florina are a respectable hotel and a number of taverns where the cooking is excellent.

Before reaching Edessa, make a halt on the shores of Lake Ostrovo. It would be a pity not to sit down for a moment in a tavern in Arnissa —a small village beside the lake—to enjoy a dish of eel prepared in Greek fashion, of course, or a huge portion of giant crayfish. On a

Parga

little island there one may glimpse the remains of a mosque which, if tradition is to be believed, was once the centre of a village which is now completely under water. One point in favour of the legend is the fact that the level of the lake varies very precisely every seven years.

Edessa is highly picturesque. Brooks flow right through the town, to meet in the east where they form waterfalls, one of which is 230 feet high. Quaint old houses rise on either side of the streams, which are spanned by delightful little wooden bridges. Clumps of trees grow on all sides, casting a deep green shadow across this dream city. Apart from being a fashionable summer resort, Edessa is also an industrial town where the most beautiful material is manufactured. The esplanade, leading from a wide avenue to the public gardens, commands a marvellous view of the plain of Salonica, Mount Athos, and the sea. The mountains of Olympus block the horizon to the south. In this unique setting, in the year 336 B.C., King Philip II of Macedonia, father of Alexander the Great, was assassinated, just as he was preparing to march against the Persians.

Naoussa is likewise renowned for her textiles. Strolling through narrow little streets hemmed in by 18th- and 19th-century houses, we suddenly emerge on a lovely promenade shaded by plane trees. But it is time to leave Naoussa and visit the extraordinary Jewish quarter in Verria, built on the brink of a ravine.

History informs us that St Paul preached here beside a mosque, the minaret of which may still be seen. The churches are all hidden in the depths of courts, and we should never be able to find them without a guide. All the houses are corbelled, making the streets look even narrower than they really are. Situated at the foot of Mount Vermion, the town is undoubtedly more picturesque than Salonica now that all the minarets have been removed, but she cannot compete with the capital of Macedonia when it comes to historic monuments.

Salonica (Thessaloniki), the most important town in Greece after Athens and Piraeus, boasts an extraordinary number of Byzantine monuments and exquisite churches ornamented with very ancient Byzantine mosaics. Since the big fire which destroyed the centre of the town in 1917, Salonica is a green and white haven of wide avenues, esplanades and parks designed by the French architect Hébrard, who directed reconstruction. But her houses are lacking in elegance and inspiration, and the use of

reinforced concrete gives the town a rather dismal appearance. Tourists who come to visit Mount Athos will certainly not stop to visit the modern town. A coach will convey them to the small town of Trypiti, from where a motor-boat continues the journey to the port of Daphni.

MOUNT ATHOS

OUNT ATHOS is famed throughout the world, and people come from all over the globe to visit this extraordinary monastic republic where, for the past ten centuries, neither women nor children have been admitted, and even female animals are banished.

Consequently, despite its debonair appearance Mount Athos is one of

Turkish Ramparts in Salonica

the most closely guarded spots in the world. Access is possible only on presentation of a permit issued by the Ministry of Foreign Affairs in Athens. Before the war, the Greek Government merely provided a personal letter of recommendation, on the strength of which the Archbishop of Trebizond, representative of the monastic republic in Athens, issued a permit to visit the monasteries of Mount Athos. He used to extend a cordial welcome to tourists in his residence in Patissia, in accordance with the familiar, moving rites of Greek hospitality, needless to

Edessa

say. One hardly had time to admire the archbishop's *zostico*, or wide-sleeved robe of black silk, and cylindrical, rimless headdress known as a *scouffia*, before a servant appeared with a tray laden with glasses of ouzo, cups of Turkish coffee, cold water, and a pot of jam. According to custom, one had to take a spoonful of jam, swallow a mouthful of cold water, and then the glass of ouzo, before sipping the coffee. Once this was accomplished, the permit was issued.

In the Ministry of Foreign Affairs, the procedure is far less ceremonious, but the precious paper permitting you to land with a clear conscience in

Daphni, the regular port of the Holy Republic of Athos, is delivered more quickly. There are only five or six little houses in the port, and one of them belongs to the carabineers maintained there by Greece to protect this miniature Free State. The others are inns which accommodate travellers who arrive in Daphni too late in the day. Monks often stay there, as well as tourists, and in fact it is most unusual not to make the journey in the company of a monk, or *caloyeros*, who will be only too willing to talk to you about his mysterious mountain home.

No one knows the exact date at which monastic life began in this peninsula washed by the Gulfs of Haghion-Oros and Rendina, and the Aegean Sea. But a Greek tradition maintains that Jesus made a journey there which is not mentioned in the Gospel, during his travels round the Phoenician coast. According to another legend, it was not Jesus, but the Virgin Mary

Working-class District in Salonica

who visited Mount Athos. One thing is certain: since the beginning of the reign of the first Christian emperors, the Holy Mountain has attracted an endless flow of pilgrims.

Peter the Athonite was said to be the first hermit to settle on Mount Athos, where he reputedly lived in a cavern for fifty years. Others followed his example, and tiny communities, or *lavrai*, were eventually formed. Athanasius the Athonite, tutor, friend, and adviser of the Emperor Nicephorus Phocas, immediately undertook to organize them. In 963 he built the monastery of the

Rotunda of Saint George in Salonica

Great Lavra, which became the capital of the small monastic republic. The valleys of Athos gradually became populated by hermits, who regularly increased in number throughout the Byzantine Middle Ages. Recluses secluded themselves amongst the rocky crage, whilst the coenobites built monasteries in the middle of forests or beside the sea. Isolated as they were from the rest of the world, the monks of Mount Athos remained aloof from events which only too often steeped the Greco-Slav peninsula in blood and, in the twenty great monasteries of their republic, they continued to live in the same way as in the 7th century. Latins, Catalans, and Turks

Little Port of Daphni

occasionally raided their territory, but never succeeded in hampering the advance of the monastic republic, which reached its apogee in the 15th century.

Whilst the Vatican never gained the slightest influence over Mount Athos, the Russians definitely left their mark there, particularly between 1830 and 1890. Every year, a number of Russian peasants made a pilgrimage to Jerusalem to attend the Easter festival, and on their way back they invariably stayed in Mount Athos.

During the Balkan wars in 1912, Mount Athos was invaded by the Greek Army, and in 1913 its neutrality and independence were recognized by the Conference of London.

During the 1914 war, the allied armies despatched a scientific mission and a handful of soldiers there. Since 1920, Mount Athos constitutes a theocratic republic under Greek suzerainty. The peninsula itself belongs to Greece who, for the sake of appearances, maintains a small constabulary there, headed by a governor holding the rank of prefect, appointed by the Ministry of Foreign Affairs. But in actual fact, the monks are self-governed. Karyes is the seat of the Holy Community of twenty representatives—one per monastery—elected every January, and wielding almost absolute rule over all the monks in Mount Athos.

On arrival in Daphni, before actually visiting the monastic republic one has to undergo certain legal formalities and have one's passport stamped by the Greek constables who, incidentally, have had no occasion to use their rifles against pirates since 1712. They make no bones about the fact that they would be the happiest men in the world, were they not completely deprived of women. For all that, they have not lost their good humour, and

Spring in the Forest of Haghion-Oros

Russian Monastery of St Andrew near Karyes

they welcome tourists not as intruders but as friends.

Karyes, the capital, has to be reached by mule. There tourists are obliged to pay a call on the governor—a hardened bachelor, as one would expect—the Holy Community, and the Constabulary.

It is a small town centred round a monastery, comprising a few shops run by monks, selling crucifixes, stoops, rosaries, etc. also made by monks. There are, besides, several stores run by laymen—grocers, druggists, tailors, and cobblers.

A detail to be remembered is that smoking is prohibited in the street leading to the Protaton. The seat of the Holy Community is guarded by soldiers wearing traditional white kilts. On presentation of your permit you will be admitted into the Council Chamber, a spacious room with divans on either side. Twenty little labels are attached to the walls, announcing the names of the twenty convents on Mount Athos. A raised wooden seat is reserved for the "First Man of Athos". Beside it is his secretary's desk. A servant-monk immediately brings you ouzo, with jam, and Turkish coffee. Then the four epistatai (civil service attachés) appear, followed by the secretary, who writes you out a kind of certificate of registration bearing the seal of Athos.

It only remains for you to take leave. You can then venture forth without qualms: all the monastery doors are open to you—an important detail, since there is nowhere else to stay in Athos. Every evening at sunset, the porter-monk raps loudly on the door with an iron bar. This means that it is time to close, and it would be wise to hasten your steps (unless you want to spend the night in the open). Once the door is shut, it is impossible to have it reopened, and you would have to stay out-of-doors until dawn.

There are two categories of convent in Athos: those of the *coenobites*, who abstain from eating meat all the year round, and those of the *idiorrythmic* monks who are allowed to eat meat, and live on their own resources. All the monks, without exception, have to pray for eight hours out of twenty-four. There are also anachoretes who live in complete isolation, usually in inaccessible cells; *sarabaitoi*, or groups of two or three hermits; and *gyrovakoi*, or roving, mendicant friars.

Each convent is headed by a *higoumenos*, elected either for life or for a set time, two or three *epitropoi*, and a council of elders. All the monks are not compelled to do manual labour; this is reserved for the *pamicroi*, who are the regular servants of the *proistamenoi*.

On entering the monastery, for the first three years the monk, or *caloyeros*, is a novice, designated by the same name as his black robe—*dokimos* or *rasophoros*. Then he has the right to wear the petty habit, becoming a

Artist-monks in Karyes

stavrophoros or *microskhima*. Finally he becomes a *megaloskhima*, entitled to wear the grand habit for communion, embroidered in white with the symbols of Christ—skull, crossbones, and inscriptions. All the monks are obliged to wear beards and long hair piled up in a bun beneath their scouffia.

Three hours' mule ride from Karyes, the idiorrhythmic convent of Vatopedi rises up in an extraordinarily beautiful setting. Legend has it that the monastery was built by Theodosius' son, Arcadius, who, as a child, fell into the sea during a journey from Naples to Constantinople in the company of his mother and his brother Honorius. A violent tempest blew up and battered their ship so violently that Arcadius slipped into the waves. Hermits from Mount Athos found the young boy under a raspberry-bush, where he had been washed up by the sea, and took him to Constantinople. On being crowned emperor, Arcadius decided to build a monastery on the spot where the sea had cast him ashore.

In Vatopedi, as in all the monasteries on Mount Athos, the monks' timetable is regulated to the sound of a curious instrument composed of a long piece of wood struck by an iron mallet. The *simandre*, as it is called, rings out as loudly as metal, but not as clearly, and it can be heard all over the monastery and even further afield.

The old 11th-century church of Vatopedi is particularly remarkable for its mosaics and paintings. The external ambulatory is decorated with pictures representing Theodosius the Great and his two sons Honorius and Arcadius, who founded the monastery. Beside them is a fresco evoking the siege

Father Proigoumenos of Vatopedi

Monastery of Coutloumoussi

by the Arabs in the 11th century. Behind the altar you will be shown objects of immense value used in worship, offered in the past by Orthodox princes and dignitaries such as John Cantacuzene, tutor to John Paleologus, from whom he usurped the throne in 1341. When defeated by the latter in 1354, he retired to the monastery of Vatopedi, on which he had already heaped donations. The library contains 8,000 volumes or manuscripts, including that of *Ptolemy's Geography*, illustrated with coloured maps.

On leaving Vatopedi, you should take what is known as "the Monk's Walk", in the lovely forest surrounding the monastery. Then, after a hasty visit to the monastery of Esphigemenou, proceed to the convent of Iviron, where churches and a host of small buildings are grouped round a huge tower, giving the monastery the appearance of a veritable little village. There is nothing really remarkable about Iviron except that, like the majority of monasteries on Athos, it boasts a very fine library and a rich collection of relics and ornaments. Moreover, one of the small chapels contains the miraculous Panaghia Portaitissa ikon which the Archangel Gabriel retrieved from the sea, and thanks to which he was able to walk miraculously on the waters.

It would be tedious to visit all the monasteries on Mount Athos since they are all alike, but you should not miss the Great Lavra monastery, the biggest and most beautiful on the Holy Mountain. Its buildings, dominating the sea, are situated beside a tiny port from which the monks embark for the neighbouring island of Thasos.

The entrance to the Great Lavra lies beneath a vaulted passage protected by several invincible iron doors. One has the impression of entering a fort. The residential buildings extend to the right and left, forming one with the surrounding walls. The most outstanding features of the monastery are the frescoes; those in the catholicon were painted by Theopanus, and those in the refectory by Frangos Castellanos. The latter also decorated the Saint-Nicolas Chapel, which should likewise be visited. But the pride and joy of the monks is their collection of

Entrance to the Monastery of Vatopedi

Father Higoumenos and Proistamenoi Monks of the Great Lavra

relics and ornaments, including a large fragment of the Holy Rood said to have belonged to Constantine, an extraordinary quantity of Byzantine plate, pictures ornamented with chased gold, and the most beautiful 12th-century ikons. Needless to say, there is an immense library, rich in treasures.

THASOS

FROM Iviron, Vatopedi, and the Great Lavra, three islands may be seen—Thasos, Samothrace, and Lemnos—forming a kind of non-clerical suburb of the monastic republic. The French School of Athens has been carrying out most successful excavations in Thasos for the past twenty years. The monks go there frequently, and the charm of the island, the beauty of the girls, and the sweetness of the wine have given rise to a number of dubious stories.

What is the secret of Thasos' charm? It is difficult to say. Immediately one sets foot on this blessed isle, one is tempted to linger there—not so

Monastery of the Great Lavra and Mount Athos

much to admire the archaeologists' discoveries, but to while away the happy hours in a delightful setting, amidst a wonderfully friendly population. Hardly has one sat down at a café terrace in the square, beneath the shade of plane trees, to taste the local wine—a little too sweet for my liking— than the local adolescents cluster round to inspect the newcomer. And none of them needs to be asked twice to sing lovely Greek melodies or, with befitting solemnity, dance rounds strangely reminiscent of the

Catalan *sardana* which is, in fact, a sacred dance from the Bay of Scardana in Delos.

The Isle of Thasos has always been considered the most fertile in the Aegean Sea, producing wine and cereals in abundance. Olives and tobacco are also cultivated there. In the past, the inhabitants enriched themselves from the gold mines. Nowadays they live handsomely by tilling the soil and fishing. Is it their affluence that makes them so serene? The air is full of the joy of living. One feels at ease there immediately, without the slightest desire to do anything other than let life roll by.

Thasos witnessed the birth of one of the greatest painters of ancient times, Polygnotus who—according to Pliny—was the first to paint women with glittering clothes and place variegated mitres on their heads. And Pliny added: "He greatly contributed to the progress of painting, for he was the first to depict open mouths with teeth showing, and introduce expression into his faces instead of the former stiffness. He painted the Temple of Delphi, and the portico in Athens known as the Poecile." We should specify that Polygnotus lived 420 years before Christ, and none of his works has been handed down to us.

SAMOTHRACE

I T was Christianity that ruined the Isle of Samothrace, the highest
in the archipelago (with Mount Phengari over 5,250 feet above sea-
level), for in the past Samothrace owed her renown to the religious
mysteries of the Cabiric gods, which were also performed in the neighbouring islands of Imbros and Lemnos. Little is known about these Cabiric
gods, beyond the fact that initiation into their divine mysteries—the oldest
in the world of mythology—was a highly coveted favour. The initiates
were not permitted to reveal the mysteries on any account, and very few
of them ever betrayed the secrets. All we know is that during the initiation
ceremony the postulant underwent ordeals which were not particularly
dangerous. Then, attired in a sumptuous costume and seated on a throne
lit by a myriad lights, with a crown of olive leaves on his brow and a
purple girdle round his loins, he watched the other initiates perform symbolic dances.

Some claim that the cult of the Cabiric gods originated in Egypt, where

Monks' Kitchen in the Great Lavra

they had a temple in Memphis. According to others, the Cabirians were Vulcan's sons who exploited the iron mines and forged metals.

But nowadays Samothrace owes her renown to the statue—now in the Louvre—discovered in 1863 by M. Charles Champoiseau, French Consul in Andrianople, whilst directing excavations beside the great portico of the Cabiric sanctuary. He noticed an exquisite fragment of white marble, emerging from the earth—it proved to be the breast of *Victory*. The statue was unearthed and transported to France.

Deprived of her mysteries and her *Victory*, Samothrace has little of interest to offer travellers.

Monastery of the Great Lavra

LEMNOS

SAMOTHRACE is separated from Lemnos by Imbros, a fertile island rich in game. The islanders lead a carefree life, farming or ship-repairing. But as Lemnos boasts none of those monuments that provide information on a country's past, travellers tend to overlook her. The Treaty of Lausanne (1923) again placed her under Turkish domination.

Lemnos is still seldom visited. The island, which used to be devastated by volcanic eruptions, produces excellent wine, cereals, and vegetables in abundance. But what made her glorious in the past was her famous sigillate soil which, so Pliny avers, was used above all "against wounds inflicted by earth and sea snakes". Even today, Lemnos soil is used in the Greek islands to heal viper bites and cure certain cases of poisoning.

Legend has it that it was on Lemnos that Hephaistos (Vulcan) landed when Hera (Juno), ashamed of her son's deformity, hurled him out of the heavens. Being received with open arms by the inhabitants of the island, Hephaistos set up his forge there. Later he married Aphrodite, who betrayed him with Ares (Mars). Hephaistos took them by surprise, and enchained them. The women of Lemnos who, so the legend runs, "were still virtuous" in those days, rebuked them so severely that Aphrodite became enraged. She avenged herself by inflicting a scourge on the women, which made them smell so unpleasant that their husbands deserted them. This in turn infuriated the women, who thereupon committed the first of the "Lemnian crimes" by massacring all the men on the island whilst they were celebrating the mysteries of Dionysos.

When the Argonauts landed in Lemnos, the women detained them there, and the island was thus repopulated. Later, during the Median Wars, the Lemnians swept down on the Attic coast and abducted a number of Athenians. But as the children born of this union despised their half-brothers, the Lemnians massacred both mothers and children. This was the second of the "Lemnian crimes" which won the islanders their proverbial reputation for cruelty.

THRACE

ON leaving Mount Athos for the islands, we strayed a little. We could perhaps have returned to Salonica and taken the train for Serres —which, though one of the most important towns in Macedonia, like most new towns holds little interest for tourists—and then ventured on to Drama in the centre of the "golden plain", and the tobacco capital, Cavalla, situated on the north shore of the Aegean Sea, opposite the Isle of Thasos. But once we have seen the Roman aqueduct and the remains of the Acropolis at Cavalla, our best course is to leave this joyless town, cross the river Nestos, and reach Orpheus' homeland, Thrace. The region is very wealthy, thanks to the tobacco, cereals, vegetables, and fruit.

Kimmeria Market in Thrace

Xanthi has little to offer tourists, since she owes her importance to her tobacco plantations—the best in the entire Orient. A more unusual sight is the lakeside city of Vristonis, famed for the preparation of botargo—made of pressed, salted fish roe (mullet or tunny-fish)—which is as great a delicacy in the Orient as caviar.

However, if you travel through Thrace in the month of May, you will perhaps have the good fortune to witness the ritual *anastenaso* dances on St Constantine's Day. Bearing ikons of dancing saints—including St Constantine and St Helen—to the sound of little bells attached to the ikons, the officiants begin to sway to a slow rhythm, to the left, to the right, backwards and forwards, uttering deep cries of ah! ah! oh! oh! eh! eh! Then the spectators form a serried circle round them, uttering cries in rhythm. Some of them go into a trance, leap barefoot on the cinders, and dance there until they drop from exhaustion. Most of them emerge without a burn, and this is considered a sign of grace. The dance goes on throughout the night. The next day, a young bull is sacrificed on the same spot, and morsels are distributed to the dancers as we distribute holy bread. And the dances continue every night for a whole week. When the ceremonies come to an end, everyone goes to church to attend mass. But strangers are not permitted to take part in these ceremonies and in olden times sacrilege was punishable by death.

THE PELOPONNESE

THE PELOPONNESE

O̤N leaving Athens for the "Isle of Pelops", one enters another world. That severe beauty, that superior order, that intimately harmonious communion of the earth, mankind, and the heavens, that "Nothing superfluous" is the apanage of Athena's tiny kingdom, Attica.

The Peloponnese is an extremely ancient, chaotic, disorderly land, rife with legends and fables; a pandemonium in which innumerable centuries of history are inextricably entangled.

If you look at the map, you will see a bare, jagged peninsula right in the middle of the Mediterranean, precariously linked to the mainland by the fragile, mutilated wrist formed by her isthmus, passionately extending the fingers on her hand towards Asia, Africa, and Italy. That rather monstruous hand, eaten away by salt, spattered with spray, bulging with convulsive brawny nodes, has exercised a fascinating magnetic power throughout the ages. The names the Peloponnese now bears or has borne in the past, and the names of the regions into which she is now divided, perpetuate memories of the great human alluvions that submerged her, sometimes simultaneously, sometimes one after another.

There is not just one Peloponnese but a dozen at least, superimposed on each other and stratified by time. The most ancient is the mythical domain of the gods, demi-gods, and their children, who are now transformed into stars and constellations. They glow in the highest heavens, watching immortally over the mountains, forests, and springs which were, and still are, consecrated to them.

We do not intend to sketch the history of all the successive Peloponnesian civilizations—from the Pelasgians to the Pelopidians, from the Perseids to the Heraclidae and the Atridae; from the Achaeans to the Dorians; from the Sparta of Lycurgus to that of Lysander; from the Roman conquest to Byzantine domination; from Frankish Morea to Venetian Morea and Turkish Morea—until the present kingdom of the Hellenes .... On our way, we shall have plenty of opportunities to remember great feats and

Corinth Canal

great names. But it will not always be easy to find our way through this magma of history. A single spot often groups tokens of the past which are centuries apart: a Byzantine church rising above the debris of a pagan temple, a Roman wall encircling a Turkish mosque, a Frankish citadel resting on Cyclopean walls. . . . But the immutable beauty of the landscape allies and reconciles these disparate relics which archaeology has, for the most part, respected up to now.

The joy of the Peloponnese is that, like Sicily, her wastes, wild though they may be in many places, are not just one long line of excavation fields scraped bare, where one has the disappointing feeling of visiting an open air museum. From Epidaurus to Mistra and Olympia to Bassae, Mother Nature has innoculated youthful blood into the ruins; and in spots such as Mycenae and Acrocorinth where the soil is reduced to ashes, the despotic splendour of the light casts huge shimmering mantles of gold, purple, and icy-blue on those dismal expanses, to perpetuate their regality.

Let us cast a final glimpse at the map, to sketch an itinerary: the seven provinces into which the Peloponnese is administratively divided correspond to the cradles of her history. Six of them are bordered by the shore: Corinth, Argolis, Laconia, Messenia, Elis, and Achaia. Each is a petal attached to the heart of a flower—Arcadia.

Shall we surrender to this geographical layout? It is the ideal solution, since it is impossible to envisage a "tourist" itinerary without some form of continuity. To travel from one spot to the next, we shall in turn have recourse to the few existing railways and roads, the coastal routes from cape to cape and gulf to gulf, and the pathways and tracks which can only be followed on horseback or mule.

We shall leave Athens at dawn. Have no hesitation about rising early: the beauty of Greek landscapes is dependent on the light. They are at their best when contemplated at the beginning or end of Phoebus' course: when his rays beat the mountains horizontally or obliquely (or caress them), diffusing deep zones of wandering shadows which accentuate the planes and diversify the effects.

From Athens to Corinth at daybreak, the Gulf of Megara, hemmed and arboured by the road, offers twenty gradations of monochrome blue blandly spread between sea and sky. Only a virtuoso such as the Attic heavens can produce such subtly shaded modulations—the virgin breath of Pallas . . . . Scarcely have we reached the isthmus separating the Bay of Megara from that of Corinth, when it disperses.

Peirene Spring in Corinth

275

CORINTH

FAR from the places they designate, names themselves conjure up a picture in our minds. But preconceived pictures such as these are often far from true, and such is the case of Corinth. One imagines an opulent fertile land, abounding in vineyards, bubbling with springs, and haunted by the spectres of the courtesan-priestesses "whose renown and merits were so great that Pindar himself was not ashamed to extol them. . . ." Alas! Corinth is a desolate waste of burning rock, impatient to unite her flames to the fiery sky.

From the Homeric era until her destruction by Rome, one of the richest and most highly populated towns of the ancient Mediterranean flourished there. Corinth was not so much a Greek city as a cosmopolitan town, a crossroads of nations and races, auspiciously situated at the controls of the main trade routes. Her fortune depended on that narrow tongue of land that made her two ports an invaluable transit wharf. This explains why the Corinthians never encouraged the "cranks" who, from Periander

Corinthian Colonnade in Roman Times

Corinth

to Caesar and Nero to Herodes Atticus, planned or actually undertook to pierce the isthmus. Now that the canal exists, the little modern port of Corinth piteously vegetates. And we have to go nearly five miles beyond the morose town of New Corinth, right into the country, to find the remains of the ancient city where, amidst the outlines of Greek, Roman, and Byzantine porticos, the seven Doric columns of an extremely ancient temple stand undaunted, despite the tide of invasion, pillage, and earthquakes. These venerable monolithic pillars probably date from the first half of the 6th century, and age has imparted to them the mimesis peculiar to certain plants and insects. In their early days they were carefully painted, but now, to slumber in peace, they have adopted the colour and even the consistence of the earth on which they rest. They do not look as if they had been constructed, but rather as if they had been secreted like some giant seed, producing mysterious stalagmites. The sight of those stubborn outgrowths, with something organic about them, inspires a vague feeling of uneasiness—not to say fear.

Radical excavations have been undertaken there by archaeologists from America. They stride across Ancient Corinth as on a colossal blueprint, life-size, and easily legible. Disinterred relics (fragments of architecture, sculpture, and pottery) are scrupulously assembled in a model museum. The contents of the showcases and the steles are mostly rubbish. However, a few small torsos of nude maidens—mostly in Hellenistic style—carved with care from flesh-white marble, evoke the strange legion of courtesans to whom the un-warlike Corinthians entrusted the protection of their town. According to Strabo, in major calamities these priestesses attended the sacrifices and marched in procession with their fellow citizens, singing hymns. With the advent of Xerxes, they were detailed to defend the city, and once the danger was past, their glory was assured. A triumph such as this swelled the ranks of priestesses, and rich citizens anxious to assure success for their undertakings promised to offer Aphrodite a certain number of courtesans whom they brought from the heart of the Orient . . . . Hence the proverb: *Non licet omnibus adire Corinthum*—"Everyone cannot take the liberty of going to Corinth."

ACROCORINTH—The centre of this "sacred prostitution" was the little temple of the Sidonian Astarte, Venus Melania (Venus of nights of love). It was a

Corinth

The Road from Corinth to Patras, near Sikyon

kind of cavern overflowing with riches, surrounded by innumerable annexes and cells which formed a kind of "red light area" probably on the
same lines as the one that used to exist in old Marseilles.

This temple crests Acrocorinth. So little remains that it hardly merits a
rather painful climb, on mule-back, up that gigantic rock 2,300 feet high,
through a picturesque maze of crumbling fortresses (Frankish, Venetian,
and Turkish rather than Greek). But the effort is rewarded by a "sensational"
view (one of the most deservedly renowned in Greece). The beauty lies
not only in the mountains suspended between sea and sky, but also in the
glorious names they bear: Parnassus, Citheron, Helicon, Cyllene, Erymanthus, Hymettus, Pentelicus—and that "sublime promontory" of Sounion,
cloaked in the mists of the Orient .... At sight of a landscape such as this,
one cannot but believe in the immortality of the Myths. And, to confirm
the psychological shock, a hollow in the rock discloses an irrefutable "piece
of evidence"—the Peirene Spring which, in the days of the gods, spurted
forth from the hoof of Pegasus. She is still there, gushing her miraculous
refreshing spray from the deep dark well that imprisons her. And here
again, thanks to the golden brake with which Athena provided him, the

hero Bellerophon, radiant with youth, daunted the great winged horse, bestrode him, and flew off towards the Chimera. . . .

Mercantile Corinth was never ashamed to adopt this divine steed "who lends his back only to poets", as her emblem and trademark. She minted coins bearing his effigy, and flooded the markets of the known world with them. So many of these staters have survived that, on seeing the "noble foal", one is inclined to evoke an erroneous picture of Corinth. Having enriched herself without effort, her sole thought was to enjoy herself and amass a fortune. Her manufacturers and craftsmen produced utilitarian objects and more particularly luxury wares—coffers, goblets, urns and mirrors of bronze, scent-bottles of clay, and bedding beyond compare. Her well-to-do merchants and big bankers were "enlightened connoisseurs", but not a single name has survived to ennoble the memory of a city that produced not one great poet, sculptor, or artist of any kind.

SIKYON—This privilege was reserved for her next-door neighbour, Sikyon, who shone uneclipsed in all the arts. Governed by cultured, peace-loving princes, she resembled a Greek Florence. From the archaic period to the decline of the classical era, Sikyon produced an endless series of masterpieces in which Dorian, Ionian, and Athenian influences were harmoniously reconciled. Some have survived to our day: the metopes from her Treasure (Delphi Museum), the wonderful *Piombino Apollo* (Louvre) and the great

The Temple of Apollo, with Acrocorinth in the Background

figures, known through Roman replicas, sculptured by Polycletus and Lysippus, both of whom were Sikyonians.

As for her painters, they were so renowned that Apelles himself went to work beside them, "not so much to profit from their lessons as to share their reputation." All that remains of them is their names.

The countryside round Sikyon was extremely fertile. Virgil extolled the succulent olives produced there. The horses bred in the region, reputed for the excellence and pureness of their strain, were so costly that "only the most extravagant squanderers from Athens could afford a pair ...."

Nowadays, all that remains on the broad plateau where this "second Athens" used to rise is a series of grooves in the rock worn by chariot wheels, and the eroded tiers of a theatre which (like all Greek theatres) was admirably situated with a "backcloth" formed by the limpid summits of Boeotia, Phocis, and Locris, outlined against an infinitely gentle sky, beyond the blue waters of the gulf.

The Road between Mycenae and Nauplia

ARGOLIS

AFTER this outing to the west on the fringe of Achaia; we turn south and enter Argolis by way of a narrow pass where, far from any dwellings, there is a little station with a great name: Nemea.

NEMEA—This is our first encounter with Herakles, the beneficent Peloponnesian hero. Six of his Twelve Labours were accomplished in the peninsula. When still a beardless youth, he made his debut here by stifling an enormous lion, reputed to have fallen from the sky. The lion's grotto still exists on the heights, and in a valley overrun with huge tortoises one can discern the remains of the stadium where the Nemean Games (one of the four major Hellenic festivals) were performed every other year. Nearby, on a desolate heathland, rise the three surviving columns of a temple dedicated to Zeus of Nemea. Only yesterday, the other columns still lay beside them, ready to be re-erected. This lovely building in Doric style, dating from the 3rd century B.C., could easily be restored. Tourists would then be incited to visit Nemea, rather than rush on—as they usually do—to the mouth of the pass, to visit the three pre-Hellenic cities of Mycenae, Tiryns, and Argos, the major curiosities in the region.

The fascination of these spots is perhaps due not so much to the dramas enacted there, as to the genius of the poets these dramas inspired. Would the Pelopides, the Danaides, the Atridae—those sinister families who killed, betrayed, and even devoured each other in hideous feasts, and those kings and queens who, one after another or at one and the same time, committed parricide, fratricide, infanticide, incest, and adultery—have left so indelible an impression, had their crimes not been transfigured in Ancient times by Homer, Aeschylus, Sophocles, and Euripides? Thereafter, from century to century, and from country to country, these families were adopted, with a constancy savouring of fatality, by hundreds of authors, great and small, from Seneca to Jean Giraudoux.

MYCENAE—On approaching the ruins of Mycenae by way of the famous

Lion Gate (so unspectacular a sight, choked as it is by a narrow passage), the first impression is one of disappointment and confusion. And then, in that immense, inhuman setting of scorched mountains, a miserable parcel of leprous soil cruelly scarred by archaeologists' scalpels imposes an oppressive sensation of wandering through an accursed spot, trampling a soil which emanates a heavy smell of blood. And suddenly one

The Lion Gateway in Mycenae

is obsessed by the thought of the fifteen royal corpses that lay for thousands of years beneath the dust and rubble, forgotten and unsuspected, attired in gold, crowned with gold, armed with gold, masked with gold—until the day (less than a century ago) an obscure Cimmerian barbarian by the name of Schliemann, enriched by banking, came in a burst of fanatic inspiration to profane their tombs. Scientifically laid out in cold glass cases, this "heap of gold" is now exhibited in Athens Museum. It is regrettable that it was not left where it was found, like the

The Treasury of Atreus in Mycenae

treasures of Olympia and Delphi. One can imagine those weapons, jewels, and crowns assembled beneath the great vaulted rotunda known as the "Treasury of Atreus", where they would glitter in the glow of artificial light. Stripped of their fabulous gold, the ruins of Mycenae are reduced to an empty cocoon, a chrysalis from which the soul has flown.

Were the corpses really those of the Atridae, as Schliemann claimed?

Professional archaeologists shrugged their shoulders, disinclined to take this autodidactic *confrère* seriously, since he did not know the first rules of the game. Confronted with an entirely new world, revealing an unknown civilization, they put forth all kinds of hypotheses quite as bold as Schliemann's, and often equally preposterous. The problem continued to arouse discussions and suppositions until twenty years later a second archaeologist, the Englishman Evans—also a "rich amateur"—made another no less sensational discovery: that of an even older civilization now known as Minoan (from the name of King Minos). Affinities between the two discoveries proved without a doubt that Argolis had been occupied by Cretan colonists. According to the experts, this Minoan-Mycenaean (or, perhaps, Meso-Helladic) art dates from two thousand years before our time, i.e., prior to the (supposed) age of the Wars of Troy.... And thus we are authorized to delve even further into the past than Schliemann, and envisage (chimerically) that those gilded corpses were not the Atridae, but the Perseids, the first kings of the city.... And why not the corpse of Perseus himself and that of his wife Andromeda, the beautiful negress which the hero snatched from the monster and brought back from Ethiopia?

On leaving this fearsome lair beneath a torrid, fiery sun, you will be tempted to quench your thirst in the convenient little inn halfway down the hill. It used to go by the frivolously Offenbachian name *Auberge de la Belle Hélène*, but I understand that it has now been replaced by a "tourist guesthouse". Drink the "resinated" wine there, preferably the rosy variety, *kokinelli*. And if its bitter, balsamic flavour brings spots to your eyes, as it probably will, bolster up your courage reminding yourself that this selfsame wine, symbolized by Bacchus' thyrsus—entwined by a vine-shoot and crowned by a pine-cone—intoxicated Silenus in his day.

The guest-house commands an extensive view across the sea, looking out towards Nauplia and Argos, beyond the plain of Argolis,

Entrance to the Tiryns Citadel

Nauplia: Bourzi in the Morning

which is richer in legends than in corn. Nearby, the track crosses the dusty
bed of a dried-up river, now called the Panitza. This is the ancient river
Inachos, the father of the nymph Io with whom Zeus fell in love. And
suddenly Io herself is conjured up before your eyes, transformed by Hera
into a heifer. Argus, the shepherd with a hundred eyes, watches over her,
whilst Hermes plays on his flute a lullaby which closes two hundred eyelids.

And then a magnificent athlete appears on the horizon, advancing erect
despite the weight of his hideous, gory trophy. It is Herakles, returning
from Lerna (a stone's throw away), bringing his master, King Eurystheus,
the still twitching heads of the Hydra of which he has just rid the putrid
marsh. He is on his way to Tiryns—and so are we.

TIRYNS—There is no denying it, the ruins of Tiryns are quite devoid of
charm. Undoubtedly, those penitentiary casemates—formed by an overwhelming conglomeration of "cyclopaean" blocks (some of which weigh
over 30,000 pounds and are piled one upon another to form walls fifty to
sixty feet thick), intersected by low narrow corridors through which one

laboriously weaves one's way in the dark—produce an ineluctable impression of might. But the buildings themselves are shapeless and lacking in grandeur. Can this giant molehill really be described as architecture? The layout itself is unintelligible. It is less a work of art than a document, and the French writer Louis Bertrand was not far wrong in saying "this jumble of stones is no more eloquent than a heap of geological matter...." It resembles a series of shells, cast off by some species of animal that one visualizes trembling with fright, captive in his own prison, run to earth in this dungeon. And yet, according to the ancients the inhabitants of Tiryns shared with the Megarians the reputation of being the gayest people in Greece. "They were so playful by nature that they were incapable of attending to serious matters...." Nowadays, only young donkeys, kids, and lambs are left to frolic on those dead ruins, hidden by the tangle of tall grass.

NAUPLIA—After Mycenae and Tiryns, it is a relief to reach the charming little city of Nauplia, which was for a brief while the capital. On the quaint, bustling wharf, a suitable hotel extends a friendly welcome, and it is pleasant to find oneself back amongst real live people of flesh and blood. Tourists would be well advised to break their journey there. In this sheltered

Little Inn on the Road to Argos

288

Acroargos and Greek Convent

bay, the Mediterranean is transformed into a lake of calm water. The city has a western exposure, and in the late afternoon the setting sun, shining down from a purple sky, gilds the mountains and the sea. This exquisite scene resembles a painting by Claude Lorrain, so perfectly copied by Mother Nature that one expects to see a galley appear in full sail, gliding pompously towards Argos, carrying Iphigenia to Aulis. A mighty fortress composed of six bastions with high-flown names (Achilles, Phocion, Mithridates, Epaminondas, Themistocles, and Leonidas) arrogantly occupies the steep rock at the foot of which Nauplia is built. Its stones have a long story to tell, from Palamedes to Guy de la Roche, and Morosini to Capodistrias. It was here that Palamedes, the craftiest of all the Greeks (if you remember the *Iliad*) introduced from the Orient the calendar, the alphabet, dice, chess, and playing-cards; in the 13th century Guy de la Roche, a French lord from Franche-Comté who became Duke of Athens, battlemented the

Peasants in Argos

walls on which, four hundred years later, the Venetian Morosini sculptured his statue of the Winged Lion. As for Capodistrias, the first head of the Hellenic Government, he was assassinated in Nauplia on the 9th October, 1831, when the heroic War of Independence nearly degenerated into anarchy.

LERNA—In less than an hour a sailing-boat speeds you from Nauplia to the little town of Myli on the other side of the gulf, which serves as port for both Tripolis and Argos.

Nearby the murky waters of the Lerna Marsh stagnate, fed by three springs. The largest ("the Alcyonian lake") is treacherously camouflaged by dense rushes swarming with mosquitoes. Despite modern damming, the setting is still extraordinarily wild. The waters are so deep that the depths have never been sounded; Nero himself failed in the attempt. This is one of the numerous gateways to Hell, through which Hades swept Persephone into his kingdom. The fetid breath of the many-headed Hydra still infests the marshes, where Chateaubriand spent a loathsome night "in the midst of harvesters who resembled wild beasts, lying on sheep dung." He caught a fever there which he shook off only in Egypt.

ARGOS—Argos, a couple of miles inland, no longer lives up to her great name. The few surviving ruins of the Acropolis are strewn over the slopes and summit of Mount Larissa (derived from a Pelasgian word meaning *citadel*). The tiers of a theatre are hewn out of the rock, as are the steps of an endless staircase which is not worth climbing: all that remains at the top are the walls and towers of a Byzantine-Franco-Venetian Kastro, similar to many others in the Peloponnese. A vague excavation there is reputed to be the prison where Danaea was held captive by her father, and secretly impregnated by the Golden Rain from which Perseus was born—an event commemorated by a temple dedicated to "Zeus of the Rain", which has

Muleteers in the Mountain Pastures

since disappeared. But where are the fair Argians famed throughout legend and history? Homer extolled them; Aeschylus represented them lamenting in chorus in *The Suppliants*, and in the 4th century B.C. the poetess Telesilla sang of their prowess as impromptu warriors saving their besieged city from the Spartans. In the days of Plutarch, this mighty deed was still celebrated in Argos by a procession in which the men had to file pitifully by in frilly female garb, whilst the women strode past in male attire, complete with armour.

EPIDAURUS—Nauplia is also the starting-point for a visit to Epidaurus.

The sun was getting low on the horizon when, many years ago, one matchless afternoon in May, we set forth for Epidaurus for the first time. Sunset in Greece is never preceded by haze, and the light is as pure at the end of the day as at the beginning. But the waters which sparkled at dawn are changed into oil, heavy, golden and syrupy, yet wonderfully transparent.

The road from Nauplia to Epidaurus is bordered by meadows watered by sources in springtime, and girt by forests.

Rotunda of the Sanctuary of Asklepios in Epidaurus

The Stadium in Epidaurus

In this rich atmosphere, the peasants' gay costumes glistened like enamels. The peasant-women paused in their haymaking, to watch our caravan go by, and serenely raised one arm, opening and closing the fingers in a solemn, friendly greeting.... To our right, the hills sloped down towards an invisible sea. As if he were saying the simplest thing in the world, Mario Meunier (my travelling companion) murmured: "We are only a stone's throw from Troezen .... We are passing through the woods where Hippolytus used to hunt." Forearmed in this way, I was not so much surprised as relieved to reach the lovely vale of Tempe where Epidaurus slumbers. The Greeks had a secret genius for discovering settings which in some way or another visualized the powers personified by the gods to whom they were dedicated. The moving grandeur of Delphi put pilgrims to a nerve test, sending them into a mystic trance—magnetizing them, in fact. The eurhythmic Athenian landscape, precisely outlined against the most subtle sky in the world, is the mental realm of Minerva, the Goddess of Wisdom. Epidaurus, the shrine of Asklepios, is a haven of grace, a tabernacle of well-being. The mere sight of the landscape is in itself an exhortation to better health. The mountains (called "Hera's Breasts") curve so gently upwards that their rhythmic rise and fall resembles the beat of a perfect heart or the breathing of flawless lungs. Even though the temples which made Epidaurus resemble Lourdes, and the springs that turned it into a watering-place like Bath, have completely degenerated, Dame Nature continues to say: "Revive your hopes; rely on my intercession; I have everything you need to cure you . . . . Surely you are feeling better already?"

There is nothing sad about the ruins of Epidaurus, and her theatre (the largest and most beautiful in Greece, if not in the world) has survived unscathed in all its stark nakedness. It coils into the mountain, like a gigantic fossil in a limestone shell. The architecture is so much in keeping with the landscape that it is hard to imagine the theatre is not one with nature. The breathtaking beauty of the sight defies all description.

On another visit to Epidaurus—also towards the end of a spring day— we witnessed an unforgettable little miracle in this theatre. The young girls who had accompanied us were scattered about on the tiers (which are delicately shaded like pearls). One of them had a flute. Inspired by the twilight and the setting, she began to play on it without a trace of affectation. The

notes were infinitely pure and discreet, yet eloquent in the extreme. We gathered round the graceful musician, moved by the beauty of the melody which seemed to be full of inexpressible promise. The music stopped, and almost immediately after, from the distance behind us, in the bushy heights of the hillside where the theatre was scooped out, we heard the

Port of Poros

294

The Port of Hydra

sound of another flute (less silvery, and a little raucous this time). It was so unexpected, and yet so unconsciously desired that at first we were not over-whelmed with astonishment: it crept upon us gradually in a slow wave of wonderment.

In so hallowed a spot, a prodigy such as this was hardly surprising. From the ancient groves of green oak, wild laurel and mastic, it was surely Pan himself replying to the artless provocation. Hardly had the invisible flute died away than the girl began to play again by ear, repeating the enchanted air. The melody alternated two or three times, and each time the sound of the magic flute became louder and closer. . . . What fabulous creature, half-human, half-divine, was about to emerge from the depths of the tangled forest? First a kid leapt out, then a second, and a third. To our mingled disappointment and relief, they were followed by a young shepherd. With his short flute still to his lips, and his face sparkling with mischief, he sat down beside the girl. Then, thanks to her skilful musical instinct, the alternated song was transformed into a duet in which the fruity rustic sounds of the pan-pipes harmonized with the liquid sounds of the flute. The magic of the dual melody echoed throughout the theatre and overflowed beyond the "secret contours of Silence".

It is now nearly a century since the Sanctuary of Asklepios was first prospected by the Greek Society of Archaeology. As one might expect, the magnificent mutilated statues of Amazons and nereids that came to earth were transported to Athens; but the "second best" was left in a modest local museum nestling behind a copse. On my first visit to Epidaurus I ventured inside. And there, without transition, I could not help but recollect that this was once the site of an entire city, one of the most famous pilgrimages of ancient times frequented for centuries, until the end of Roman domination, by an endless stream of fanatics.

The museum offers a bird's eye view of the Sanctuary as it once was, reconstructed by architects who were too conscientious and too competent to be far wrong. And yet, could this incomparably peaceful vale really have contained that incredible welter of buildings —all those temples, porticos, propylaea, altars, baths, thermae, dormitories, this library, that prytanaeum, this palestra and stadium, and more besides—all serried together into a space less than a mile square seething with a giddy mass of humanity?

I felt little inclined to visualize these buildings—beautiful as they once were—in the setting from which time had evicted them. Nor was I tempted—despite their inestimable documentary value—to devote more than a moment to those steles, found intact, and relating grossly fraudulent healings (extraction of worms, teeth, warts. . . . the tale of the bald man whose hair grew again. . . . and the blindman who was cured but lost his sight again because he refused to pay the god for the miracle . . . . and the broken goblet that the god stuck together again to amuse himself). Was I going to waste the little time I had to spend in Epidaurus with those old wives' tales of sordid witchcraft, when outside . . . .

Outside, framed by her shell of hills, the excavation site welcomed me, and I feasted my eyes on her silent solitudes. All the wounds inflicted on her in the past by archaeologists' picks have now been bandaged. I wandered about as if I were in a park, amongst architectural foundations which in no way hampered my movements, across a waving sea of grass dotted with

Fort of Palamedes in Nauplia

thousands of tiny flowers—all the "simple things in life" which man has left untouched since the day of creation, and which have lost none of their healthful virtues. The setting sun made the whole sanctuary sparkle with light—the lights of Paradise.

It was time to leave .... On the hillside below, the sublime theatre, filled with a vaguely phosphorescent shadow, had ceased to belong to a set period of art or history. In its incorruptible purity and its almost abstract perfection, it was the God of Epidaurus in person.

TROEZEN—At present there is only one route leading to the Sanctuary of Asklepios—the road from Nauplia. In the past, pilgrims used to land on the east coast, in the gulf of Myrtos, where they had a choice of three ports: Epidaurus, Hermione, and Troezen. There is practically nothing left of Epidaurus, and nothing at all of Hermione, but Troezen has retained a few traces of her great past. One has to look for them on the fringe of a plain, half-swamped, half clad in lemon, olive, and fig trees, at the foot of huge rocks forming a bay which has not changed since the fatal day when, to satisfy Theseus, Neptune created the monster described by Theramenus.

Fisherman from Caminias in the Isle of Hydra

Mount Taygetus and the Plain of Sparta

Ancient Troezen was excavated by the French School of Athens. The French archaeologists failed to find everything Pausanias described, such as the seat from which Pelops' son Pittheus dispensed justice, or the house where Theseus was born, or the one where Hippolytus lived. However, the debris of the sanctuary dedicated to that unhappy athletic prince are scattered across the fragrant heath, beside the floor of his temple where the maidens of Troezen laid their tresses on their wedding eve. And then, in all good faith, tourists are shown the wood consecrated to Venus where, nervously driving a needle through the myrtle leaves, Phaedra followed with her eyes a chariot fleeing through the quarry.

In the Middle Ages there was a Frankish stronghold here—the barony of Troezenia or Damalat, named after the town of Damala whose port, Vidhi, is so humble that ships plying along the Peloponnese coast disdain to put in there. Since we are reliant on these ships to take us from Troezen to Gytheion (the port of Sparta), we have to charter a small bark to the neighbouring port of Poros on the little Isle of Calauria, a favourite holiday resort for Athenians. There, in a well-located hotel facing the roads, our only course is to wait patiently for the local steamship from Piraeus.

Pantanassa Monastery in Mistra

HYDRA—After going around the headland of Skylla (the easternmost tip of the Peloponnese), we soon reach yet another island, Hydra.

Her little port is almost hidden away in a natural shell, forming a perfect oval. Palatial homes of white and gilt rise one above another on the steep slope of the reddish-brown rock. They were built by powerful families of buccaneers who, like the corsairs of St Malo, amassed fabulous fortunes there in the time of the Turks. But "gold had not succeeded in stifling in the soul of these uncouth mariners their love for their country and their passion for independence; nor had it softened their character, and when the signal for revolt was given in 1821, they were the first to take up the cause of freedom." Heroes such as Kondouriotis, Miaoulis, and Tombazis went to their destruction. Transformed into men o'war, their 150 racing galleys were sacrificed in heroic battles, and nowadays the descendants of the ancient corsairs are reduced to fishing for sponges.

Hydra would be completely dead, were it not for the fact that every year the Greek Government offers hospitality, free of charge, to young foreign painters. They while away blissful hours in the shade of a huge baroque cathedral, built entirely of white marble, flanked by an elegant campanile pierced with orifices—identical to those in Venice.

LACONIA

ONEMVASIA, the first port of call in Laconia, is also reminiscent of Venice. Byzantium transformed this former peninsula, 160 feet from the coast, into a fearsome rocky island, 975 feet in altitude, with a sheer drop on every side. At the foot, in what remains of the once impregnable fortresses there is an attractive group of Renaissance houses, deplorably neglected and falling into ruins. The wings of the Lions of Saint Mark, sculptured on the façade, have long lost their power. Monemvasia emerged from a long trail of siege and counter-siege. Three times this "Greek Gibraltar" was captured, lost, and recaptured by the Venetians. Prior to that, Guillaume de Villehardouin succeeded in taking the town only after three years of blockade. The citizens' long resistance was explained by the fact that the rock was overrun with cats and rats which multiplied incessantly. Tired of living on them, the Monemvasians capitulated.... It is also interesting to know that in the days when Monemvasia was called

Mistra

301

Malvasia, she gave her name to a famous wine which was so greatly appreciated by medieval tipplers that, so legend has it, when George, Duke of Clarence, was condemned to death by his brother Edward IV, he insisted on being drowned in a butt of Malmsey wine. But one can hardly imagine a single vine-stock growing on this arid rock, and Malvasia was doubtless a depot where the islanders from the Archipelago brought their wine. Nowadays, under another name one can drink excellent Malmsey at Santorini—a dense, syrupy, dark golden wine which gives the impression of being sweet at first sip, but leaves an after-taste that burns the palate.

CYTHERA—On leaving Monemvasia, we have to round Cape Malea (or Holy Angel Cape), the southernmost tip of Greece and Europe, and the terror of sailors in ancient times. The sea winds battle furiously between the dizzy cliffs of the cape and the hills on the Isle of Cythera which, though not quite as lofty, are equally forbidding. Sailing ships have every reason to fear the crossing. Lamartine prided himself on having ventured there and narrowly escaped the boulders that the gale winds often wrest from the cliffs and hurl on  the ships below. He saw a hermit with a long white beard, who knelt precariously on a step in the cliff and prayed continuously as long as the poet's frigate was in sight.

Three other French poets—Nerval, Gautier, and Baudelaire—have left disconsolate descriptions of Cythera (now called Kythera). All three were

Landscape in Laconia

enchanted to see a solitary monument—the gallows—still standing above the fallen temples of the kingdom of Venus. Baudelaire adorned it with a swinging body "already ripe", which "ferocious birds . . . . gorging themselves in hideous delight, were tearing apart." I have skirted the desolate island twice, and I feel safe in asserting that those romantic gallows no longer exist.

On the Way to Sparta—The only port of any importance in Laconia is Gytheion. Nestling in the gulf that authoritatively forces its way between Cape Malea and Cape Taenarus, it has little to offer. On the other hand, the small isle of Cranaea protecting the roads conjures up legendary memories. Having persuaded fair Helen to follow him, handsome Paris found a good hiding-place there for the night, before fleeing to Troy. Later, guided by their flair for business, the Phoenicians established large factories in the vicinity, where they extracted a precious and highly appreciated purple dye from the *murex brandaris* (a shellfish that teems on the shores of the gulf at this particular point).

The road from Gytheion to Sparta winds up and down round the wild mountains. That morning in May when we made the climb, the mountains too seemed to be dyed purple, since they were clad in a dense cloak of tiny vivid red anemones (the violent colour is derived from the ferruginous soil). Even the cloudless sky above was not blue, but a mysterious reddish violet, as if reflecting the fiery earth below. The very landscape thus confirmed our preconceived idea of a pugnacious city; and when the gigantic mass of Mount Taygetus suddenly loomed up round a bend, rearing its dread bronze wall to the West, we no longer had the slightest doubt that at the end of our journey a town withdrawn into her hostile might was waiting to drive us back rather than welcome us . . . . And yet—at first we could hardly believe our eyes—at the foot of the brawny, heavily armoured Taygetus, the Valley of Eurotas appeared unexpectedly like a Paradise Garden of meadows, orchards, and copses! Springtime in Sparta breaks suddenly through, liberating springs and foliage in a bubbling of sap, a blossoming of flowers, and a twittering of birds.

There is not a single swan left on the banks of the Eurotas, but, in the place of hoplites manoeuvering amidst a rain of javelins and a glitter of helmets, clusters of oleander conjured up two irresistibly beautiful ghosts—first Leda, and then Helen. How delightful a tryst! But what of Castor and Pollux, Lycurgus, or Leonidas. They were withdrawn into manlier retreats in Mount Taygetus, from which we failed to oust them.

Sparta—Modern Sparta, dating from the reign of King Otto, is a flat monotonous chessboard of rectilinear streets. The only pleasant thing about the town is the multitude of gardens surrounding low houses, all alike. The museum is full of trifles, but it does possess a delightful cemetery of old

Interior of the Metropolis Church in Mistra

tombstones surrounded by flowers, beneath a golden shower of laburnum. As for ancient Sparta, she was parsimoniously disposed towards the British archaeologists who laid her bare, since she had been barbarously raided throughout the ages by Byzantines, Franks, and Turks for whom she provided a convenient quarry. Consequently only a few traces of the so-called tomb of Leonidas have survived; all the tiers of the theatre have been removed, and the Lacedemonian Acropolis is reduced to a handful of fragments, most of which are Roman. Where is the austere, obdurate city of Sparta? She is certainly not to be found on that attractive little island caught between the Eurotas and its tributary the Magoula. This disconcerting island, clad in a green mantle of trees reminiscent of our own more temperate clime, is called Platanistas. There the Spartan youths and maidens used to wrestle, naked, biting one another, tearing out each other's eyes, eager to hurl their opponents into the river. And there, in an enclosure consecrated to Diana, young children used to be assembled, to be whipped until the blood streamed whilst they stoically held back their screams. Nowadays one goes to Platanistas not to sample the black broth but to laze in the shade, sipping coffee and ouzo, to the cooing of turtle-doves in the poplar trees.

Ares, the God of Battle, has ceased to reign there. An hour's pleasant stroll through the peaceful, smiling kingdom of Flora and Vertumnus leads you from Sparta to Mistra by way of dawdling paths between thriving vegetable plots and orchards bordered by straggling hedges. Beneath dishevelled olive trees and fig trees as tall as oaks, tangled vine-shoots brush against your head, and water ripples on all sides, weaving through the short grass and racing along the clay ditches. Then the plain comes to an end and the mountain begins. For a moment ancient Sparta thrusts herself into your memory: this deep narrow gorge that suddenly appears, roaring with furious waterfalls, must be the famous rock of the Apothetes from which prisoners of war and deformed children were hurled. Yet here again a refreshing little café in an arbour invites you to forget such sinister pastimes.

MISTRA—The town is perched on a tall spur, jutting out from Mount Taygetus. This huge natural amphitheatre is overrun with perennial plants and dotted with terraces where, amidst cypress and orange trees, cupolas straight from the *Thousand-and-One-Nights* (the colour of coral, turquoise, and jade) rise up on all sides; seen as a whole, from below, it does not give the impression of being deserted in any way. And in actual fact, Byzantine Mistra is not quite dead. The sight of her slow mortal agony would be heartbreaking, were it not for the fact that the laborious ascent by way of narrow, zigzag streets paved with loathsome cobbles is relieved now and then by a chapel, a church, or a monastery still towering above a chaos of crumbling houses. A few priests or nuns remain to welcome you in their dignified yet affable way, quick to show that hospitable spirit one comes across everywhere in Greece.

These churches are almost all that remains of the town built on the lower reaches of the hill. Founded in the 14th century by the "despots"—the Palaeologus and Cantacuzene sons and brothers of the emperors of

Despots' Palace in Mistra

Byzantium—Latin Mistra endured two hundred years and numbered fifty thousand inhabitants. The six or eight churches are more or less dilapidated, but the interior walls and vaults are decorated throughout with frescoes of a relatively late style. They are not masterpieces by any means, but how can one fail to be moved on contemplating them in the company of an old priest who takes a naïve pleasure in playing the guide, in the fragrance of incense and wax, whilst the bells ring on a nearby belfry? These frescoes, seven hundred years old, possess the indefeasible beauty of works of art that remain obdurately faithful to their duty and their destiny.

Halfway up the slope, beyond the last monastery, there is total devastation. The climb continues between the immense ruins of the Palace of the Despots, later occupied by Islam who installed mosques, baths, harems and bazaars. Here and there walls and lookout towers may be discerned. And then comes another climb across a difficult stony zone, which terminates in another series of ramparts surrounding the mighty redoubt where Guillaume de Villehardouin reigned as feudal lord over the Frankish dukes and barons amongst whom his father Geoffroy had parcelled Morea.

This "gilded borough" dates from the middle of the 13th century. At that time, for nearly two hundred years France had been the uncontested mistress of the Eastern basin of the Mediterranean. The history of those Frankish empires, which lasted from the founding of the kingdom of Jerusalem in 1099 until the fall of Cyprus in 1571, has fallen into oblivion. In the days when the world was still very small, when America was unknown and one had to sail round Africa to reach Asia by sea, medieval France possessed a great Empire in Greece and Asia Minor. As far as Morea is concerned, we cannot do better than quote from a book—which it is now almost impossible to find—by the scholar Alexandre Buchon who visited Greece over a hundred years ago, with the sole purpose of tracing the steps of the French Knights and Crusaders:

"Geoffroy de Villehardouin—who became Prince of Morea or Achaea thanks to his bravery and ability—immediately introduced modern customs into his State and had money minted in his name. On the model of the

Gipsy Camp in the Peloponnese

308

kingdom of France, his principality was divided into large fiefs, entrusted to barons who came under his suzerainty .... The principal voice in the council fell to the Duke of Athens, from the de la Roche family of Franche-Comté. The Duke of Naxos or the Cyclades, the Palatine Count of Cephalonia and the other Ionian Isles, and the three tertiary Barons of Oreo, Chalkis and Carystos in Euboea, were entrusted with naval defence. The Baron de Caritena guarded the mountains. The Baron de Passava, of the House of Neuilly, whose camp was pitched in the very heart of the warring territory of Maina, was invested with the hereditary dignitary of Marshal of the principality. De la Trémouille, de Toucy, de Brière, de Charpigny, de la Palisse, du Périgord, de Courtin, de Ligny, de Brienne, de Bussy, de Lusignan, de Bracy, d'Agout, d'Aunoy, and many other lords, and also the Knights of St John of Jerusalem and of the Temple, received fiefs of varying importance at different times.

"The countryside bristled with fortified castles: the Prince's castle for the general guard; barons' castles in the centre and on the extremities of the baronies; and castles for the lord-bannerets .... In rediscovering the customs of their homeland beneath the lovely sky of Greece, the French became attached to the conquered country. Many of them brought their sisters and part of their families there, and Morea soon became—to quote Honorius—a New France. But unfortunately the knights began to fight each other over questions of rivalry. First the Greeks and then the Turks recaptured Constantinople. Meanwhile France had almost forgotten her possessions in the East, for the kingdom was in dire distress. The only enemy that counted was the English, who had occupied France. The principality of Morea was unable to hold out for long, whilst Greeks, Venetians, and Florentines quarrelled over the scraps. Barely ten years after Mahomet conquered Constantinople, Morea fell prey to the Turks, and Greece as a whole was divorced from civilization for nearly four centuries."

The wonderful adventure of the Frankish Knights in Morea was transfigured by the visionary lyricism of a poet of genius. Those ruins lying beneath a thick shroud of ivy buzzing with bees were brought to life again by Goethe in his *Second Faust*, in which, through the mists of Weimar, he filled his invincible old age with enchantment. He selected this lofty spot as the birthplace of Euphorion, born from the last love of the Swan's Daughter and the Germanic hero. Maurice Barrès saw him surge up there, leap forth, and fade away in a devastating glow of light, like a mirage between heaven

Corn Threshing

and earth. From this "beautiful volcano of history and poetry" he brought back his most precious memory of Greece: "The universe will never be a lonely place for me, since I carry the memory of those dazzling pictures in my mind's eye. I recall them without ever wearying, like a shepherd on Mount Taygetus who perpetually whistles the same three notes. Those beautiful moments of my journey come dancing back. With motionless features and impassioned movements, they adorn my past and hide my coffin from me."

ON TO MESSENIA— From Sparta, Messenia may be reached either by land or by sea. Although it is not really dangerous, the journey by land calls for prudence, endurance, and contempt for vertigo. It can be undertaken only on horseback or mule, in the company of *agoyatai* (native guides). It entails crossing the compact Taygetus mountains by way of the *langada* of Trypi, the sole gorge which cuts right through the range (and a veritable labyrinth). Those impressive wastes are a magnificent sight of nature in the raw, only too often masked by dense mountain fog. (The above should all be in the past tense, since I am told there is now a road right through Mount Taygetus.)

To go there by sea you have to return to Gytheion, whence a second steamship conveys you to Kalamata-Nisi, in the hollow of the Gulf of Messenia. Between the two havens, the ship skirts the arid Mani peninsula sufficiently slowly to give passengers a glimpse of a region which is justly claimed to be the most archaic in the Peloponnese.

THE MANI—Mount Taygetus narrows into a fierce, long rocky spine, all scrag and bone, terminating abruptly in the sharp tip of Cape Taenarus (now called Matapan), where Herakles emerged from the Nether Regions with Cerberus noisily straining at the leash. The Mani is "the end of the Greek world". The proud race that has survived there jealously regards itself as the sole authentic line descending from the Spartans. In a Christianized world, the Maniotes long remained faithful to pagan beliefs and customs. Ancient authors claim that in the 7th century B.C. horses were sacrificed to the Sun each year on the summit of the cape.

The Maniotes were unshakeably independent and warlike, and neither Romans, nor Franks, nor Turks (nor the Greeks themselves) ever succeeded in subjugating them. The Mani has conserved her feudal character to this day. The countryside bristles with fortified cities. Each family defends itself against a neighbouring clan; as in Corsica, family feuds are hereditary. In olden times, a single village often contained twenty or thirty square towers, within which one could climb from storey to storey only by way of indoor ladders which were removed at night. Bitter enemies though they may be, the Maniotes unite instantaneously in the face of common danger, devoting themselves body and soul to the head of some ancient family whose ancestry and authority are uncontested. Thus it was that in 1821 the famous Peter Mavromichalis, known as the "King of Mani", raised ten thousand Maniotes against the Turks, whom they decimated mercilessly. Once they had driven out the Turks, they returned to their favourite pastime of warring amongst themselves so boisterously that Mavromichalis found himself in prison. However, the "King of Mani" later became a senator and personal adviser to King Otto.

Like a monstruous madrepore, the shores of Mani are indented by innumerable creeks and grottoes where the Maniotes from the coast used to hide out as pirates a century ago. Hermit-monks, on the lookout in the crags, reputedly acted as surreptitious sentinels on their behalf. Nowadays there are neither pirates nor monks. But, although they no longer assassinate

castaways, the Maniotes now indulge in another form of massacre. At the end of the autumn great flights of quail flutter down there so exhausted that they are caught by the thousand in nets or even in the hand. Once they have been dried in the sun and pickled in salt, there are enough quail—supplemented by the produce of the sea—to satisfy the hunger of the coastal population, and there is even a surfeit for export throughout the Mani where it is considered a delicacy. In fact, the small pier on the tip of the cape is actually known as Quail Port.

MESSENIA

KALAMATA, the port of Messenia, is the most important town in the Peloponnese after Patras. Suburbs over half a mile from the sea link it to the "ladder" where passengers land on a quay dating from the end of last century, built by French engineers.

The lower (modern) town is pleasing to the eye. It too, was designed by the French at the time of the War of Independence. A wide, lively street separates the new quarter from the old, built on the slopes of the abrupt incline at the top of which the French again (the Knights this time) built a sturdy fortress in times gone by. Guillaume de Villehardouin, who was born in Kalamata, made it his capital. The steep little streets are still bordered by gloomy medieval houses. Some of the doors are blazoned with the *fleur de lys* of France or the *Croix Ancrée* of Villehardouin. A few ancient Greek families in Kalamata are of French origin.

From the top of the Kastro, one has a general view of the widespread plain of Messenia which is so fertile that the Ancients named it Makaria—the Happy Land. To the south, the plain opens on to the sea; to the east it is protected by the Taygetus range, and to the north by the mountains of Arcadia. Opportune cliffs to the west protect it from the winds blowing in from the Ionian Sea .... But alas, the peaceful Messenians derived little benefit from their natural advantages. As early as the 8th century, their highly undesirable neighbours, the Spartans, seized this Promised Land. They remained there almost without interruption for five hundred years. It required a Greek "Washington" (as historians readily call Epaminondas) to drive them out when he invaded the Peloponnese. After turning the capital of Messenia into a fortress, the valorous Theban overcame the stubborn Lacedemonian phalanges at Mantinea, where he paid for his victory with his life. The fortifications of Messene were famed in ancient times, and they still arouse the enthusiasm of the connoisseurs, who regard them as the "masterpiece of Greek military art".

It is an easy trip from Kalamata to Messene, across the Happy Plain, through a tangle of thriving blackberry bushes, olive, orange, and pomegranate trees. The fields of maize look as if they were sewn to the vineyards. Here and there haughty plane trees cluster round fountains reminiscent of Islam, and the pathway runs between rows of gigantic aloes and imperturbable cactus shrubs, forming African vaults of prickly pears and aggressively defensive spears which the hottest rays of the sun are powerless to penetrate.

Landscape between Olympia and Pyrgos

315

MESSENE—Amply protected by the foot-hills of Mount Ithome, Messene nestles in a wide basin reputed (erroneously) to be the crater of an extinct volcano. The masterly walls of Epaminondas unfurl over an expanse of five miles and more. They date from the 4th century B.C., and considerable stretches are in a remarkably fine state of preservation. The walls are built of magnificent blocks of white stone that looks like marble, and so skilfully hewn and assembled (many of the almost invisible joins are still intact) that they are far more pleasing to both the eye and the mind than the clumsy crumbling bricks of Roman ruins. There exists a hierarchy in materials, independent of the work of art itself: those wonderful stones surviving from the utilitarian walls of Messene put the Greek mason on the same footing as the Greek architect; they are quite as moving as a fragment of a frieze or metope, or a broken column in a temple. Sturdy wild bay trees stand watch over the noble corpses. The bitter aroma of the Apollonian plant tickles the nostrils like incense.

Leaving Kalamata and continuing to coast westwards, the steamer now skirts the arid, graceless shores of the headland that forms the fourth finger of the Peloponnesian hand on the map (a thick, spatulate finger—not to say deformed). After rounding Cape Gallo (or Akritas), we encounter the heavy swell of the Ionian Sea (which we follow mentally as far as the shores of Sicily); and then we head due north, hugging an abrupt, monotonous coastline suddenly broken by a high, narrow doorway. It opens on to a quite unsuspected inland lake, or rather, roads—the theatre of a memorable naval battle on the 19th October, 1827, which inspired young Victor Hugo to write his ode, the *Orientales* (which is now of little interest).

NAVARINO—The Battle of Navarino, entered into by surprise, decided the freedom of Greece . . . . It was an odd encounter, in an odd place: 192 ships —Turkish, English, French, and Russian—were crammed into an enclosed space about two miles square. They were not assembled in this "eel-pot" with a view to fighting each other, but on the contrary, in order to negotiate a truce ("without hostility or bloodshed"). But a shot from a Turkish ship was fated to kill a British officer, giving rise to a general conflagration. It was a long and terrible battle, unleashing a hurricane of fire for three hours. Serried one beside the other, the ships formed a huge mobile dais. The crews fought hand to hand, in a blinding volley of thunder produced by 3,714 cannon, firing their broadsides point-blank. It was a long time before

Olympia

the smoke concentrated in the closed roads cleared away. In the evening, when the wind had at last swept it away, it became evident that the Turkish squadron was totally defeated: 58 ships had been sunk. And long after, the huge black hulks could still be discerned, bogged down in the white sand, ten fathoms deep.

The now-deserted roads of Navarino have become a naval cemetery, watched over by half-a-dozen memorials, by way of which as many European countries stake their claim to a forgotten doughty deed. The modern town, built by the French, slumbers in the stillness of its empty port. At the other end of the roads, the ancient city of Pylos—where Nestor the Sage used to reign—is completely dead. The fabulous grotto where Hermes hid the oxen he had stolen from Apollo in nearby Arcadia is still there; so are the oxen, petrified in a forest of stalagmites.

THE gulf of Argolis, nestling against the eastern flank of the Peloponnese, is matched by the Gulf of Arkadia on the western flank. The low, gently curving shores are composed of rich alluvial soil washed down from the mountains by the Arcadian rivers. The Messenian town of Kyparissia, in the south of the gulf, is green with orchards of apricot and almond trees, and groves of mastic (the resin from which is used to flavour raki and ouzo). Vines are cultivated in Elean Pyrgos north of the gulf; her port, Katakolo, exports currants by the ton. A debonair train, whinnying gaily as its smoke curls round the cypress trunks, conveys tourists from Katakolo to Olympia.

OLYMPIA

NEARLY all cruises which leave for Greece from Marseilles or Venice call on the way out at Katakolo, so that Olympia is the first sanctuary anyone arriving from France or Italy visits on Greek soil. There is no risk of feeling out of one's element. Olympia is essentially western, not only in its geographical situation but also in general appearance. Surveying these mountains which are neither particularly high

Olympia

nor particularly striking, beside the river with its wide bed of pebbles and
sand, in the shade of those pine, olive, and cypress trees, one might well be
in Southern France or Italy. As for the ruins themselves, they do not have a
dominant part to play: there is not a single "specially manufactured"
monument. The main merit of the vestiges is the way they harmonize so

intimately with nature that one could swear never an archaeologist or contractor had been this way, everything having been created by Father Time. . . .

And yet, since the 18th century this illustrious sanctuary has been the archaeologists' paradise. In 1766 the Frenchman Fauvel recognized the ruins of the Temple of Zeus, which his compatriots were the first to excavate during the Morean expedition. And then in 1875, fulfilling the prophetic vow of their compatriot Winckelman, German scientists undertook the total excavation and methodical exploration of the *Altis*—the Sacred Wood—which until then had been buried under silt fifteen to twenty feet thick. The work took six years (from October to May each year). 130 statues or bas-reliefs, 13,000 objects of bronze, 6,000 coins, 400 inscriptions, 1,000 objects of clay, and the remains of 40 monuments were brought to light. It was decided not to exhibit the ruins like corpses in a morgue: without undergoing any abusive restoration, they were left in natural surroundings. The grass and the trees were allowed to grow around them, so that on present-day Olympia handsome pine trees of varying ages (the eldest being seventy years old) form a sacred wood which, though certainly vastly different from the original sacred wood, is pervaded with charm and poetry which immediately cast their spell on the visitor.

In the past, the *Altis* was wooded with olive and plane trees; nowadays it is a pine forest. The pines grew up of their own accord from seeds which an auspicious wind carried across from the nearby hill. Saplings big and small found their niche from which they could keep company with some re-erected column, watch over scattered shafts, cast their shadow over the substructure of a temple, or accentuate perspective. The excavation site at Olympia naturally has a style of its own; one has the impression of wandering through a picture by Poussin (or rather, across the free sepia drawings sketched from life, in which Poussin gives a hint of the picture to be born therefrom).

It is not so much the colour as the light that brings trees and stone into communion with each other. Polychrome is replaced by a gamut of bronzes and golden hues, soberly allied by subtle, delicate shades without a trace of affectation. It is a bewitching sight, and the air is fragrant with the balm of pine trees and carpets of red needles, whilst thousands of tiny nameless flowers scent one's steps with a pleasant smell of honey.

In this little wood, nestling at the foot of a modest hillock, before these aged stones, broken and scattered, or tenaciously rooted into the soil, is it possible to imagine what this famous sanctuary must once have been like, when the various people of Greece used to foregather there for peaceful feasts every four years, under the patronage and in honour of the gods, in the pride of their might, the consciousness of their unity, and the cult of their race? Unaided, imagination could not venture in this domain. In this *Itinerary*, Pausanias scrupulously enumerates and describes the wealth of monuments in the *Altis*: he also gives details of the rules and the regulations

Olympia

governing the various trials of the famous gymnastic and equine competitions. But Pausanias lived in the 2nd century A.D., by which time the Greeks had long ceased to be a great, free people. Subjugated by the Macedonians, and then by the Romans, although still on home ground in Olympia, they were no longer amongst their own people. "Barbarians" were now participating in their games, which, since the foundation of the sanctuary, had been open only to full-blooded Hellenes; the *Altis* (and its environs) was littered with arrogant monuments, erected by the "occupants", from Philip to Nero, and Mummius to Hadrian.

The heyday of Olympia corresponds to the period following the victories of Salamis and Platea. Until then, the wood of wild olive trees remained almost intact (within the limite defined by Herakles). Two highly archaic edifices of small proportions (the Heraeon and the Pelopion) loomed up almost alone. All Zeus boasted was an altar in a clearing. The victors of the Persians decided to dedicate a temple to him, larger and more beautiful than those which then existed in other Greek sanctuaries. Built between 468 and 457 B.C., the Temple of Olympia is senior to the Parthenon and the temples of Delphi and Epidaurus. It is over 200 feet long by nearly 90 feet wide, and to make room for it in the *Altis* (which covers less than 2,150 square feet), a large proportion of the sacred olive trees had to be torn up. When it was erected in all its magnificent newness (sheltering the colossal chryselephantine statue, Phidias' masterpiece and one of the Seven Wonders of the World), the character of the sanctuary was completely modified.

The apogee of Olympia lasted little more than a century and a half. After the defeat of Cheronea, a slow decline began, (which was to endure seven

The Temple of Zeus in Olympia

hundred years). The games lost none of their popularity; they continued to attract a fanatic public, but the religious, civic, and political prestige of these "sacred truces" had vanished forever. Olympia was nothing more than the great profane crossroads of Mediterranean cosmopolitania. It became at one and the same time a race-course, an amusement park, a fairground, and a festival hall where people went to amuse themselves, out of curiosity, and doubtless for more snobbish reasons—probably the way one goes to Deauville or Nice during the "season".

The last Olympiad was held in 393 A.D. The following year the Christian Caesar Theodosius I prohibited the practice for all time. Nonetheless the buildings of the persecuted cult remained standing—and it is probably that pagan priests continued to officiate in the abandoned sanctuary. In 426 a second Theodosius, just as fanatic as the first, ordered it to be burnt down. For all that, the Temple of Zeus was not to perish by the hand of man: in the 6th century it was overthrown by an earthquake.

The columns are still there, prostrate on the grass, for the most part lined up side by side exactly as they fell in one swoop. There is talk of re-erecting them, but is this advisable? All those shafts, hewn out of a rather coarse tuff, have been somewhat exfoliated by the years; restoration would entail considerable reinforcement with cement.... The way in which the Parthenon was similarly restored some twenty years ago is hardly encouraging.

The two frontons of the temple and twelve of its metopes were decorated with sculptures. With the exception of two metopes which were unearthed by the French in 1829 (and are now in the Louvre), the German scientists found large fragments of the decorations, of inestimable worth. The stones are now assembled in a museum which, though unattractive to look at, was happily built off the track. With Paeonios' *Victory* and Praxiteles' *Hermes*, they make up the main attraction at Olympia. Unfortunately these magnificent and highly precious stone carvings, which were intended to be seen from below (the frontons were 40 feet above the ground) are exhibited almost at eye-level, thus accentuating the sculptor's intentional deformation and betraying his purpose.... His, or theirs?—Indeed, the sculptures would seem to be the work of several hands: Peloponnesian hands, heavy at times, but controlled by austere minds, wedded to truth and greatness. We are confronted with a transitional style of art. These frontons and metopes (attributed to 460 B.C.) still betray the expressive gawkiness of Aeginean

Vitina

archaism (of about 480 B.C.), and yet already hint at the liberal style and poetic force of Attic classicism as it was to blossom forth less than 25 years later in the Parthenon.

It is a moving experience to dally in that immense gallery between strolls through the *Altis*. Paeonios' radiant *Victory* is exhibited there on the original stele 30 feet high which used to be placed in front of the temple; she seems to be descending from heaven through the untrammelled light, to take her place amongst the olive trees. Unfortunately the statue was discovered in pieces, and it cuts a sorry figure with its ridiculous remains of a skull barbarously attached to the shoulders by a hideous iron stem. Although the goddess has lost her wings, invisible wings still bear this youthful body, vibrant from head to heels, scorning captivity in the museum, despite mutilations.

On the other hand, Praxiteles' *Hermes* is perfectly in harmony with the small gallery where it is displayed. This world-renowned statue was discovered almost intact (with only the left arm missing) in the ruins of the temple of Hera which was small, ill-lit, and congested with other statues, vases, coffers, tapestries, ex-voto offerings, etc. In the midst of those motley treasures, this marble polished with such loving care must have looked more like a luxury article than a work of art. Its value lies in the nature and quality of the medium, and the subtle, refined craftsmanship. No cast can give any idea of the beauty of the original; it emanates a gentle golden phosphorescence which seduces the eyes in somewhat the same way that the smell of tuberoses charms the senses.

ARCADIA

ARCADIA—that ancient country which time and mankind have left so unscathed that it still seems to cradle the childhood of the world—was still practically impenetrable at the beginning of this century. Travellers ventured there only in the company of a courier (or *dragoman*) supplied guides, mounts, and food. He also assured accommodation—of a kind—in a rudimentary *khan* (inn for horses), the home of a dignitary, or in a convent. Nowadays the exceptional natural beauty of Arcadia have won her fervent admirers; but they are still few and far between; and I doubt whether any of the tourist agencies make regular excursions as far as the frigid springs of the Styx or the barren wastes of Lake Stymphalus. However, a carriage road now crosses Arcadia from west to east, making it possible to travel without difficulty from Pyrgos to Tripolis (the present capital of the province). Climbing over hill and vale, it also links several small summer resorts recently established in the heights

Langada

(Alonistania, Vitina, Maguliana, Ipsus), where one is sure of accommodation and from which one can radiate further afield.

The secondary roads are hardly more than tracks. They soon peter out, compelling those who explore on foot to undertake perilous mountaineering feats in the bottom of deep gorges and on the sides of steep mountains culminating over 6,500 feet above sea-level. They isolate Arcadia on all sides, making her an immense fearsome fortress in the middle of the Peloponnese, which, throughout the centuries, has frequently offered a haven but seldom been violated. To the north, Mount Cyllene, the Aroanian Mountains, and Erymanthus form an intransigent wall parallel to the southern shore of the Gulf of Corinth. The Menalian chain breaks off in a series of ramifications and unites in the south with the imposing Lyceum Mountains, which rival in height with Taygetus.

Even in the height of summer the tallest summits are capped with snow. The mountain slopes are often clad in pine-forests which cast an icy shadow. Were it not for the paradisiac limpidity of the Grecian sky, one could imagine one had strayed into the Tyrol. In the well-watered valleys below,

Byzantine Church

326

Farms with Painted Façades, near Tripolis

these hyperborean pines give way to groves of plane trees, beech and oak, pastures, and lavender shrubs; then, just above the foot, grow myrtle and bay, pomegranate and turpentine trees, enormous cacti, fig, mulberry and orange trees—not to mention olive groves and vineyards.

MOUNT LYCEUM—The Arcadians used to claim they were "born before the Moon"; they prided themselves on being the only indigenous inhabitants of the Peloponnese, and situated the cradle of their race on Mount Lyceum (where Saturn and Zeus confronted each other before the birth of the world). There the Earth had given birth to their ancestor, divine Pelasgus, "the first man who gave up eating green leaves and roots and—according to Pausanias —taught his fellow men to live on acorns."

It was also on Mount Lyceum that King Lycaon, the son of Pelasgus, sacrificed a newborn child to Zeus, to put him to the test, and sprinkled the altar with the blood. He had cause to rue it, for Zeus was outraged and promptly transformed Lycaon into a wolf. Since then, on the anniversary of the crime, certain Arcadians likewise become wolves, but not necessarily for life since "if, as wolves, they abstained from eating human flesh for ten years, they became men again. . . . If they ate any, they remained wolves." These werewolves used to roam throughout Arcadia terrifying the inhabitants who have been shepherds for the most part since time immemorial. And finally, it was on this same Mount Lyceum that the selfsame Zeus fell in love with the daughter of the king-wolf, young Callisto, the beloved companion of Artemis. Two sons were born of their union: Arcas, whom Hera, out of jealousy, transformed into a bear, and Pan of the illustrious cloven hooves. One gave his name to the country, who appointed the other as her divine patron. Arcadia was dotted throughout with altars, statues, temples, and sacred woods dedicated to Pan. For the naïve Arcadians, Pan was not so much a god as a good genie and invisible friend, fond of hunting and hunters—and treated so familiarly by the latter that they whipped his

Shepherds Leading their Flocks to the Mountain Regions

image when, instead of driving the game into their nets, Pan forgot himself in pursuit of a nymph.

One could unfurl a never-ending roll of fables here .... Arcadia's extraordinary mythological wealth is said to be the richest in Greece. This antique folklore emanates a poetry composed purely of instinct and imagination, inspiring a feeling for nature which, throughout the ages, remains primitive and immaculate. Although the Arcadians were neither artists nor poets, they were all good musicians, and they dedicated to their gods "the songs of the tender, credulous lyre" and of the rustic flute, both lyre and flute having been invented in Arcadia. On his native Menal, with the shell of a tortoise and the guts of a sheep the infant Hermes fashioned the first lyre; and, with his hirsute arms from which the nymph Syrinx slipped to be transformed into reeds, ingenious Pan assembled seven of the hollow stems and, blowing into them, sent up a bewitched air to his prey who was now no more than a shadow. Two other native nymphs reiterated

the air—plaintive Echo and Pitys, who was changed into a pine tree, and with her Aeolian harp infused a soul into the murmur of the wind. . . .

Charmed by tales such as these, from one age to the next poets and painters all agreed to regard Arcadia as the land of dreams, the fanciful kingdom of idyll and pastoral . . . . And indeed, certain fertile hilly regions on the outskirts of Elis, sloping harmoniously down towards the Ionian Sea, confirm the impression Virgil and Horace, Anacreon and Ronsard, and all the other poets formed of that Arcadian land which they visited only in dreams. The noble, peaceful foliage which casts its shade on the banks of the Ladon resembles the leaves surrounding the rustic cenotaph where Nicolas Poussin's shepherds enviously decipher the four magic words: "*Et in Arcadia ego. . . .*" but it goes without saying that the insipid settings, in which the gallant shepherds of Florian offer their hearts in nosegays of roses or thrushes' nests to shepherdesses with beribboned crooks, are but poor imitations, inspired by artifice and convention . . . . The real Arcadia is a wild country with an austere, impressive, earthly beauty chilled by long icy winters—a frightening labyrinth of mountains rent by ravines and precipices at the bottom of which waterways flow untamed. In a series of torrents, rivers, and waterfalls, they disappear suddenly and mysteriously, snatched into eerie caves or swallowed by fathomless gulfs, to reappear lower down, unpredictably, spurting from the soil in huge bubbles like blood from a cut artery, or divided into thousands of baby winds, restored to their original state as springs. Thus from *katavothre* to *katavothre* (the Greek name for these gulfs), over and under Arcadia, then over and under Elis, and finally over and under the sea as far as Sicily, amorous Alpheus frenziedly pursues the swift nymph Arethusa, the poetic explanation of a natural phenomenon.

Apart from Tripolis, which is simply a wide crossroads (the "turntable" of the Peloponnese); apart from Tegaea and Megalopolis, both of which cities are dead and buried, there are few towns of any size in Arcadia; however, there are innumerable villages, big and small, on the mountains and in the plains, frequently dominated by the medieval ruins of a Frankish castle. The houses, swarming like bees round a hive, servilely flaunt the gold and russet tones of the rocky slopes to which they cling. Here and there in a hidden vale, a chapel or tiny convent, more or less abandoned beside a fountain, between sharp cypress trees, rounds the crevassed clay with its Byzantine cupolas.

Little Square in Tripolis

BASSAE—The famous (although rarely visited) Temple of Bassae is even more hidden (or at least it was in the past, since there was not a trace of a road leading up to it). The inhabitants of antique Phigalia dedicated this temple to Apollo Epikourios, the charitable. For centuries it slumbered in its high rustic solitudes, 3,900 feet above the sea, until it was accidentally discovered in 1764 by the French architect Bocher.

One can enviously imagine the stupefied wonder the architect experienced on coming abruptly and unexpectedly face to face with this divinity in stone that loomed up almost intact in a prodigious silence, in the heart of a wide hemicycle of mountains rising heavenwards in tiers like swoops of a wing, from the first bushy waves of holly oak, broom and briar to the solemn summits—naked, wooded, or sparkling with snow—of Mounts Ithome, Taygetus, and Lyceum.

Nowadays, explorers who undertake the ascent—which takes several hours on mule-back—set out not in expectation of a surprise, but a promise. And yet the moment the voices of that sublime choir of columns rise in unison to greet the visitor, the excursion becomes so breathtaking an experience that it is prudent to qualify it as indescribable.

The Temple of Bassae is unique not only on account of its picturesque, poetic setting, but also because of the originality and perfection of its proportions, the delicacy and rarity of the grey-blue limestone veined with lilac and rose, and lastly (or perhaps primordially) on account of its miraculous state of preservation, unequalled by any other temple (in Greece, at least, since Segesta and Paestum should not be overlooked). Although the frontons have disappeared, the architrave remains in place, supported by columns that did not even have to be re-erected, as did most of those in the Parthenon, its blood brother—both temples having been designed by Ictinos, the most famous architect of ancient times.

The Phigalians resolved to dedicate a mountain and a temple to Apollo, since he had protected them from the plague. The mountain was Kotylos; as for the temple, eager to boast a building as beautiful as the Temple of Olympia (which was hardly completed, and where Phidias created a statue of Zeus), they commissioned the artist who had collaborated with the great sculptor on the Acropolis. This took place in about the 26th Olympiad, i.e. about 420–415 B.C. The Parthenon had then been finished for barely twenty years. In Bassae, Ictinos in no way repeated himself. To crown an illustrious and mighty city, the Parthenon imposes an impression of majesty and might, whereas the Temple of Bassae—which is far more modest (120 feet by 45 as against 230 feet by 100 feet)—aims solely at grace, elegance, and refinement. With the slender Doric style of the 38 exterior columns Ictinos audaciously associated 10 Ionic columns inserted in the wall of the *cella*, and—for the first time in a Greek temple—placed a Corinthian column all alone in front of the statue of the god.

At the beginning of this century, the walls of the *cella* were rebuilt; nearly all the stones were still there, scattered round (thanks to its haughty solitude, remote from towns and highways, this monument escaped being used as a quarry, as befell so many others). The cella was decorated with a frieze composed of 27 bas-reliefs of white marble, representing the war between Centaurs and Lapithae, and that between Greeks and Amazons. At the beginning of last century these sculptures were still in place, or remained where they had fallen nearby. But in 1812 two Englishmen, Cockerell and Foster, laid hands on them. The pasha intervened. It was then that Elgin's emulators had the entire frieze secretly removed at night "by sixty men who set out from Zante and corrupted the peasants into assisting them in this act

Mountain Village of Goura

of brigandry." Four years later, having been purchased for £35,000 by the Prince Regent of England, these precious remains were placed in the British Museum, London, where they remain on exhibition to this day.

ACHAIA

THE modest, peaceful province of Achaia, which attracted attention only at the beginning and end of the history of ancient Greece, nonetheless conferred its name upon the entire Peloponnese on two different occasions (under the Romans and under the Franks). Although devoid of natural beauty spots or sensational monuments, Achaia contains innumerable vestiges of medieval citadels; but this is not enough to distinguish it from other regions in the peninsula which abound in similar relics.

MEGASPILAEON—It was also in Achaia, on the southern slopes of the Aroanian Mountains, that the Megaspilaeon, formerly the richest convent in Latin Greece, survived its departed glory. The façade, in which eight storeys of galleries and balconies are superimposed, conceals an immense and very ancient grotto. From century to century and generation to generation an image of the Virgin Artemis and a statue of the Virgin Mary attracted an endless flow of pilgrims and gifts. This oddly picturesque spot, with its gigantic rock beetling over a valley of thriving olive groves, is reminiscent of Rocamadour in south-western France. Alas! Some twenty years ago the Megaspilaeon was burnt down, and in its presentday state of pennywise reconstruction, tourists pass it by. It is decadent in every way: its renowned cellars, which used to be lined with kegs each containing 4,400 gallons of wine, are empty; and the cells in which 400 *caloyeri* used to live on the fat of the land are almost empty too, since they now house barely a dozen inhabitants.

PATRAS—Patras, the capital of Achaia, is the third largest town in modern Greece (the second, after Athens, being Salonica). The port, which lacks both character and beauty, is the great centre from which currants (whose name is derived from Corinth) are exported, together with sultanas from Smyrna, to fill our Christmas puddings. Patras is an extremely ancient town, founded by the Eleusian Prince Triptolemus (who blessed mankind with the gift of corn). She conceals the fact most successfully, or at least she is not dead by any manner of means. One could hardly say as much for her legendary rival Helike, which used to rise on the same shores further west, almost opposite Delphi, and was often extolled by Homer for her wealth and might. She lived up to her reputation until two years before the Battle of Leuctra in the 4th century B.C., when she was destroyed by an earthquake even more merciless than those which recently wrought havoc in the Ionian Isles. Buildings, inhabitants, and even the soil itself were ferociously swallowed up. . . .

In the days of Pausanias, the ruins of Helike could still be discerned beneath their limpid watery shroud; and, according to hearsay, the seamen used to make a wide detour to avoid being dashed against a colossal bronze Poseidon which fabulously survived on the surface of the water, above its submerged base. . . . Who knows, this Helikonian god may one day be recovered, clad in seaweed and shells, like the wonderful statue known as Zeus of Histaia which was retrieved a score of years ago near the shores of Euboea, and is now the pride of the National Museum in Athens.

ΘΕSEVS

CRETE

Fresco from the Palace of Knossos

CRETE

WHENEVER the subject of Greece forces itself into the conversation, a kind of divine tenderness pervades the atmosphere. Wits are clarified; senses are sharpened; complexes fade and eyes begin to sparkle. This narrow country, attached to the wrist of the world like a sparkling bracelet, sheds its pearls in the form of islands. The traveller has the impression that the bay trees rustling as evening descends, and the ships setting sail as the sun climbs in the sky, give him an insight into his own soul.

Crete is a network of evident mysteries, averted dangers, and lifted hoodoos—a thorny enigma. But long processions of maidens returning from olive-picking, as in Southern France, introduce a happy note of reality.

Crete is the heart of Greece, outlined in red and black—using heart in the anatomical sense of the word. And then again her red soil, arched and jagged, resembles a cockscomb. The bull, the cock, and the colour red are all battlesome objects which stir the patrician's blood.

Mycenae and Eleusis are steeped in tragedy or mystery. Crete bathes in gilded drama. But have no fear: the drama—as befits it—is yet to come. It smoulders like fire beneath a burning place. In Mycenae there are phantoms. In Knossos, beneath fuming debris, there are men who are not quite dead. We know we shall never hear the final strains of this mighty, thundersome opera.

Every landscape is humanized in some way or another. If certain spots attract us, it is because man has lived and died there.

Whilst Knossos is overrun with shadows, Delos is a desert. Men who have reached their paroxysm, devoured by the gods, reign in Knossos, whereas Delos contains the god who has no need of man to reveal himself.

CANDIA—Crete, which the Venetians called Candia (a name which has remained in Herakleion) and the Turks Kirit, is the largest island in the Archipelago. In the map she seems to detach herself from Greece like an

The Fountain of Morosini in Candia

elongated boat, or a long stroke underlining the flotilla of other islands. It is the immense hyphen joining East to West, and on setting foot on the pier of Candia one is immediately struck by the variety of types encountered there. Whilst the orange-vendor is a fat, heavy Turk, the waitress in the restaurant is slender and graceful like that famous *Parisienne* smiling behind the walls of the museum.

When I first arrived in Candia, I saw a tall boy of about twenty years old, stretched out on the pier deep in sleep. The feet of the passers-by brushed against his outstretched hand, which was full of drachmas. I naïvely asked my companion what this meant. "That's a beggar," he replied, with a smile.

And I found this animal confidence in fate and this insolent yet tranquil scorn of effort so beautiful that I too pitched in my drachma.

It should be made plain from the outset that Crete is a human island, endlessly seething with battle. Some build forts, others tear them down— everyone must have his turn. This produces beautiful ruins, just as the mingling of hot blood produces beautiful children. The Cretan is as proud as a Greek, as charming as a Venetian, and as cunning as an Oriental. But, human though she is, the Island of Crete did not escape the notice of the Gods: since the beginning of time she has been battered by geological catastrophes which have left deep scars on all sides. It was probably because the people made too much noise—think of the atmosphere of the "caravan-serai" of Knossos in wartime!—that the Gods took so much trouble to maltreat her. Being equidistant from the Cyclades, Rhodes, and Libya she has always been a port of call between Europe, Asia, and Africa. The name alone evokes brigands weighted down with silver pistols and smoking long pipes, bearded old men fingering amber rosaries, and barefooted pirates with pale pink scarves round their heads.

Immediately on arrival in Candia from Athens, for instance, one has the impression that something has changed. The light has become heavier. A gaudy range of colours shrieks of the Orient. There is a medley of voices, languages, and skins; a smell of fried fish, hot orange, and skinny dog; the rapaciousness of Shylock and the sumptuousness of Venice. Wherever you go you are sure to find an unemployed youth who will beg you with tears in his eyes to ask him to do something for you. He will show you whatever you wish, and take you where you will. If you want to see the loveliest teeth in the world, offer him a cigarette.

The most charming spot in Candia, to my mind, is the little square where the Fountain of Morosini sings. Morosini had the leisure to complete his fountain during the siege of Candia by the Turks, which lasted 22 years. Once it was finished, the *proveditore generale* was doubtless at a loose end (since his sole passion was for fountains), and decided to capitulate. He surrendered to the Grand Vizir Achmed Kemprulu. All this took place during the reign of Louis XIV, who despatched troops under the command of the Duc de Beaufort. 500 men perished, Arab influence filtered into the town.... and the charming fountain continued to flow.

In a corner of the square there is a delightful church, St Mark's. You will probably see huge coloured photos of your favourite stars on either side of the porch—I forgot to mention that it had been converted into a cinema. This little world is enclosed within solid Venetian battlements. The duration of the sieges had one advantage: it allowed time to reinforce the ramparts.

The treasures of the Museum of Antiquities, buried during the war, are gradually being brought to light. After being shamefully interred in the bowels of the earth, the gods of marble and bronze are now being restored to their rightful place. Let us hope they will long remain there.

If you go into the heart of the town—and what better could you do?— you will still find a delightful juxtaposition of the Orient and Venice. Beautiful façades with Venetian blinds and portly balconies conjure up scenes from Mozart and Elizabethan drama at one and the same time. Candia is a subtle prologue to Crete—it represents the Comic Opera, or rather the Opera Bouffe preluding the Grand Opera.

KNOSSOS—But the heart of Crete is Knossos, and it is already time to leave the market-places where the loveliest fruit from the plain is heaped. One always feels a little sad on leaving Candia. For all that, you hasten southwards along the road to Pyrgos. Your companion, for whom—if you are reasonable—you have refused to enlist the help of a guide, is bound to ask you the name of "that mountain over there, on the right." You reply astutely: "A word of three letters, as in crossword puzzles." Without thinking she will open wide her eyes and exclaim: "Ah! Is that it?"

Yes, that is Mount Ida. Almost immediately after leaving Candia, you find an ancient Turkish road which descends into a ravine and rises on the other side. There you will discover the magnificent tomb of Isopata.

The road to Pyrgos passes several little villages such as one comes across everywhere in Greece—villages with whitewashed walls and sleepy streets.

Butchers' Street in Candia

Some two miles on, beyond the remains of a Roman amphitheatre the wonder of wonders comes into sight.

On a plinth at the junction of two little valleys between hills whose baldness appears intentional, as if to set it off, the Palace of Knossos appears. A first encounter with the Parthenon strikes straight to the heart. It imposes calm and serenity on the spectator. It is an order (in every sense of the word). One has the impression nothing can be changed in this wonderful equation in marble, and that there are no two ways of solving it. On first contact with the Palace of Knossos, one realizes it is the opposite pole. If, as a Chinese philosopher said, "tranquillity in disorder is the sign of perfection," the Palace of Minos will give you a perfect image of perfection. The tranquillity is overwhelming, and the disorder absolute. For one single instant, you will forget the divine rigour that reigns in Delos and Olympia. The Palace has been remarkably well restored, and gives an exact idea of its past glory. It is a kind of charivari of courts, big and small, joined by stairways of plaster-stone and lit by wells of light—the whole forming a sort of improvisation in oriental style, surrounding a central court. The columns are of painted wood supported by stone shafts. The walls are neither of marble nor porphyry but of plaster-stone or stucco, and it was doubtless the poorness of the medium that gave rise to the wonderful frescoes that dazzle our eyes. It is not just a labyrinth—it is The Labyrinth.

The impression experienced is religious in nature, but totally different from that created by the Parthenon. Here it is not the gilded whiteness of marble imposing itself on reason; it is not the torrid solitude and implacable silence that drives one into oneself, but an emotion full of colour, so to speak, which penetrates the secret depths of one's being. The candour of the Parthenon contrasts with this maze of lies. Labyrinth spells Game of Illusion. In the Parthenon, one feels lost at the outset; here, one feels afraid of being lost.

The Minoan palace is horizontal and this doubtless accounts for the uneasy, overbearing feeling it inspires. The Palace of Knossos was built without weights or measures. The materials of which it is built—wood, stucco, and brick—and above all the colours, produce a tangle of haunted

District beside the Ramparts in Candia

342

houses. Mystery overpowers light, which gives up the struggle. Hence that kind of terror which pervades us, even if we are not very familiar with mythology. The people in groups lower their voices, whilst lone visitors draw close together. There must be someone living here, since the big jars are ready to receive oil and grain. One could hardly imagine the ground of the Parthenon being swept, whereas in Knossos domestic life seems to continue unperturbed. And so does religious life, with its altars and lustral baths. In short, the dual anguish of man, who needs life, and knows that death has need of him.

The throne of Minos is still there, in the Griffons' Gallery. The terrible king is coming to take his seat there, and the suspense is overwhelming.

Let us flee, rejoicing because he will not come after all. At the spot where the modern road is intersected by a Minoan causeway which evidently led straight from the Palace to the port, there is a small café where one can drink the best wine in Crete. From its shady terrace, at a distance of about a hundred

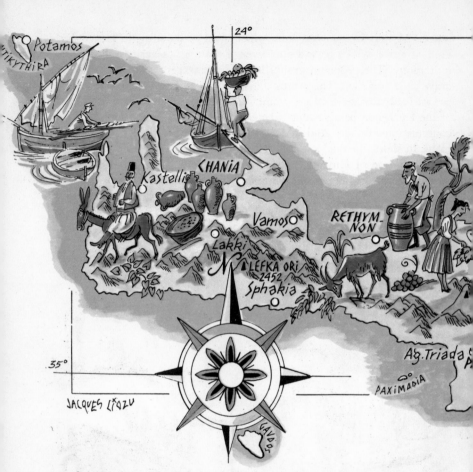

yards one can see the delightful "fresco house", the original home of the beautiful paintings we saw in the museum in Candia, without really understanding what they represented with their blue monkeys and blue bird— that strange blue which pervades all the Cretan frescoes. We should take another look at them, and imagine them in their intended setting. We daydream in front of a glass of ouzo or wine, and the evening descending —also Cretan blue—reposes our minds from the tumult occasioned by our visit to the Palace. . . . And tranquilly through the stillness we conjure up one of the most disturbing—though not the loftiest—spots in mythology.

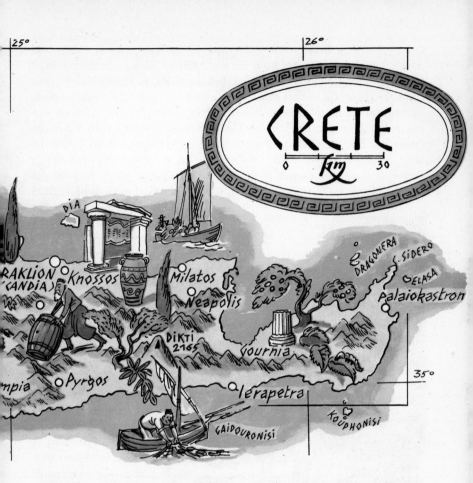

In Crete one does not seek perfection and balance, as elsewhere in Greece, but rather a justification of the "barbaric" side of the soul. Greek temples, even in ruins, outline a definite plan and a definite purpose; it is impossible to devise a supplementary ornament of any kind without making the edifice topple over, whereas one can well imagine the Palace of Knossos spreading its winding staircases, angular corridors and cellars of all sizes in an immense flow of red and black lava, relentlessly submerging villages and orchards all over Crete.

To breathe a less oppressive atmosphere, one should go to the summit of

345

nearby Mount Iouktas, commanding one of the finest views in the world over a boundless expanse of plain and sea. At dawn, clouds cover the mountain with their moving veil. Villages, hedges, fields, and boats glitter in the crystalline light. Of all the Greeks, the Cretans were the only ones who dared to mention the death of Zeus, and according to their legend, his tomb was situated at the summit of Iouktas. The wonderful precision with which the Greeks selected their hallowed spots is once again to be admired. Just as the only possible birthplace for Apollo was that narrow silver disc which Poseidon cast in the middle of the sea like a platter of purity to form the Isle of Delos, it is only natural that the tomb of the God of Gods be situated at the summit of that mountain where cypress and cedar cast their graceful shadow. At daybreak our eyes repose on the rich Mesara plain, the fields of corn, the vineyards, and the orchards of olives ruffled into silvery foam at the slightest breeze. The shepherds still play on their flutes as in the days of Theocritus. And at all times—this cannot be repeated too often—Greece reveals to us aspects of our soul to which the film we call civilization blinds our eyes. She was made to seduce the *barbarian*—meaning literally foreigner

*The Emblem of
Minos in Knossos*

346

—and restitute him to himself.

PHAESTOS—In Phaestos the spirit of Crete seems to become more human. The hills are gentler, and the Mesara plain rounds off the knoll of Haghia Photini. Mount Ida, which seems to be the pivot round which the island turns, or the mast of that great ship of rocks and leaves, beetles over you. The Palace of Phaestos looms up on a plateau straight ahead. In Phaestos I saw an unforgettable sight— a Greek storm—one of those romantic, devastating storms of which Zeus alone has the secret. At first the sky was a limpid blue and then, abruptly, a

Annexes of the Palace of Knossos

kind of uneasiness seemed to weigh down on the countryside. In a setting such as this it was easy to understand that lightning is caused by the electricity of the earth and the sky defying each other and coming to grips. One could feel the current everywhere. It quivered beneath my feet, as everything was suddenly overcast with a layer of red copper. The sight of the glow pervading the stones reminded me of cauldrons swept away by thunderbolts, to be discovered flattened into shapeless slabs. A treacherous breeze ran through the grass, the cypress plumes were ruffled, and the leaves on the olive trees

347

changed colour. The ground rumbled more fiercely than the sky. Lightning of every shape darted all round Mount Ida, and the rain began to stream down, drowning the horizon. Cretan storms do not last long. The more terrible the wrath, the less it endures, and the Palace emerged, washed, glistening and new, in a smell of ozone. The olive trees were quieted, and the cypress, temporarily taken off their guard, stood once again to attention. Then is the time to admire the lustre of the oleander leaves, and to breathe the perfume of the flowers glittering beside the Yeras Potamos.

And when those clouds of sulphur and lead stretch themselves and split to reveal a blood-red sun, one cannot help thinking of the great man of modern Crete, Dominicos Theotocopuli, known as El Greco, born (about 1550) nearby, in the little village of Phodele, east of Herakleion (Candia).

Phaestos is said to be one of the oldest towns in Crete. The youth who guided me through the Palace had eyes like hornets, with fluttering lashes. He was chewing an oleander blossom glistening with dew. I reflected that if, at his age, I had committed so rash an act (everyone knows that the sap is the quintessence of prussic acid!), someone would have violently snatched

Cretans from the Mountains

348

Phaestos

away the flower. Then, instead of warning him of the frightful danger in store, I too plucked a flower and began to suck it with relish.

Here again, as in Knossos, there is a welter of terraces, stairways, and porticos, but on a smaller, less disorderly scale. The entrance is by way of an upper terrace, from which a stairway leads down to a wide flagged courtyard where dances and games used to take place. After the storm a pleasant smell arose from the earth, and one could well imagine the slow unwinding of chains of dancers led by a coryphaeus, and the shuffle of feet brushing the ground, in a solemn yet jovial atmosphere characteristic of youth.

HAGHIA TRIADA—Crete is a country which, like a diamond or an equation, cannot be broken down. From one end of the island to the other, everything is in perfect harmony: the ruins, the foliage, and the people who saunter to and fro in the fields. This harmony is achieved by the Cretan peasant's attitude towards strangers. The simplest of shepherds seems to say that the only way for Crete to continue is by making sure that the foreigner (*Xenos*) is a guest (*Xenos*): a sacred being to whom the home and the heart are thrown

Haghia Triada. Crête - mai 1953

Excavations in Haghia Triada

wide open, and on whom every attention is lavished, even to the extent of giving him the best seat in the bus or train.

Crete resembles a symphony constructed round a sole theme—the Palace of Knossos—that magnificent overture for rubicund brasses which then continues on all sides as far as the sea, leaving increasingly "human" vestiges as one gradually moves away from the centre.

Whilst the Palace of Phaestos is a replica of Knossos, slightly less terrifying than the original, the Little Palace or Villa of Haghia Triada, some two miles away on the edge of the hill terminating the plateau, is a replica of Phaestos, one tone lower. It was doubtless the residence of a vassal of neighbouring princes. To reach it from the road, one has to ford the river. In Haghia Triada, the superimposition of two architectural periods is more evident than in Phaestos. First there was an extremely complicated palace built of rare materials and made to last, comprising—in typical Cretan style—an endless succession of staircases, peristyles, and corridors. It was totally destroyed by the Achaeans in about 1450 B.C., and on the vestiges another palace was built, from which the massive substructure of a megaron survives to this day. To the north there is a huge portico on piles, whilst shops and other debris of a village extend towards the river.

MOUNT IDA—But one should never visit Crete without climbing Mount Ida, in order to have an overall view and form a general impression. It should not be forgotten that it housed the tomb of Zeus, and it is meet to climb to the peak, to take a lesson in wisdom. At the foot of the mountain, all the ruins that sent shivers down our spines look vain and ephemeral. And indeed, they too are dead, but the thunder which assiduously haunts the summit of Mount Ida has not succeeded in splitting the rock of the God.

The route leading to the summit begins at Vori, a small village of white-washed houses surrounded by beautiful trees. It is no small matter to visit the tomb of the father of the Gods, and the roads are extremely bad. A few miles from Vori (it is best to leave at dead of night, to see the countryside emerge from the mist), we halt at Grigoria to drink the sparkling water; one has the impression of drinking a philtre that brings relief from archaeology. After a wealth of ruined splendour, we at last enter the domain of living men. A mule-path leads from Grigoria to Camares, the last village preceding the vast mountain solitudes—an extremely picturesque village whose inhabitants, accustomed to tourists, act as gate-keepers to the Magic Mount. Each house is an inn, where you will be welcomed as a lifelong friend. The local resinated wine is particularly sharp, and it is his like or dislike for this beverage that decides whether or not a stranger is worthy to be adopted by Greece. Beyond Camares, difficult pathways lead up to the

The Odeon of Gortyna

352

Basilica of Haghios Titos

Nida plateau and the grotto of Ida, where you may turn your thoughts to Plato.

It faces Knossos where the Palace of Minos is outspread in the sweltering sun, for once free of mystery. To the south you will also encounter the grotto of Camares, which is more welcoming and refreshing than the grotto of Ida; this is the last stage before the summit.

MALLIA—After a few days, our heads are less burdened with all those red and black memories, those tall oaks on the mountains and olive trees in the plains, and those vast expanses of cornfields and vineyards. Returning to Herakleion is like returning to modern life. Whilst you were at grips with mythology in the raw and nature unadorned, life was still continuing, and the port still emanates the heavy perfume of its motley life. After the "Poussin from nature" effect produced by the gorges and clearings of Ida, one returns to Delacroix. The coaches lined up beside the wharves bring one back with a bump from the sharp pebbles of mountain pathways.

A road east of Herakleion hugs the sea. It is intersected here and there

353

The Windmills of Mallia

by valleys perpendicular to the coast, and terminates at the mouth of the Kairatos where the Port of Knossos must once have been situated. There is nothing to recall its past splendour. The spot is majestically melancholic; the road rises swiftly above the coast and beetles over the sea; then it descends again, intersected by little streams spanned by arched bridges reminiscent of Provence. And, since Crete is composed entirely of contrast and vanity, a bend in the road suddenly reveals the Bay of Mallia, dotted with windmills that look like a flock of birds squatting on the plain. The bleak foothills of Lassithi contrast with the fertile plateau. Mallia is a large village slumbering amidst olive and carob trees. The Palace of Mallia, contemporary with the first Palaces of Knossos and Phaestos, rises between the village and the sea. Although smaller than the others, it gives the impression of being more serious, not to say austere, being composed not of flourishes of stucco and perishable materials, but of huge blocks of stone, ungraceful columns, and difficult stairways. It is more like the house of a wealthy merchant than that of a prince. In Knossos and Phaestos, there were certainly signs of everyday life—shops, and jars for oil and grain—but in Mallia one has the feeling that the daily cares of life took priority over religious matters. There are sanctuaries and assembly rooms, to be sure, but less numerous than elsewhere, doubtless because the Palace is older and met its death without engendering other palaces. In this respect it should be purer than the others, and give a clearer impression of Minoan architecture.

GOURNIA—We must by-pass the little villages and necropoli dotted between Mallia and the sea, and proceed to Gournia. The road is so picturesque that we should be stopping every few minutes if we dared. Beyond a succession of hills, vales, and defiles skirting the Gulf of Merabellos, we reach the ruins of Gournia. In every respect it is a typical Cretan village, built on a hill in the middle of a valley deeply indented by the sea. Like Pompeii, it gives an inkling of life as it was during the heyday of Crete. One can wander there as easily as in any modern quarter. The houses are built one above the other on either side of the hill, linked by alleys, often in the form of steps, which terminate in two parallel main streets. All the dwellings grouped round the agora are built on identical lines, and generally have two entrances, facing each other. Life must have been exceptionally calm and sweet in this little town. The small Palace of Gournia, opening on to the agora, has a provincial air. Here we are remote from the splendours of Phaestos and Knossos, in some sub-prefecture of middle-class merchants and small landowners.

CANEA—But there is so much to see in Crete! Vestiges of the past are crammed between fields and woods. Whilst the best place to land is Herakleion, if you do not want to harbour too unhappy a recollection, the best point of departure is Canea. Here one is already in Europe: the Orient has vanished .... The route hugs the Bay of Sade, protected by Fort Izzedin, a political and military prison nowadays. We sense that this is the end of the vast green expanses and poetic ruins. The present catches up with us. The streets are lively, to be sure, but not with the

Canea

"gratuitous" animation of the Orient. People come and go with a definite purpose in view. They do not dawdle round the charming little square, or pause to dream in front of the mosque and its minaret. If you ask where the Museum is, you may be surprised to hear that it is in the Law Courts. There is not much to see in it—nor in the rest of the town, for that matter. The Halepa Boulevard running towards the sea is alone worth a visit . . . . But it runs towards the sea, and you already begin to feel as if you were no longer in Crete.

One should not go only to Crete; above all one should go back. The first encounter is too brutal a shock, especially when one arrives direct from the mainland of Greece. Each time I return to Crete, I recollect Diderot's remark to Sophie Volland:

"Fifteen years ago you looked beautiful to me; today I find you more beautiful still. It is the magic of constance, the most difficult and the rarest of all our virtues."

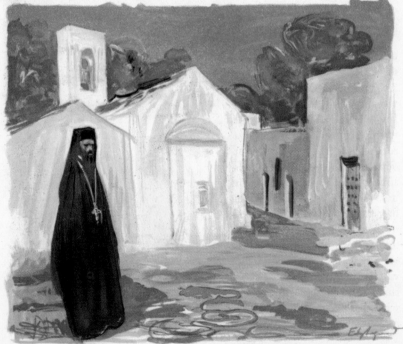

Monastery of Vrondissi, at the Foot of Mount Ida

THE ISLANDS

Piraeus

THE CYCLADES

IF the journey to Greece is one of the finest man can make in his lifetime, the journey to the Cyclades is the ·zenith. Let us, then, embark one evening from Piraeus on one of those pretty Greek steamers that sails to the Cyclades at the hour when the Parthenon glows purple on the Acropolis.

The name of these islands signifies that they form a circle—round Delos, the sacred island. The climate is pleasant even in the dog-days, thanks to the Etesian winds. The islands are, in fact, the realm of the wind, and the *meltem* or *vorias* that blows from the north often makes navigation difficult there. For the most part they are sparse in vegetation, arid, and rocky in the extreme. The white houses in the little ports seem to be inundated with light by centuries of sunshine. Some of the ancient relics found in them are remarkable, and they confirm the wealth of those homes and the role they

The Cliffs of Santorini

played in the golden age of humanity. Their feudal ruins evoke the days when they constituted the Duchy of the Archipelago under the domination of Venice.

It is the most beautiful of journeys in every way. The vision of the Acropolis dancing before our eyes soon gives way to that of the colonnade of Cape Sounion, the extreme tip of Attica. Opposite, beyond the long isle of Makronisos—formerly the Isle of Helena—we catch sight of the Mountains of Kea, the first of the Cyclades, and the first stage in our journey.

The ancient name, Keos, has hardly changed. Chateaubriand, who called it Zea, wrote a charming description of his brief stay there. In the past there were six temples to Apollo, and two to his sister Artemis, on the island: we are on the road of the Gods of Delos. The main town, which goes by the same name as the island, is built on the site of ancient Ioulis, birthplace of the poet Simonides. A curious law obliged citizens to poison themselves at the age of sixty, or leave the country: the inhabitants had no love for dotards. Not far from the Leon promontory a colossal lion has been hewn out of the rock; on the south-east coast rise the ruins of ancient Karthaia.

We resume our journey, regretful not to have seen the Orthodox bishop spinning silk in the public square, as described by our predecessor Tournefort in the 18th century. And now we veer south, by-passing the island of Gioura—formerly Gyaros—that looms up in the distant east. It was one of the most accursed spots in the Roman Empire—in fact Tiberius himself deemed it too wild and deserted to receive his exiles, even though it was then a place of banishment.

Thermia—formerly Kythnos—where we land, owes her modern name to her thermal springs, consecrated to the holy Anargyroi—literally, doctors "who would not accept money". Her main curiosities are the ruins of two ancient towns, one on a tall cliff on the west coast, the other on a similar site to the north-east.

Serfo—ancient Seriphos—is further south. After she had been made pregnant by the golden rain, Danae was washed ashore there with her son Perseus in a coffer that had been hurled into the sea; the future liberator of Andromeda spent his infancy and childhood on the island. Nowadays Serfo's wealth lies in her gold mines.

The Isle of Siphnos, beyond, boasted four towns. In ancient times she was renowned for her gold and silver mines on the one hand, and the voluptuousness of her inhabitants on the other.

The small island of Kimolos nearby used to keep Athenian fullers supplied with "Kimolian" earth.

Milos—formerly Melos, which pre-sentday geographers have named Milo—owed her name to her circular

The Port of Santorini.

shape resembling an "apple". Volcanic phenomena cut a slice out of the apple to the north, and even scooped out the largest port in the Archipelago. Of all the islands Milo is the most renowned for her beautiful women, which probably explains the origin of the *Venus* decorating the Louvre. It was in 1820 that the Comte de Marcellus, the young secretary to the ambassador to Constantinople, went to Milo with the aim of acquiring the statue for the King of France. It was one of the most romantic abductions imaginable. Whilst the primates of Milo were upholding the Frenchman's demands, the caloyer claimed the right to sell the statue to the interpreter-in-chief of the Ottoman fleet. A minor battle ensued. The frigate *L'Estafette*, in which *Venus* had been stowed, set sail for Constantinople with the Ottoman fleet hot on her trail, and the abductor breathed again only when the goddess had been transferred to the gunboat *La Lionne* which carried her to France. The magnificent statue of Poseidon in Athens Museum, with a naked torso and the lower half of the body veiled like *Venus*, also came from Milo.

Veering south-east, we first strike Polykandro—onetime Pholegandros—where there was once a temple to Artemis, and Sikinos, where there is still a temple to Apollon Pythios, converted into a Panaghian church.

Nios—formerly Ios—slightly to the east, used to pride herself on sheltering Homer's tomb.

SANTORINI AND ANAPHI

SANTORINI—formerly Thera—our southernmost port of call, derives her name from her patron Saint, Irene. Whereas all the other islands we have visited are more or less similar in type—composed of barren rocks rent by creeks—Santorini is unique. We are suddenly confronted with a prodigy—a sheer cliff 650 feet high, revealing all the secrets of Mother Earth like a geological cross-section. White veins of pumice run through the middle of brown rocks, black cinders, and red earth. It is the wall of a volcanic crater, with roads flowing through the centre. The Isle of Therasia opposite is another residue of the same crater. Moreover, although the volcano is under the sea, it is still active and asserts itself by making islets appear and disappear. The Kaimeni group, dotted across the roads, was formed by this volcano.

At the top of the cliff, the modern town of Phira displays white houses and cupolas at the end of a zigzag path. A small museum contains some of the

Santorini

treasures from the town of Thira. The ruins, which are about three hours distant, were explored by the German School. They revealed a selection of archaic, Greek, Roman, and Byzantine vestiges. A sanctuary in the rocks, protected by a tall doorway silhouetted against the whitewashed rock, has been converted into a chapel. Inscriptions have been engraved on the rock near the gymnasium of the ephebi, extolling the young dancers who used to participate in the festivals of the gymnopaedae. In the sanctuary of Apollo, on the threshold of the court, the footprints of ancient pilgrims are engraved, recalling the famous footprint in the *Quo Vadis* chapel on the Appian Way. Below, the hemicycle of the Roman theatre stands out against the sea. Here and there the insignia of Priapus may be seen decorating a column or a strip of wall. A meagre palm tree beside a beautiful Hellenic wall, a gnarled pine beside a marble basin, and another beside the isolated chapel of Evanghelismos, are the only trees in Santorini. The sole plant is the vine, which produce a wine of repute.

I shall never forget my visit to Anaphi, a night's journey from Santorini. I had hired a caique—one of those small boats that are so convenient for travelling from one island to the next when one wants to take one's time and not be confined to the brief halts made by the steamship. The sombre wall of Santorini loomed up anew with the lights of Phira glittering on the summit; the sky was riddled with stars; the water lapped gently against the hull; the skipper hoisted his red sail and glided serenely towards the open sea. At sunrise we were in the roads of Anaphi, where I was anxious to see an oracletemple to Apollo, renowned in the past and since converted into a church, like the one in Sikinos. It rises up near the shore, within the walls of the monastery of the Panaghia Kalamiotissa (the madonna of the "bulrushes").

AMORGOS AND NAXOS

RETURNING northwards, on a level with Nios—which we have already visited—we come across Amorgos. Like many of the islands, which are always picturesque but not always highly populated, it would appear to have been more prosperous in the past than it is today. It used to have four towns, the most important of which was Minoa on the north coast, where excavations have been made. The inscriptions revealed the existence of six temples, three of which were consecrated to Apollo. The present capital is quite far inland. For want of an ancient oracle, she boasts a modern

Night Stop in Syra

one—that of Saint George the Valsamite—which would seem to mean "balm". One of the loveliest, tragic-faced female busts in Athens Museum comes from Amorgos, as do the heads of Asklepios and Hygeia which are equally fine. Despite these signs of wealth, Amorgos was also a place of exile in the days of Tiberius: Tacitus recounted that the proconsul of Spain was banished there "on account of his atrocious morals."

Beyond a sprinkling of islands we reach Naxos, the largest and loveliest of the Cyclades. It is cut from north to south by a chain of mountains which drop sheer to the east and slope down gently on the west, where the principal villages and farmlands are situated. The white houses of Naxos, on the site of an ancient town, extend from the shores as far as a rocky peak crested by the ruins of the ducal castle. At the entrance to the port on the islet of Palati rises a marble gateway—the remains of the Temple of Dionysos. The island's wine was renowned in ancient times, and the God of Wine was the guardian of Palati. But that was not the sole reason for building temples there: after Theseus had abandoned Ariadne in Naxos—

—Ariadne, my sister, how deep were the wounds of love
To which you at last succumbed on the shores where you were forsaken—

Dionysos consoled her there before she died on the island. The god found her sleeping on the shore, and their meeting is the theme of innumerable Pompeian frescoes and a number of bas-reliefs. In addition to painters, sculptors and poets, "Ariadne in Naxos" likewise inspired operas by Monteverdi and Richard Strauss.

Mount Zia—previously Drios—over 3,250 feet in altitude, is the highest in the Archipelago. Its modern name recalls that of Zeus, to whom a grotto near the summit was dedicated. At the foot of the mountain the ruins of an ancient tower and the remains of an acropolis may still be seen. To the north, near the village of Komiaki, an unfinished colossus of Apollo has been abandoned in a marble quarry. We are, in fact, on an island of marble, and this is even more true of Paros. Naxos marble is coarser, and was used mainly for building. However, the votive lions we shall see in Delos—the offering of the Naxians—were carved of marble from their island.

Like Gyaros, the small island of Donoussa to the west was one of the most dreaded places of exile under the Roman empire, "because both isles were short of water."

PAROS

To the east, the white marble of Paros glistens from afar. The extraordinary contribution this island made to the Attic Confederation testifies to her immense wealth in marble. The famous stone is found in thick layers in the crystalline limestone forming the base of the island. It was called *lychnites* because it was exploited underground "by lamplight". The largest quarries are near the monastery of Haghios Minas, an hour's journey from the capital, Parikia. The inland village of Leukai ("the White") also lives up to its name. It was the quarries of Mount Marpissa that furnished the marble for Napoleon's tomb. The Castle of Parikia, on the ancient Acropolis, is built of antique debris; the remains of a temple form the walls of a small church. The triple church of the Panaghia Hecatonpyliani ("of the hundred doors") merits a visit. The nearby museum contains an inscription concerning Archilochus, the most biting of the Greek satirists, who was born on the island, as well as a fragment of the famous "Paros marbles"—chronological tables indicating, amongst other things, the date of Homer's birth. A little further on we find the remains of the temple and fountain of Asklepios. One of the most beautiful archaic statues

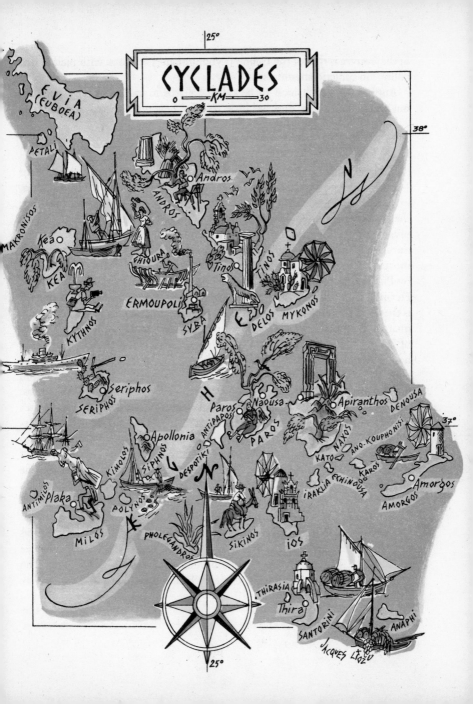

in the Louvre is that of the *Couros* ("young man") of Paros with plaited hair falling on athletic shoulders.

Antiparos—which used to be called Oliaros in ancient times—stretches out to the south-east, and has little to offer beyond a grotto of stalactites.

SYRA

SYRA—ancient Syros—to the north, is the chief town of the nomos of the Cyclades nowadays, as well as being the richest and most highly populated of the islands. In ancient times Syra was relatively unimportant; she owes her fortune to the fact that in modern times, until Piraeus was revived, she was the main port of call for ships sailing from the West towards the Black Sea. Syra is the homeland of the swine-herd Eumaeus, immortalized in the *Odyssey*: the son of the King of Syros, who was abducted by Phoenician pirates and sold to Ulysses' father. Hermoupolis, the town of Hermes, is the capital. The houses rise on two conical mounds: to the left is the old Latin quarter, dominated by the cathedral; to the right, the Greek quarter, dominated by the Greek church. Under the protection of the kings of France, the population was exclusively Catholic—this explains why Syra has been endowed with French schools and a hospital. Greek colonization dates only from the War of Independence in 1821, and originates from Chios where the Turks were holding sway. *Loukoum* from Syra is the most renowned type of "Turkish delight" in Greece. In addition, the town's industrial activities—spinning, tanning, and smelting—are not to be overlooked. The main square, not far from the pier, is flagged with marble and surrounded by arcades. A monument to Miaoulis recalls one of the heroes of the struggle for Independence. The Syriots' favourite stroll is along the coastal road leading to a cliff prettily bordered with windmills. An hour's journey away lies the fashionable town of Delle Grazie, which is much frequented in autumn, whilst Kyni beach is preferred as a summer resort.

None of the poets of ancient times ever extolled Syros, and in fact she was not even mentioned. But the French poet André Chenier righted this injustice by using the island as a setting for his famous bucolic *L'Aveugle*, in which he described Homer cast up on the coast by brutal merchants, and rescued by children.

A Street in Mykonos

TINOS AND MYKONOS

I N Syra we are not very far from Delos—in fact, the isle of Apollo and Artemis is on the horizon. But before we go there, let us first cast a glance round this horizon where larger islands await us. Tinos—previously known as Tenos—is dominated by two mountain ranges whose terraced slopes are clad in vineyards and fields of grain. In ancient times she boasted three temples, one of which was consecrated to Hyacinth. But none of them ever knew such renown as the Church of Panaghia Evanghelistria now enjoys, thanks to the miraculous image discovered there in 1822. The name of the church means "Good News", and in fact the image seemed to herald the "good news" of Independence for which the Greeks were then striving. Two annual pilgrimages—on 25th March, the national holiday, and 15th August—bring tens of thousands of pilgrims there, avid for miracles. They call upon the image to cure certain illnesses or infirmities, and the sight of that imploring crowd crushed together in the church is perhaps the most extraordinary that modern Greece has to offer us. A host of ex-voto

Chapel in Mykonos

The Port of Tinos

offerings in silver testify to the might of the Panaghia Evanghelistria.

In the middle of another little bay slightly south of Tinos Bay, the ruins of a great temple to Poseidon and Amphitrite evoke the gods of long ago. This is doubtless the temple that was rebuilt in the days of Tiberius, as Tacitus informs us: to escape from certain dues, the inhabitants of Tinos availed themselves of an oracle of Apollo inciting them to build a temple such as this, and it is highly probable that Tiberius' senate moderated their religious zeal in favour of the imperial Exchequer. The Venetian town was situated much further north, on the granite slopes of Exoburgo, where the citadel, a pretty fountain, and three churches may still be seen. Tinos was Chateaubriand's sole port of call in the Cyclades after Kea. He described it as "a tall island, resting on a marble rock." It is not particularly high; nor is it composed of marble.

Mykonos, to the south, is, so to speak, the port of Delos. This is where the steamships put in, and where one can hire a caique for the brief crossing to Delos. Herakles battled there against the giants; and in this same port Datis, the Persian general vanquished at Marathon, dreamt that he received

"Cleopatra's House" in Delos

orders to restore to Delos a statue of Apollo that his soldiers had stolen on their way through. Apart from this, according to a Greek saying, people used to go bald in Mykonos. The main attractions of this white city dear to painters and holidaymakers are the fig trees, vines, and windmills decking the hillside. The most modern hotel in the Cyclades has just been opened there.

DELOS

THE little island of Delos round which we have been circling since we left Syra is at last under our feet. It is not always easy to land there, since the *meltem* often blows that way. The most sheltered port is the creek of Gourna, on the same side as the ancient stadium, whereas the sacred port near the temples and the town is less easy of access. There are also two other anchoring berths: the merchants' port and the slaves' port.

With her mountain 370 feet high, this island, less then three miles long, is one of the most celebrated spots in the world. The name means "the apparent", Poseidon having made her emerge from the waves so that Leto (Latona), pursued by Hera's jealousy, could bring the fruits of Zeus' love into the world. In the shade of a palm tree on the island, the goddess gave birth to Apollo and Artemis. The god was washed in the waters of the Inopos, and fed on nectar and ambrosia from Mount Cynthus. This legend, which thus made Delos the cradle of one of the most highly venerated gods of the Greeks—the god of light, of the Muses, of beauty, of healing, and of the flocks—earned that sorry island an extraordinary fortune, despite the fact that even the homeric hymn to Apollo of Delos qualified her as

"sterile" "Here", in the words of the ode, "Apollo will build a magnificent temple that will become one of the most renowned of all the temples with which mortals honour him under so many different invocations .... and the altar will ever be laden with victims." There are no more victims nowadays, but the ruins of the temple are still there.

In the 7th century B.C. Delos was the religious hub of Ionia. The heyday of her prosperity was doubtless the 4th century B.C. Every four years the Athenians sent a delegation there to bear gifts and sacrifice

Cisterns in Delos

oxen. Capital punishment was suspended until the delegation returned, and
this custom earned Socrates several more days of life. Later, important
societies of foreign traders—such as the *hermaistai* from Rome and the
Poseidoniastai from Merytus (Beyrouth)—established their headquarters
on the island. Later still, the town was laid waste by Mithridates, and
then by pirates. In 200 A.D. Athens put her up for sale, but was unable to
find a buyer. "Woe upon me!" Delos exclaimed—in the words of the poet
Antiphilus—"How many Greek vessels have I seen pass by without stopping?
What then! Is Delos, once an object of worship in Greece, now no more
than a desert? Hera, you have avenged yourself tardily but bitterly upon me
for sheltering your rival." Julian the Apostate made the pilgrimage to
Cynthus, but the Oracle was deaf to his questions. Like the great Pan, Delos
was quite dead. She was still dead when Marcellus visited her in 1820, and
he found "the sole inhabitants were a herd of goats and a goat-herd." The
ruins of Delos have, however, been resuscitated since the end of the 19th
century, thanks to the excavations of the French School of Athens. She has
become one of the most important frameworks for ancient life in Greece,
like Delphi and Olympia, but in an even deeper solitude. Contrary to the

Statue of Cleopatra in Delos

Lions of the Naxians in Delos

other two, she reveals not only a collection of places of worship, but also
the basis of an entire town, like Pompeii. Nowadays the sole inhabitants are
the guardians of the excavations, a handful of fishermen, and the several
employees of the small Tourist Pavilion, where hospitality is extended for
stays of short duration.

It was in front of the great Temple to Apollo—the vast foundations of
which may still be seen near the sacred port—that the gymnastic competitions for Athenian youth were held in pilgrimage years. Not one of the
columns is still standing, and grass has grown up in the place of the pavement,
but those dazzling flagstones outlining the precincts of the temple still
prove, twenty-four centuries later, that the homeric hymn did not lie.
Another temple nearby was consecrated to Apollon Pythios: the god went
to Delphi to slay the serpent Python that had pursued his mother. Artemis
also had two temples in the neighbourhood. The entire region is dotted
with the foundations of small religious edifices, confined within the more
imposing ruins of the porticos of Attalius and Philip. The tiniest stone and
the slenderest of objects has a name. This rim, for instance, resembling the

brim of a well—pompously called the "sekos of Tritopator"—is a monument to some deified ancestor of an illustrious Athenian family. That other circular base is the *hieron* (sanctuary) of Hermes and Maia. Those stone dice and square foundations are the altar to Zeus Polieus and that to the Sotiric gods. This jumble of stones is the monument to the hyperborean Virgins. Here is the pillar of Antiochus, and there is that of Vulcan.

Beyond the sacred enclosure we find ourselves face to face with the white lions of the Naxians, opening their jowls and stretching themselves like greyhounds on their pedestals. Near the Temple of Rome, where the mutilated statue of the goddess is to be found, rise the four columns of the portico of the merchants of Beyrouth. A sun-dried wall of stone indicates the site of the sacred lake, and a palm tree planted beside the ruins of the nearby Temple to Latona reminds us of Ulysses' gallant compliment to Nausicaa, comparing her to the "magnificent young palm tree" he saw at Delos near the altar to Apollo.

In the sanctuary of Dionysos, the curious monument to the choragus Karistios is decorated with symbols of the Dionysiac cult, reminiscent of those we saw in Thera. There is a dazzling statue of a nude, lying on his belly, with a himation (rectangular garment) draped over one shoulder. Further on in the museum we shall see other effigies of Apollo, Artemis, an ephebus, a winged Victory, and a highly amusing satyr.

The ruins of the town extend on the other side of the sanctuary of Apollo. There are innumerable mosaics, of exceptional quality. And there too we may see the masks of the "swashbuckling soldier", the "chagrined dotard", a pecking bird, and vases decorated with palm trees and garlands; another scene depicts the drunkenness of Silenus, and Dionysos seated on a panther, clad in a rich oriental gown, with a thyrsus in one hand and a tambour in the other; or again, the most elegant of tridents decorated with dolphins, other fish, and a knot on the shaft. Most of the houses have colonnades; some of them were several storeys high, as indicated by the one that has been rebuilt. The main public monument in the region is the theatre which, although in ruins, commands a magnificent view of the Isle of Hecatus opposite. Before the last war, an ancient fig tree used to cast its shade on one side of the theatre; it has since disappeared, and the palm tree of the French school is the only tree now standing in Delos.

Following the shore, we first stumble on the marketing district, where the "shop with the columns" and the "shop with the bathtub"—a marble

Excavations in Delos, on the Edge of the Sacred Lake

bath similar to our own—are to be found, as well as another house devoted in rather a special way to the worship of Aphrodite. Further on, the oracle-temple of Glaucos outlines the hemicycle of the consultation chamber on the very edge of the water.

The ruins of the Temple of Aphrodite are on the lower slopes of Mount Cynthus, which we have yet to climb. The goddess had another temple near the sacred lake; it was called the Temple of Aphrodite of Inopos, being built beside a small stream (one of the most attractive groups in Athens Museum is that of Aphrodite and Pan from Delos: the goddess is raising one of her sandals to strike her over-venturesome companion). A tiny theatre

A Port in the Cyclades

nearby was situated within the precincts of the goddess. Being higher up, it commands an even finer view than the big theatre looking down on the Isle of Rhenea—also known as Greater Delos, as distinct from the island we are now on—with the sanctuary of Apollo to the right. Rhenea played an important role for the people of Delos: since birth and death were forbidden on Apollo's isle, people about to die and women in labour were carried to this nearby island.

The Inopos, on the banks of which we are now standing, is of course dried up; however, in the past there was evidently no dearth of water since it sheltered the sanctuaries of Syrian and Egyptian gods, and water played a major role in the latter cults. The two columns of the façade, the fronton, and a decapitated statue from the Temple of Isis Pankale ("the all-beautiful") rise up before us. Slightly higher up, the small precincts of the Temple of Hera show how concerned the people were to pacify Latona's enemy.

An ancient path hewn out of the rock leads straight to the summit of Mount Cynthus. It is a steep climb, but not a long one, and whilst Homer and Euripides give us the impression of a real mountain by referring to "the bluff tip" of Cynthus, the geographer Tournefort likewise exaggerated in qualifying it as "unpleasant". How could it be other than pleasant, even under the fire of Apollo's most piercing darts, to climb Mount Cynthus? It gave the Romans one of their prettiest feminine names, Propertius having immortalized his mistress Cynthia in our memories.

On the way, we catch sight of an oracular cavern, the roof of which is composed of two enormous blocks of stone that have hardly been squared. It was consecrated to Herakles; the round base of his statue may be seen inside; it again commands a magnificent view of Delos. But it is from the summit of Mount Cynthus—dotted with ruins denoting the sanctuaries of Zeus and Athena of Cynthus, Zeus the Highest, Baal, Zeus the Sun-God, and others—that one should "see the golden Cyclades emerge out of the blue".

ANDROS AND SKYROS

ANDROS, on the other side of Tinos, is a prolongation of Euboea. It is a pleasant contrast to Delos, which is even balder than the inhabitants of Mykonos used to be. Veritable forests of lemon trees and mulberry bushes are fertilized by perennial torrents; vines flourish in the region, and mineral water from Sariza is despatched all over Greece. Here and there the square towers of pigeon-cotes rise up. The present capital is on the east coast, whereas the ancient capital, Palaeopolis, was located on a far less lovely setting on the west coast. The remains of the walls and the port may still be seen, and the famous Hermes in Athens Museum was found nearby. In the vicinity there was once a Temple to Dionysos beside a fountain whose waters tasted of wine for seven days a year. Near Gavrion, to the north looms up one of the most beautiful Hellenic towers still standing in Greece—five storeys, 65 feet high.

Skyros lies outside the Cyclades. It is the southernmost of the Sporades, but a visit there forms a picturesque conclusion to our little trip. It has two summits, and two legends. Having chosen the island as a place of rest from his labours, Theseus was put to death there, and Achilles, dressed as a girl, was concealed there by his mother. We all know how Ulysses discovered the hero amongst the maidens of Lycomedes by showing him a weapon—a theme that has inspired a multitude of painters ancient and modern. Atalanta, whose feet were as fleet as Achilles' heels, was the daughter of a king of Skyros. The island numbers two villages: the little port of Linaria,

near which Rupert Brooke is buried, and Khora to the east, built round a
kastro. Although no doubt the island can no longer provide an Achilles or
an Atalanta, it now supplies modern Greeks with decorations for their
houses. Those little low tables, those small chairs with naive sculptures and
cord seats, the faience, and all those drawings of two-headed eagles, animals,
and cypress trees seen in shop-windows and homes in Athens come from
Skyros. Let us buy something here so that, after visiting so many of the
islands that supply the most wonderful statues in our museums, we can bring
back something more than immortal memories of our journey to the isle
of marble and sunshine.

THE DODECANESE
AND THE SOUTHERN SPORADES

ASIA—EUROPE: the two continents scatter their sparse islands across the
sea to testify to the days when they were welded together, and when
Indian elephants and Siberian megatheria used to come down to
leave their huge bones on the Aegean shores.

In the past the summits emerging from and rising into the blue used to
tower over wooded countryside; nowadays they float on the sea. The islands
stretch out beseeching arms to each other, like loving couples heartbroken
at being separated.

Providence seems to be more concerned with geography in her minutest
details than with history and her great men. The Aegean Isles form a rear-
guard where a civilization long forgotten by the mainland constantly lags
behind. They continued to believe in Athens' might when the latter was
no more than a Roman colony; they still referred to Byzantium years after
the Turks had changed the name of the illustrious capital; and they remained
Ottoman half-a-century after Greece had liberated herself and become
European.

Seen from the air, or on an atlas, the Greek isles look as if they had been
thrown into the sea like stepping-stones in a ford, systematically laid out in
places (the Cyclades), and scattered haphazardly in others (the Northern
Sporades). As for the Dodecanese, they are dislocated from head to toe.

ASIAN GREECE—On leaving the kindly harbour of Alexandretta, I recollect
the time I returned from Beyrouth to Italy on a steamship that hugged the
Anatolian coast. I was enraptured by the wonderful view of the sea shimmer-

An Alley in the Knights' Quarter in Rhodes

ing like a heavy drapery of watered silk, and the milky moats in which the red cliffs of Taurus are entrenched, like the foundations of a keep. In those valleys of Asia Minor a civilization grew up which is, perhaps, more important for us than that of insular Greece. Caria in the south, Lydia in the centre, and Mysia in the north gave birth to the greatest of the Greek genii: Homer, Thales, Heraclitus, Pythagorus, Herodotus Hippodamus, the first town-planner. The names of Pergamos, Ephesus, Smyrna, and Miletus are undoubtedly as worthy of merit as Athens and Sparta. On those shores Homer scanned the most ancient songs in the world; philosophers laid the foundation-stones of human thought there; Anaximander and his school drew the first maps; Hippocrates created medical science; and Ionian art reached divine perfection there.

Until the days of Byzantium, the Dodecanese represented the furthest tip of our civilization. "There," in the words of Curtius, "a few leagues from Asia, more history was enacted than in any other space as narrow."

Hardly had my ship rounded the arc of the sickle formed by the Asiatic continent than I began to feel at home. That corner of the Aegean was like the corner of my street. I could have embraced the first island that hove into sight—Castellorizo (ancient Megisthi), bringing me greetings from the west—a welcome relief after the cheerless reception extended by the Anatolian coasts.

RHODES

A n hour later the snowy Tairos—ancient Atavyros—loomed up before my eyes, towering over Rhodes and her capital.

The Colossus no longer surveys the entry to the port. The man of bronze was short-lived; he died at the age of fifty, shattered by an earthquake. It took him twelve years to grow to the height of 104 feet. I involuntarily imagined him as he appeared in my schoolbooks, holding a lantern in his right hand to light the pilots, and straddling his legs to let the big sailing-boats pass underneath. Scholars disagree as to whether the statue was erected at the entrance to the pier, or in the middle, in front of the town. Nor are they in agreement as to the name of the sculptor (Chares?) who hoisted his bronze plates right to the summit, crowning his statue with a diadem of spikes (from which Bartholdi drew his inspiration for the Statue of Liberty in New York harbour).

This Colossus was not alone: a hundred statues of the Sun, 100 feet high, were dotted round the isle like the monoliths on Easter Island. Long before

The Port of Rhodes

it spread to Germany, America, and Russia, passion for all that is colossal was rife in Egypt and Oceania. The great epochs were not content with constructing gods of their own stature: they wanted them to be even bigger still. But even gods fall: the giant, eighty cubits high, collapsed, and all that remained was the legs; his entrails of rock piled up inside to give him a more solid base, were scattered over the ground. Athens, who had always rankled with jealousy, had the Oracle of Delphi forbid restoration of the

Lindos

monument. The children used to amuse themselves by climbing up the legs, and they had to open their little arms to the full in order to clasp a toe. Once she was rid of this competition, Greece began to build other titanic models on her own soil. The statues of Minerva in Athens, and Zeus in Olympia, were imposingly massive, but they were never in the international class, worthy to compete for the championship of the Seven Wonders of the World.

I have always enjoyed visiting islands, and I spent two weeks in Rhodes, devoted partly to fishing for sponges. Never having been to Djerba, to console myself I went to Himia armed with harpoon and trident to fish for the animal-plants that were already sought after in ancient times—in fact, if I am not mistaken, they were used to wash the banquet table on Ulysses' return. As underwater goggles were not then in common use, the fishermen used to pour oil on the water to make it easier to see the bottom, and by peering down I could distinguish those strange shrubs that intrigued Aristotle in his day: the shaggy golden heads attached to the rocks were fluttering like mermaids' fans. The ship, laden with sticky gelatine, returned to the "brand new antiquity" of Rhodes, which had been restored to the last stone by the prodigious skill of modern architects, who had done their utmost to put an edge on those rusty old blades. With their winding stairways, overhanging towers and battlemented crests the rosy ramparts seemed identical with those built by Hippodamus, to the envy of Athens. In a few days Italian polishers had given them a better patina than the Greek climate achieved in centuries. I returned to the hotel to take a sunbath on the white marble terrace, in homage to the tutelary god of the city Pindar (even before the Incas) had called the Wife of the Sun.

Like the other islands in the Dodecanese, Rhodes began by buttering her bread on both sides. Long prosperity and a magnificent civilization ended in sieges, destruction, depredation, massacre, emigration, and deportation. Her fleet, once the greatest in the Aegean, was reduced to fishing-smacks; her docks, which Strabo so much admired, crumbled away; her triremes, whose prows were reminiscent of Scandinavian craft, no longer furrowed the Mediterranean as far as Gibraltar; her maritime law code, which was so remarkable that Justinian incorporated it in his *Pandectes* without changing an iota, ceded to the customs of piracy. The sea, once her servant, became her gaoler.

And yet what a cardinal position she occupied! The routes to India, the Holy Land, the Dardanelles, Italy—and a welter of other great sea routes

Bazaar Street in the Old Greek Quarter in Rhodes

Rhodes Seen from the Ramparts

—meet there. And that is why Greeks, Persians, Romans, Franks, Saracens, Arabs, Venetians, Genoese, and Turks succeeded each other in Rhodes, the martyred sentinel. . . . Even the Russians played their card, since in 1770 Catherine II sent Orloff there to incite the Greeks of the islands to rise against the Turks—an abortive prelude to the War of Independence that liberated Greece in 1821.

At the beginning of the 20th century a new—and yet extremely ancient—Greece was revealed to the world. She bore very little resemblance to the

BEUVILLE

classical land of our school days, and was therefore all the more enchanting in our adolescent eyes. I can still see the octopus friezes that appeared in the *décors* of the first Russian ballets, imitating Cretan motifs. Now this Greece, which Schliemann and Evans suddenly popularized, had not been discovered in Crete but in Rhodes, half a century earlier. In the Victorian era, Anglo-French excavations in Camiros (1853–1863) brought to light a hitherto unsuspected civilization.

In Camiros—which, with two other cities, preceded the town of Rhodes

—gold masks, pottery, jewellery, and vestiges of architecture heralding Troy and Mycenae were discovered. No ceramic tradition ever outvied this one in duration: the vases decorated with serpents in Berlin Museum, the *oinochoes* with friezes of animals in the Louvre, are the first signposts along a road which terminated only in the 16th and 17th centuries with the famous Rhodes faience, of which the Cluny Museum in Paris, the Galdiano Museum in Madrid, the Ariana in Geneva, and the Victoria and Albert in London have amassed the treasures, and of which the small town of Lindos was the cradle.

It was not just golden rain that Zeus poured down on Rhodes, but a shower of nautic art, science, and poetry with which the Father of the Gods inundated the city. The basis of the famous Library in Alexandria came from Rhodes; in 272 B.C. it was purchased by the Philadelph. Little remained of the actual town; after being sacked from top to bottom by Cassius to punish her for siding with Antony, in the Middle Ages Rhodes was laid waste even

Hippocrates' Tree in Cos

more thoroughly, and definitively this time, by the Frankish knights, whose brutal valour provoked so many holy catastrophes in the name of Jesus.

The Bibliothèque Nationale in Paris possesses a magnificent manuscript: the Codex of Caoursin, Vice-Chancellor of St John of Jerusalem, the order that had been occupying Rhodes for the previous two centuries. Caoursin, who witnessed the siege of the island by Mahomet II, related this final phase of the Frankish venture, and had the text illuminated; by that stage, only a handful of knights remained on the island, and, under orders from their sovereign master, Pierre d'Aubusson, they left with relics and galleys for Cyprus and Malta. In 1522, nearly half-a-century later, Soliman besieged Rhodes for the second time.

In this phase, German artillery opened fire, to succour the English redoubt attacked by the janissaries—in short, in a miraculous Christian accord, a babel of tongues and a hotchpotch of people united under the banner of the West.

OTHER ISLES IN THE DODECANESE

THE other islands are called Kasos, Karpathos, Saros, Tilos, Nisyros, Cos, Astypalaia, Halki, Symi, Kalymnos, Leros, and Patmos; then they have other names that the Italians gave them to make them forget Greece: Karpathos is called Scarpanto, Patmos Palmosa, etc. To complicate the picture still further, they also have a Turkish name; and to simplify matters, they are grouped as the Isles of the Dodecanese and the Southern Sporades.

Most of them are minute and so much alike that, as often as not, the guides do not even deign to mention them: they all have whitewashed arcades against the background of the sea, a monastery clinging to the rock, an anchorite's grotto, an ancient Turkish cemetery, vague ruins surrounded by vineyards, a Kastro—which is an acropolis, or if you prefer, an alcazar converted into a Frankish castle—terraces to bank the sloping ground, and cafés where, imitating the locals, I used to try to read the Athens Daily and drink a glass of water as they do; and lastly, a Customs office and a mutual security society known as a *hetairie*. Fishermen and market-gardeners who grow melons and figs for export to Egypt vegetate on the shores. It is hard to imagine these islands rich with fleets and warehouses, mobilized in the alliance of the King of Kings, sending vessels without number to attack Troy, as Homer described them to us. The gods themselves were not ashamed to patronize them, Apollo honouring Kalymnos, and Poseidon Nisyros. Before becoming Turkish—even more Turkish then the others, in fact, since they were nearer the Dardanelles—they formed the fringe of the Empire, or *theme* as it was called in Byzantium, meaning the frontiers of civilization, or the *romania*.

Cos—I have always had a passion for medical science and medicaments which amuses my cronies and incites a doctor friend to send me a complete set of the latest pharmaceutical creations every birthday. I should therefore take off my hat to Cos as the cradle of medical science. The Temple to Aesculapius-Asklepios and the first regular hospital, the Asklaepion, were erected there; the Arabs went to Cos to derive the principles of their renowned medical skill; and the great Hippocratus lived there. In 460 B.C., 23 centuries before Freud and Jung, this wandering doctor sensed the *vital principle* (libido), and named it. He became illustrious not so much for refusing to collaborate with Artaxerxes, or for curing Perdicas II of Macedonia from lovesickness, but because, by watching animals lick themselves, he realized that saliva is antiseptic, and on seeing waterfowl syringe their anus with their beaks, he deduced therefrom that the intestines could be purged by douching; and lastly, because he was the first doctor bold enough to undertake dissection by sacrilegiously laying searching hands on dead bodies.

He offered the Oracle in Delphi a golden skeleton—science's last tribute to magic, whom she was about to dethrone. His family came from Cos on his mother's side.

In ancient times, Cos boasted another product besides medicine: her audaciously transparent textiles. The picture of Bilitis standing naked beneath that flimsy material haunted our adolescent years, and

Monastery of Patmos

The Port of Patmos

for the first time in our lives made the name of a Greek island familiar and dear to us. The transparency of the cloth caused a scandal amongst the censors: Juvenal rebuked Creticus for appearing at the tribunal in a toga from Cos. "I cannot stand the July heat," Creticus objected. "Then plead stark naked—it's less dishonouring."

If he so wishes, in Pyli the tourist may visit the ruins of the ancient town of Isthmos, brought to light by excavations. As one might expect, they comprise protective walls, porticos, and a Temple to Aesculapius, the demi-god worshipped by the Dorians, the founders of the city, on whom Aesculapius bestowed a medicinal spring which dates back to the 6th century and is still in existence. Cos is a town favoured by springs, which are rare in the Dodecanese; they spurt up on all sides, and others are conducted there from Mount Prion by an aqueduct. This charming spot was also the adopted homeland of the painter Apelles and the poet Theocritus. The Ptolemies were brought up there. Nowadays Cos, like Rhodes, is a highly popular summer resort.

PATMOS—This is the last of the Dodecanese; Lesbos, Lemnos, Imbros, and

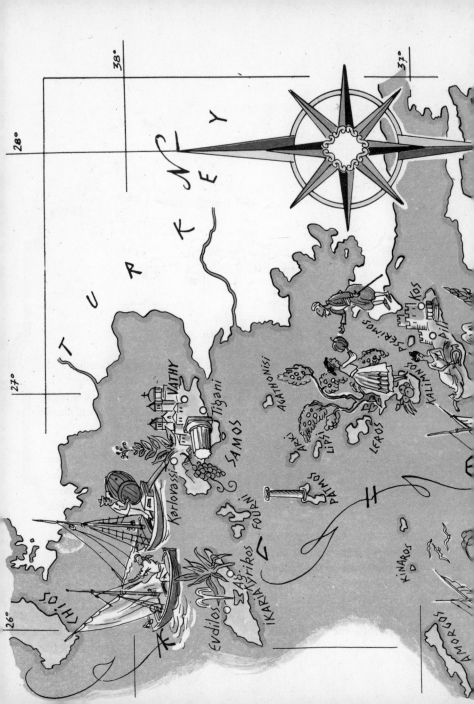

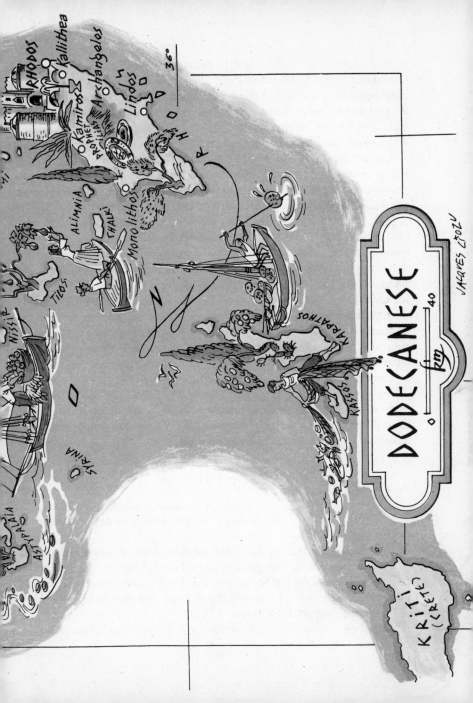

Ikaria do not belong to the group: in 1915 the Allied fleets headed for the Dardanelles swept north across these islands, bringing them into the lime-light again for a moment, before their fall into oblivion. For a long time Patmos was no more than a name: this place of exile was itself exiled by Baedeker. Cruises visiting the neighbouring isles of Naxos and Mykonos overlooked it and hastened on towards the Peloponnese or Constantinople.

And yet the island where St John had his vision of the end of the world merits more than a passing glance. One imagines the apocalyptical isle devoured by infernal flames and sulphurous clouds, beneath a terrible moon resembling a goatskin bag filled with blood; on the contrary, it is a vision in pink, white, and blue. After being captured in Ephesus, led to Rome and cast into boiling oil, St John was finally relegated to Patmos. There, ac-cording to the monks who show you a grotto in the St Anne chapel in which the apostle used to prostrate himself, he heard the voice of the Trinity rising out of a cavity and dictating the Apocalypse to him. But a visit to the fortified convent known as St John of Patmos is more interesting; it contains a magnificent and extremely renowned Gospel according to St Mark, illuminated throughout in gold and silver on purple parchment. The con-vent also boasts another rare and precious museum piece—the Islands' letters patent of nobility—the bull of King Alexis Comnenus. Patmos holds an elevated rank in Orthodox mysticism.

The soil is so sterile that barely a score of cypress grow there, and the shafts of marble columns from the acropolis serve as bollards to attach the ships. These are now more numerous than in the past, since Patmos is linked to Piraeus more frequently than before.

LESBOS

The globe of the radiant moon rises into the sky, letting her silvery rays flow down on the dark land of man....

I AM about to set foot on this island, the homeland of Sappho whom the Greeks proclaim as their greatest poet; I should like to recapture those features inspired by the Muses; but the island's crude coins only present them to me in a defaced and desecrated form, like her poems, of which only sublime vestiges have survived.

Nowadays Lesbos is called Mytilene; it is a large island detached from

Asia and extending towards the Hellespont. But what do we care about her modern name, her modern destiny, her 14 mosques, her 7 churches (one of which is a cathedral), her port of Malea, and her Hill of Olympus 3,250 feet high? We forget that she was founded by the Pelasgians, and reached the height of her prosperity under one of the Seven Sages of Greece. That jagged shore where gnarled olive trees grow; those torrents, vehement and thirsty; those mild May evenings when I had the good fortune to slip in between the squalls of the Sea of Marmara and the arrival of the Etesian winds—everything is in harmony with Sappho's violent yet tender soul. She wandered there, lovingly entwined with Anactoria (who inspired

Swinburne's lascivious poem), until "black-eyed sleep" came to lower their lids. There she wreathed Atthis with violets until the moment when—in her own words—"softly cushioned in my arms, thou slakedst thy parched lips."

And there again, she reigned over the feminine schools, or *thiases*—the last vestiges of an intellectual matriarchy brushed aside by invasions.

What exactly were those thiases?—High schools for girls? Convents for courtesans? Conservatories? —Doubtless a mixture

*Woman
from Astypalaia*

On the Deck in Third Class

of them all, as befits a free and exquisite civilization. To find all the accomplishments united to so high a degree of perfection—dancing, poetry, music, technique of the heart and the senses, moral and aesthetic culture—one would have to await the advent of the Chinese courtesans under the Sung dynasty, or the Venetian women of the Renaissance—and even they could hardly compare! In the Nymphs' Garden and the House of the Muses, Sappho used to teach; she became enamoured of Erinna of Telos and Darnophile of Pamphylia, and sang of them in passionate, frenzied verses:

"*I am glowing with perspiration and seized with trembling; I become as green as grass and feel about to die. . . .*"

The poem broke off there, but is it not more beautiful to resemble a mutilated statue?

"*The cajoler swept me off my feet. . . . I would give all the chariots of Lydia, all the armour that glitters in battles, to contemplate thy graceful gait and the glow of thy radiant face.*"

She knew all the anger of jealousy: "*What uncomely hag has thus bewitched thee? A woman unfit to lift her skirts above her ankles. . . .*" (A typically feminine rebuke!)

Thus unsatiated heart was obliged to alienate herself from "treacherous women": "*My heart is not of stuff soft enough to pardon.*"

One day she uttered this strange cry of anguish: "*What do the Gods desire of me? I have two souls....*"

She loved silent, mysterious Phaon, the Albertine of the 6th century B.C.; and, having written: "*If death were a boon, the all-knowing Gods would have chosen it rather than life,*" the poetess flung herself from the Leucadian rock.

SAMOS

I HAVE been there, to be sure; was it in 1922, during my first trip to Greece, or in 1932 on that small yacht lent by a Greek friend, thanks to which we made a tour of the Isles? My memory is just as hazy about the date as it is about the spot itself. I conjure up a confused mental picture of frenzied gesticulations accompanied by abuse.

Through an odd caprice of memory, I stumble on the following quotation: "Egypt does not cultivate tobacco; she imports it from Samos to make Egyptian cigarettes"—and the penny drops. Of course, Samos is the island of light tobacco! I see myself striding through the capital, Vathi, one day, and emerging into tobacco plantations: the golden spirals of ripe tobacco perfume the air, and the huge golden leaves sway beneath the sky in nets slung on boats bound for Alexandria.

We made an impromptu landing in Samos, having exhausted our water supply. "*Néro, néro!*" (water, water!) shouted the captain. "No, no," the Port Authorities exclaimed, and a swarthy little man with an admiral's cocked hat shook his head. "*Krassi, Krassi!*" (wine, wine!) shrieked the mob. The Eupalinos tunnel, which was supposed to bring water from the reservoir in Hagiades, was empty, but wine from Samos was unladen on the deck—wine from the Catholic mission station, wine from German houses, wine from Dimitrelos, wine from Goldstein, in bottles, demi-johns, and hogsheads. For lack of water, I washed my hands black with grease in wine from Samos, and they became blacker and stickier than ever. And on going ashore I was surrounded by a sumptuous procession of flies, wasps, mosquitoes, butterflies, and other insects—far worse than in Central Africa—doubtless attracted by the fragrance of the Samos vintage, which cured me from dessert wines for the rest of my life.

The Ship of the Isles

CHIOS

THIS paradise was created by man; he dug through the arid rock of fat blue marble crystals and antimony until he found water; it flows down from Mount Haghios through deep crevasses, beside a scarlet border formed by the most beautiful oleanders in the world.

Once beyond those serried streets hemmed in by the old walls of harems 12 feet tall where a captive lemon tree poked through, the view opened on to the plains of Cambos, Calamoti, and Cardamyla. Olive, palm, mastic and turpentine trees wafted their unforgettable perfume into the very depths of the gorge. It was mid-May, and harvest-time already; broken by the skeletons of norias, vast expanses of barley and corn fell on all sides, reaped to the accompaniment of prayers and songs that cannot have been very different from the hymns to Ceres or Cybeles, for there is still an altar to the goddess—a kind of bench scooped out of the rock and ornamented with lions. Against the blue and grey stones, the tufts of oleander formed a mosaic of colour. The pistachio-mastick tree wept tears of golden gum—that precious material known as *masticka* which is cooked in *sherbet* or masticated

398

as chewing-gum. Mastícka was highly appreciated by the Turks, whose gardeners were Chiots, and it was despatched to Stamboul to perfume the breath of the sultans and fortify their gums. There were three qualities of mastícka, corresponding to the category of civil servants and court officials (just as there are three types of caviar behind the iron curtain).

The history of Chios was alternately brilliant and pitiful, comprising periods of prosperity interspersed with invasions, sackings, earthquakes, and massacres. She gave birth to Homer—so she believed; she belonged to the Ionian Dodecapolis; she had her Homeric poets, her Homeric school, and, under Byzantium, her Arvisian wine, her figs and her liqueurs, which were all sources of wealth; but Byzantium ceded her to the Genoese who ruled the people severely; they shut them up in fortified villages—veritable prisons with closely guarded doors—lest the precious production of mastícka be diminished through smuggling or theft. Paradoxically, the island was happy under the Turks; considered as the sultans' dower, Chios supplied the Padischah with supple, wily, high-ranking officials who surreptitiously governed the pashaliks, and she would have continued to enjoy her privileges in peace, had that admirable Greek spirit of patriotism not thrown her into the War of Independence. The reprisals were terrifying; Victor Hugo and Delacroix immortalized the horrors: 25,000 massacred, 45,000 human-beings led into slavery, whilst famine and typhus decimated the survivors. Of the island's hundred thousand inhabitants, only two thousand unhappy victims emerged, half dead. But nothing can destroy the sturdy Chiot race, nor stifle its genius for building and seafaring. Chios was rebuilt; from her shores those mighty Greek families I came across in Trieste, Leghorn, Marseilles, London, Bucharest, and Bombay set sail.

We went up to the village of Pyrghi by way of the Haghios Loukas road; on the way we passed a group of lovely girls, with eyebrows meeting at the root of a nose welded to the brow as on ancient statues of Venus. They stared at us with big round eyes like those in icons; they resembled the Virgin in mosaic in the apse of the convent of Nea Moni, built in the 2nd century by Constantine Monomachos.

Pyrghi bore no resemblance to any village I knew. Her two-storeyed houses were neatly aligned; the ground floor was inhabited by sheep and a donkey, the upper storey by the family. Strange old women with turbans twirled round their heads like diadems were seated on their doorsteps, bolt upright; Hecuba must have had that same set expression, and that haughty, despairing look. We advanced through the mighty silence: who said Greeks were talkative?—In Athens, perhaps, in cafés; elsewhere, they are extraordinarily taciturn. We entered a tiny pitchblack church, weakly gilded by its iconostasis; children followed on our heels. "Beware of fleas," the guide whispered. His words were calumnious, for the children were clean. Together with the Jews, the Greeks are the most slandered people on earth. Even their courage has been discredited. "I shall believe in the bravery of the Greeks when I see their kilts fluttering in a volley of grape-shot!" said Anna de Noailles. Their heroic conduct in a long series of wars, and the infinite patience with which they supported a permanent state of mobilization have put an end to such stupidities.

Chios is my last lap—my last farewell to the Aegean Isles; I bring all their savour away with me, in bottles: that miraculous jam, *nerandzaki*, lilliputian oranges, *limonakia*, minute lemons, and other citrus fruits beyond compare, roses, and those *sherbets* of masticka which as long as I live will remind me of the Paradise of the Archipelago.

GREECE

GREEK

THE GREEKS

TOWARDS A BETTER UNDERSTANDING OF
GREECE–GREEK–THE GREEKS

Yesterday and Today—Greece attracts us by her past, and holds us by her present—or rather, by the natural way in which the present continues the remotest past. The spinner guarding her sheep against a background of olive and cypress trees or the youngster driving his donkey along a bumpy road are just as evocative of Greece of ancient times, yesterday, and always, as the shaft of an ancient column.

The Greeks are proud of their courage and their love of independence, but they would rather discuss their resistance to invasion during the last war than the feats of Leonidas in the Battle of Thermopylae. Does that surprise you? If you mentioned the Battle of Britain to a foreigner, would you not think it rather bad taste should he reply: "I'd rather hear about King Alfred —now there's a man who really incarnated the spirit of your race!"

If you will only allow your Greek friends to remain 20th-century men and women, they will show their gratitude by welcoming you to their homes, introducing you to the charming gaiety of their daily life, escorting you through their old quarters, their markets and inns, their shops, and even their museums and ruins. Needless to say, they are well aware that the legacies of Ancient Times compensate their country for the gold and uranium mines that enrich more economically favoured regions.... and most of them are born ciceroni.

Apart from very rare exceptions, the hotels are extremely clean. In certain large tourist centres (Nauplia, Mykonos, Delphi, etc.), the government has built—and is continuing to build— "tourist hotels" which are models of comfort, elegance, and refined taste.

If you mentioned to a foreigner....

402

If you stay in the same hotel for several days, it will be worth your while to take "half-board", which will permit you to take one meal a day in the restaurant or tavern of your own choice (in Greece a tavern—TABEPNA— like our "country pub", is a place where one can eat the innkeeper's cooking served by the daughter of the house under the supervision of mine host, who has the knack of giving all his clients the impression that they are friends in the making. And in the evening you will hear popular Greek folksongs sung in these taverns).

Even in luxury restaurants in Greece there is one person who is unusually tactful compared with his counterparts all the world over—the wine-waiter. Greeks drink very little wine, beer, or spirits of any kind, and they do not expect foreigners to be any less temperate. So if you care to wash down your meals with water—which is usually excellent—don't be afraid of being frowned upon. For all that, the maître d'hôtel will be just as attentive to your needs, and the proprietor just as amiable.

On the other hand, it would be a pity not to take the opportunity of tasting Greek wines—red, rosy, and above all white, heavy and light, natural or "resinated". However, tread warily in regard to the last speciality, which —even amongst the Greeks themselves—has as many adamant disparagers as fervent enthusiasts. As you probably know, the Greeks have the habit of adding resin to wine when still in the cask, as it keeps better that way and is, apparently, healthier to drink. The taste of the resultant beverage—which one either adores or abhors—is, in any case, far removed from that of the grape.

Moreover, there is "resinated" and "resinated", dependent on the dosing of the two main elements. You will drink the "real stuff" in country regions, where- as Athenian taverns tempt the tourist's palate with discreeter varieties. The con- ditions in which it is sampled also have their part to play. *Palikari* lamb is never the same without resinated wine, and it also goes down well with a dish of fried fish or a spicy sauce. As a general rule, it is pleasanter to drink with

The maître d'hôtel will be just as attentive to your needs....

ABOMINABLE! EXQUISITE!

RETSI

*The wine that has as many adamant
disparagers as fervent enthusiasts....*

savouries than with sweet dishes.

Before the meal, you may care to sample the local appetizers—*mastícka*, *rakí*, and *oúzo* in particular. They are all similar in appearance and even in taste—a whitish liqueur flavoured of aniseed, rather like weak *pernod*. The first is perfumed with syrup of lentisk *(mastícka)*; despite the name, it is deliciously thirst-quenching. These appetizers are served in tiny glasses, together with a dish of *mezés*—an assortment of titbits (triangular open sandwiches of cold meat, diced tomato, goat cheese, fat shrimps, or enormous olives which one spears with a cocktail stick)—and, of course, a large glass of water.

The coffee-cups hold only two or three sips, but the Greeks drink coffee at all hours. It would be as well to know how to order it: *Varý Glykó* if you like it strong and sweet; *Skéto*—without sugar; *Métrio*—medium.

ROAST BEEF VERSUS PALIKARI LAMB—I do not imagine you belong to the class of travellers who expect to be served with their customary dish no matter where they are! If you have a sudden yearning for roast beef, you should have no difficulty in finding it, especially in Athens. But you would probably prefer to try Greek specialities: vine-leaves stuffed with cold rice or hot meat; *palikari* lamb—i.e. roast on the spit, generally eaten at Easter and on other holidays; pilafi; macaroni with meat; stuffed tomatoes; *kokorétsi* (sausages made of offal, grilled on the spit); mutton with marrow, egg-plant, turnips, and okra *(bámies)*; and every variety of fish and shellfish, with the accent on a kind of red mullet *(barboúnia)* and more especially bream *(synagrída)*, often garnished with herbs and flavoured with the most wonderful sauces.

Dessert consists of cakes and fruit *(froúta)*. If you are not averse to very sweet pastries, order *baklavá* (a cake made of ground almonds), *karidópita* (walnut and honey cake), *galactoboúriko* (cream cake), *loukoumádes* (fritters in syrup and honey), and *kourabiédes* (biscuits made of almonds and semolina).

For the fruit course, in summertime you will usually be given a choice between water-melon *(karpoúsi)* and honey-melon *(pepóni)*. The water-melon is the real summer favourite; one sees them piled up in tottering heaps in every market-place, on roadside stalls in the country, and on every meal table; and there is no getting away from it, those purple slices glistening with black pips are deliciously refreshing. From August on, you will begin to find the most wonderful grapes, especially in the islands and the Peloponnese (where you can taste the Corinth variety before they are converted into currants).

Honey—which, according to the labels, always comes from Hymettus—is an essential ingredient in the majority of desserts. In the taverns it is served with the wax on, in the form of a cake.

And if the lack of a menu on the innkeeper's part, and the lack of vocabulary on your part, make the choice of a meal too difficult, make a beeline for the kitchen. This is quite a normal procedure, and you will be able to select your own dish straight from the saucepan.

A DAY IN GREECE—However early you rise, you will always find the streets full of life and most of the cafés and shops already open. The majority of employees start work at 8 a.m. (Greece, by the way, is an hour ahead of Western Europe), and work until noon.

The streets are alive with a picturesque world of people you will soon learn to distinguish: shoeshines, vendors of peanuts and jasmine, urchins swinging scales containing a microscopic cup of coffee and the ritual glass of water which the director has ordered to entertain a friend or reward himself for a strenuous morning's work.

In the majority of restaurants, lunch is not usually served until 1 or 1.30, and even later in private homes.

After lunch comes the sacrosanct siesta. For the first time in the day traffic slows down, trams are virtually empty, and even the street cafés are deserted. Wherever you go you will see bodies slouched on benches, chairs, and even on the ground. If you insist on ordering a drink, the waiter gets up, bleary-eyed, from the bench on which he was slumbering, and hardly waits to be paid before dropping off once more. By about 4 o'clock the towns and villages gradually come to life again, and the bustle reaches its height in the evening.

This is devoted to social life and friends in general. Greeks—and Athenians in particular—still maintain their traditional sociability. From one week to the next every evening is booked in advance, either for drinks or for a dinner party. Even foreigners need never worry about having to spend an evening on their own, as long as they have an introduction to a friend of a friend. Dinner parties begin late (about 9 or 10) and consequently go on until late also. When they are not dining at home, Greeks have a fondness for open-air restaurants with tables set out on a terrace beneath an arbour of grape-vines, or beside the water (at Phaleron we once saw diners seated literally with their feet in the sea, apparently delighted with the setting).

As a general rule Greeks are very informal, and soon put you on a pleasantly familiar footing. Friends you made only yesterday will call you by your Christian name and encourage you to reciprocate. When asked for directions, countryfolk—the fair sex in particular—usually accompany their explanations by an affectionate pat on the arm or the back. As for the children, they run after you to offer you a rose, a sprig of jasmine, a bunch of basil or verbena—or one of the other products of a land poor in corn but rich in herbs.

RELIGION AND SUPERSTITIONS—The official Greek religion is Orthodox Christianity. The priests (or *papas*) are allowed to marry and have children; however, the bishops—who are the supreme heads of the Church, which refuses to acknowledge papal authority in Rome—are selected exclusively from bachelors. The priests have long hair gathered at the nape of the neck in a kind of bun; they are held in great esteem, and it is still quite natural for members of the congregation to kiss their hand. When the Orthodox cross themselves, they always do so three times in succession.

Beside the Orthodox church there is a Greek Catholic church which comes under the authority of the Vatican. Mass is celebrated in Greek, and communion takes place in both Greek and Latin.

The countryfolk are even more pious than the townspeople. In a small island

A microscopic cup of coffee and the ritual glass of water....

such as Mykonos there are as many chapels as there are days in the year. Each chapel is visited several times daily by the incense-bearer and the oil-bearer who comes to fill the lamps that burn in front of the ikons.

Religious though they may be, do not imagine that this explains why one sees so many Greeks from every walk of life —in the street, in the tram, seated outside a café—fingering

Diners seated with their feet in the sea....

an amber rosary adorned with a silk tassel. There is nothing sacred about them at all; telling the twenty beads or so is just a game to keep the hands occupied, just as a smoker fidgets with a cigarette whilst he is talking or daydreaming. One has the impression that it would take a course of anti-toxic treatment to break the habit. As if to confirm this, these rosaries are sold in the same kiosks as tobacco.

For all their piety, the Greeks as a whole are still very much afraid of the "evil eye". To protect them from it, the children wear a string of blue beads round their necks. Similar necklaces—on a larger scale, of course—are hung round the necks of horses and mules.... for the same reason!

If, when discussing a price, you want to express the figure 5, resist the temptation to hold up your hand with the fingers outspread and the palm facing your interlocutor: this is the gesture used in casting spells. You will see faces pucker in consternation, whilst the mothers hide their children in their skirts and implore you to utter the counter-spell as quickly as you can. Since it is beyond our competence to teach it to you here, you are likely to find yourself in a predicament.

A Few Practical Tips—January and February are the only two comparatively cold months, at least in Attica and the islands. In springtime everywhere is bright with flowers. If you pick this season for your trip, in addition to summer frocks take a jacket or two and some woollies, not forgetting a waterproof, just in case.

Similar necklaces are hung round the necks of horses and mules....

In summer, even in Athens you will wear your most low-cut dresses. A bolero, a light stole or scarf are all you need to protect you against relatively chillier evenings.

Greek women protect their complexions by wearing a muslin kerchief over the face, and in country regions they wear veils with one corner drawn across the face.

You will have no difficulty in finding a taxi (ταξί) for hire (ἐλεύθερος) in which for a moderate price (2.4 dr. per kilometer) you can drive round Athens. If there are five or six of you, you will find taxis hardly more expensive than coaches, and you will be far more comfortable and independent. But if you are afraid of mis-planning your trip, there are innumerable tourist agencies in Athens to relieve you of your worries and make sure you store up a maximum of memories in the time and on the budget available. All the information you need regarding individual taxis or agencies will be given competently and helpfully at the Tourist Office (30, ὁδὸς ὁμήρου) (pronounce it *odós Omírou*, and understand Homer Street).

Before leaving, you will want to do a little shopping. If you are departing on a Thursday at dawn, be careful not to leave it until the last minute—all Greek shops close on Wednesday afternoons.

If you want to buy some clothes, take a stroll through Stadium Street *(Stadíou)*. There, between the two hearts of Athens—Constitution Square *(Syntágmatos)* and *Omónia* Square—you will probably find just what you were looking for, especially if you belong to the stronger sex. The shops devoted to masculine elegance are, in fact, far more numerous than those specializing in women's fashions. If you cannot find what you want in Stadium Street, go as far as Hermes Street *(Ermoú)* where the luxury jewellers are congregated. But if you are interested in local shopping centres, you should go along Aeolus Street as far as the Tower of the Winds. And be sure to visit Pandróssou Street, the antiquarians' corner where, for a mere 75 drachmas, you may acquire an authentic fragment of an antique amphora, a goblet or statuette. The soil of Greece brings so many to light each day that the museums would never be big enough to contain them all.

GREECE IS NOT CHINA—Whenever they have to decipher a sign, the name of a street, or the destination of a bus, the majority of tourists in Greece adopt the same sort of negative attitude they would assume in the depths of China. They make no attempt to understand, and either dispense with some useful piece of information, or trust to fortune—often kindly disposed —to produce a translator out of the blue.

And yet it is simply a question of alphabet. If the Greeks used the same letters as we did, we should

You will be able to select your own dish, straight from the pan...

have the impression—as in Scandinavia—that we were confronted with a sister language, and that with a slight effort we should manage, if not to speak it fluently, at least to get the gist and make ourselves understood.

How can one fail to feel at home in a country where a daily paper is called *ephemeridá;* bill: *logariasmós;* letter: *epistolí* (a love letter is, of course, *erotikí epistolí*); to go for a walk is *perípatos,* and when two people agree with each other, instead of muttering O.K. they simply say: *sýmphonoi.*

But alas, there is that wretched alphabet in which the letters often have no resemblance to our own either in shape or in sound. There are those disconcerting triangular capitals which all look alike, to our despair: A; Δ; $\Lambda = A$; D; L—so that a word (seldom used, it is true) such as Dalai-lamas would appear in the following attractive form: $\Delta A \Lambda A I \Lambda A M A \Sigma$.

Why not attempt right away to master these difficulties, which are not nearly as thorny as they appear? An hour's concentration, a few days' practice.... and you will be able to read Greek just as easily as English.

NOW FOR THE ALPHABET—Before we begin, it should be pointed out that certain letters (*a, z, i, o*) are very similar to our own. Others, such as π (pi) are familiar to anyone who has ever battled with problems of circles and circumference. As for the rest, it should be noted that:

(1) Despite appearances, *P* is not a *p*, but a capital *r* (Padio); *H* is not an *h* but a capital *η* (pronounced *i*), and *ω* is not a *w* but a small omega (ô).

(2) In addition to the *t* as we know it, there is a *Θ*, pronounced very much like *th* in "think".

(3) The Greek alphabet comprises three other supplementary letters, *φ* (*ph*), *χ* (*ch* or *k*), and *ψ* (*ps*). On the other hand, there is no *J*, and in order to write a foreign name such as "John", one has to use the *Z*—ZON.

The alphabet is as follows:

A	*α*	Alfa, as in *arm*.
B	*β*	Veeta, as in *veal*.
Γ	*γ*	Ghamma; the nearest sound to that in English is *y* in words like *yarn*, *yes*, *youth*, only in Mod. Gk. it is a little harsher, and more guttural (especially before *a* sound: e.g. *γάμος* sounds almost like *ghámos*).
Δ	*δ*	Dhelta, as in *the*, *though*.
E	*ε*	Epsilon, as in *ferry*.

Z	*ζ*	Zeeta, as in *zeal*.
H	*η*	Eeta, as in *kin*.
Θ	*θ*	Theeta, soft as in *thought*.
I	*ι*	Yota, as in *kin*.
K	*κ*	Kappa, as in *core*. Followed by 'ε' and all 'i's', however, it is softer. *Καί* is pronounced *kie*.
Λ	*λ*	Lamtha, as in *London*.
M	*μ*	Mee, as in *mother*.
N	*ν*	Nee, as in *nurse*.
Ξ	*ξ*	Ksee, as in *accent*.
O	*o*	Omikron, as in *ball*.
Π	*π*	Pee, as in *pray*.
P	*ϱ*	Ro, as in *rock*. Very much like the Scottish 'r'.
Σ	*σ* (*ς*)	Sigma, as in *mass*.
T	*τ*	Taf, as in *cut*.
Y	*υ*	Ypsilon, as in *link*.
Φ	*φ*	Phee, as in *phonetics*.
X	*χ*	Chee, as in Scottish *loch*.
Ψ	*ψ*	Psee, as in *Epsom*.
Ω	*ω*	Omega, as in *ball*.

*On moonlight nights
you may prolong your musing....*

In conclusion, the main irregularities of pronunciation are given below:

(1) Modern Greek suffers from "iota-cism", a simplifying disease whereby most diphthongs and vowels are pronounced *i*. The five ways of writing *i* in Greek are: *ι, η, υ, οι, ει*. The letters *a*, *e*, and *o* are pronounced as written.

(2) The letter *B* is pronounced *v*: *Ταβέρνα* tavern, is pronounced *taverna*; *Βούτυρον*, butter: *voutiron*.

To express an English *B* in Greek, the two consonants *Mp* (*Μπ*) are used—*Μπάρ*: bar; *Μπράβο*: bravo. An English *d* is indicated by *Nt* (*Ντ*)—*Ντούς*: douche.

(3) The diphthongs *αυ, ευ, ην, ων*, are pronounced either *av, ev, iv, ov*, or *af, ef, if, of* (*Basileus* [*βασιλεύς*] is pronounced *vassilefs*. *Euréka* [*εύρηκα*] becomes *eurika*). *Ai* is pronounced *e* (*Αθῆναι*: Athíne). On the other hand, *ου* is invariably *oo*.

WORD-LIST

ENGLISH	GREEK	PRONUNCIATION
Mr, Mrs	*Κύριε, Κυρία*	Kírie, Kiría
Good day, Good evening	*Καλημέρα, Καλησπέρα*	Kaliméra, Kalispéra
Good night	*Καληνύκτα*	Kalinícta
Yes, No	*Ναί, Όχι*	Né, Óchee
Thank you	*Εὐχαριστῶ*	Efcharistó
Please	*Παρακαλῶ*	Parakaló
Hullo, Good health	*Χαίρετε, Γειά σας*	Vhérete, Yiásas
A room	*Ἕνα δωμάτιο*	éna thomátio
Hot, cold water	*Νερὸ ζεστό, κρύο*	neró zestó, krio
A towel	*Μιὰ πετσέτα*	miá petséta
Bath, shower	*Λουτρό, ντούς*	loutró, doús
Laundry	*Πλυντικά*	plintiká
Breakfast	*Πρωινόν*	proïnón
Lunch, Dinner	*Γεῦμα, Δεῖπνον*	yiévma, theípnon
Tea, Coffee, Milk	*Τσάϊ, Καφές, Γάλα*	tsáï, kafés, ghála
Water, Wine	*Νερό, Κρασί*	neró, krasí
White, Red	*Ἄσπρο, Μαῦρο*	áspro, mávro
Resinated, Unresinated	*Ρετσινάτο, Ἀρετσίνωτο*	retsináto, aretsínoto
The menu	*Ὁ κατάλογος*	o katálogos
Bread	*Ψωμί*	psomi
Salt, Pepper	*Ἁλάτι, Πιπέρι*	aláti, pipéri
The bill	*Τὸν λογαριασμόν*	tón logariasmón
The tip	*Τὸ φιλοδώρημα*	to' filothórima
The street, the square	*Ἡ ὁδός, Ἡ πλατεία*	í othós, í platía
The station, the railway	*Ὁ σταθμός, Ὁ σιδηρόδρομος*	o stathmos, o sithiróthromos
Post Office	*Τὸ ταχυδρομεῖον*	to tachithromíon
The letters	*Τὰ γράμματα, Οἱ ἐπιστολές*	tá grámata, í epistolés
The stamps	*Τὰ γραμματόσημα*	tá gramatósima
The letter-box	*Τὸ γραμματοκιβώτιον*	tó gramatokivótion

ENGLISH	GREEK	PRONUNCIATION
The telephone	Τὸ τηλέφωνον	tó tiléfonon
The telegram	Τὸ τηλεγράφημα	tó tilegráfima
The bank	Ἡ τράπεζα	i trápeza
The hairdresser	Ὁ κουρεύς	o kourefs
The shoeshine	Ὁ λοῦστρος	o loústros
The week	Ἡ ἑβδομάς	i evthomás
Monday	Δευτέρα	Thefféra
Tuesday	Τρίτη	Tríti
Wednesday	Τετάρτη	Tetárti
Thursday	Πέμπτη	Pémpti
Friday	Παρασκευή	Paraskeví
Saturday	Σάββατο	Sávato
Sunday	Κυριακή	Kiriakí
What time is it?	Τί ὥρα εἶναι;	Ti óra íne
One	Ἕνας (fem. μία, n. ἕνα)	enas (fem. mía, n. éna)
Two	Δύο	Thío
Three	Τρεῖς (τρία, τριῶν)	Trís (tría, trión)
Four	Τέσσερις (τέσσερα, τεσσάρων)	tésseris (téssera, tessáron)
Five	Πέντε	Pénte
Six	Ἕξι	éxi
Seven	Ἑπτά	eptá
Eight	Ὀκτώ	októ
Nine	Ἐννέα	enéa
Ten	Δέκα	théka
Eleven	Ἕνδεκα	éndeka
Twelve	Δώδεκα	thótheka
Twenty	Εἴκοσι	íkosi
Thirty	Τριάντα	triánta
Forty	Σαράντα	saránta
Fifty	Πενήντα	penínta
Sixty	Ἑξήντα	exínta
Seventy	Ἑβδομήντα	evthomínta
Eighty	Ὀγδόντα	ogthónta
Ninety	Ἐνενήντα	enenínta
One hundred	Ἑκατόν	ekatón
One thousand	Χίλιοι, ες, α	chílioi, es, a

INDEX

413

We should like to express our thanks to the following organizations for their permission to use the illustrations on the pages indicated—

A.D.E.P.–92. ALNARI – 50, 61, 66, 81, 90, 96, 97, 99, 101, 105. ANDERSON – 46, 54, 57, 59, 71. APERGHIS – 167, 171, 173, 174, 181, 250, 333, 360. EVELPIDES – 384, 395. GIRAUDON – 42, 44, 72, 77, 79, 175. HAULTECŒUR – 113. EMILE SERAF – 98. TOUSSAINT – 110/1, 112, 160. ZERVOS – 88. ZUBER – 89.

The reproductions in colour in the chapters on *Art*, *Drama and Literature*, and *Mythology* are by JACQUES ELSER.

The other colour photographs (Kodachrome-Rectaflex) are by ROGER PUECH who took them especially for this book.

Drukkerij Holland, N.V.— Senefelder, Amsterdam

G. Jacquemot